# HEADACHE

BJ GEISLER

# Copyright

Copyright 2011, HEADACHE—How to Survive a Head Injury and Headache Caused By Insurance Companies, Doctors and Lawyers.

ISBN: 0615559727

All right reserved. No part of this book may be reproduced or utilized in any form or by any means, electronic, or mechanical, including photocopying and recording, or by any information storage, and retrieval system without permission in writing from the author. Author holds all rights to this book.

Logo: BJ Geisler

Book cover by: Holly Womack

# Dedication

This book is dedicated to the millions of people in the world who have a brain injury or are the family member of someone with a brain injury. You, above anyone else, will know what I am talking about in this book. And this is especially dedicated to those who are homeless and walking the streets alone because the system does not care enough to accurately diagnose your brain injury, to have the facilities, the therapy and the financial means to help support you in your everyday fog of bewilderment, abuse, neglect and turned-up noses of those who don't have a clue of the struggle you experience every second of your life.

This book was written to first of all tell my story and what I went through to get where I am today and, secondly, to act as a primer for those who are just beginning or are in the midst of their journey through the dark void of brain injury. It is also written for those on the outside of the patient and the family, namely, the therapists, medical personnel, police, social services personnel, legal professionals, insurance companies, friends, co-workers, neighbors, teachers, preachers and anyone else who comes into contact each and every day of your life with someone or several people who have a brain injury, even if you don't know it.

I want to thank my good therapists, doctors, attorneys, friends, family, angels and guides first and foremost. Without them I could not in any way conceivable have written this book. To my bad therapists, attorneys, and doctors, I hope we have cleared some karma….

To my children, especially Jenny, who put her life on hold to move in with me, stuck with me and kept me from numerous accidents. To my friend John who kept me from falling more times than I care to mention. Thanks to Chance for the old clunker computer that I started writing this on (it was so old that I had to use a floppy disk to transfer it to my newer computer). To Holly Womack who at a moment's notice designed the book cover for me.

Without any of you I would not have made it back from the void, or in my case, see-sawing back and forth on the edge of it. Thank you.

# Table of Contents

Title Page...................................................................1
Copyright Page..........................................................2
Dedication..................................................................3
Quote..........................................................................8

Chapter One ..............................................................9
   The Accident—I Didn't Even Get a Band-aid

Chapter Two ............................................................29
   Reality Sets In—We Shouldn't Be Alive

Chapter Three .........................................................39
   The First Signs of Traumatic Brain Injury—
   I Think I'm Okay

Chapter Four ...........................................................51
   Optometric Testing—It's All In Your Head

Chapter Five ............................................................60
   Insurance—An Alternate Reality

Chapter Six ..............................................................68
   Cognitive Testing—I Should Have Passed Out

Chapter Seven .........................................................81
   "Dr. Dapper" and The Broken String

Chapter Eight ..........................................................93
   Guided Introspection Brain Injury Inventory—
   Is Someone Reading My Mind?

Chapter Nine .........................................................114
   Neuropsychological Testing—Denial!

**Chapter Ten** ...................................................128
  The "Dizzy Doctor" and How Diligence Pays Off

**Chapter Eleven** ................................................137
  Biofeedback and Climbing Rocks With a Wedgie

**Chapter Twelve** ................................................145
  Independent Medical Exams—Prescribing Drugs to
  Fix the Problem

**Chapter Thirteen** ..............................................151
  "Dr. Satan" and "Insurance Whores"

**Chapter Fourteen** .............................................168
  Doctors Who Work For the Insurance Company

**Chapter Fifteen** ................................................188
  Grab a Gas Mask and Put On A Helmet!

**Chapter Sixteen** ...............................................199
  Miss-Managed Care—Hillary, What Were You Thinking?

**Chapter Seventeen** ...........................................224
  How to Do the Tango in 5/4 Time

**Chapter Eighteen** .............................................238
  Social Security, Medicaid, Medicare, and HUD

**Chapter Nineteen** .............................................257
  Class Action Lawsuits, Housing Snafus and NAET

**Chapter Twenty** ...............................................272
  The Mind Versus the Brain—
  Are You Willing To Drink the Water?

**Chapter Twenty-One** .......................................286
  If Your Guts Say Don't Do It—Don't Do It

Chapter Twenty-Two ................................................297
  The Lawsuit Begins—First Set of Discovery Requests

Chapter Twenty-Three................................................323
  How to Be Prepared—What I Needed to Know

Chapter Twenty-Four ................................................334
  Attorney vs. Psychiatrist—And the Loser Is!...me

Chapter Twenty-Five ................................................342
  Durable Power of Attorney—
  A Trust Fund for My Settlement Money

Chapter Twenty-Six ................................................353
  The Deposition—Now You Really Are in Hell

Chapter Twenty-Seven ................................................387
  Mediation—The End of the Nightmare

Chapter Twenty-Eight ................................................404
  Paying Off My Debt—Still More Good/Bad News

Chapter Twenty-Nine ................................................413
  New Techniques—
  Back Surgery and Nursing Home Nightmare

Chapter Thirty ................................................431
  What Does Everything Mean?—
  Finding Grace Through Humility

Indicative and Contributory Signs
  of Bad Faith................................................436
Bibliography................................................446
Disclaimer ................................................456
Author Info................................................459

...The best and most beautiful things in the world cannot be seen or even touched, but just felt in the heart.  —Helen Keller

# Chapter One
## The Accident—
## I Didn't Even Get a Band-Aid

1.5-2 million Americans sustain a traumatic brain injury each year. (See Bibliography, 1-1).

Chinle, Arizona is a magical place. It is true that the town itself is steeped in poverty with a landscape of dirt yards, tumble weeds and tumbling cans, newspapers and candy wrappers that are blown up against chain link fences. But it is home to Canyon de Chelly, one of the most spiritually, inspirational places I have visited.

My new friend Pam, her dog and I rode in her SUV to Chinle one weekend. We drove on post-snowstorm roads for hours, then through treacherous snow-packed mountain roads until we reached Arizona and the bright late-afternoon sunshine.

We marveled at the buttes and spires that turned from deep red to rose pink to denim blue as the setting-sun shadows cast their signature.

Although we had planned to arrive in Chinle sometime in the late afternoon, Pam missed the turn-off to Canyon de Chelly and we ended up in New Mexico. I kept telling her that she had missed the turn-off and needed to go back, but she wouldn't listen.

We were sixty miles out of the way and running low on gas when we finally saw the bright lights of a solitary gas station, seemingly out in the middle of nowhere. The lady at the gas station told us to turn around and go back and to turn left at a tiny brown sign that most people missed the first time by.

We backtracked through the now-eerie forested mountains and found the little carved wooden sign at an unlit junction that was the entrance to the canyon. We finally reached the town of Chinle late that evening.

When we got out of our beds on Saturday morning we ate breakfast at the motel restaurant then drove to the visitors' center at the mouth of the canyon. We hired a Navajo guide to ride with us for two hours since no one could enter the canyon without a Navajo present.

Pam drove the SUV into the canyon through the constantly shifting, tire-sucking sand that was the non-road. She was having a great time gunning the engine and fighting the wheel. She told the guide about her days as a "professional" driver and how she missed that.

The guide told us the history of the canyon's Anasazi people. We viewed the petroglyphs up close and the tiny-looking cliff dwellings from hundreds of feet below. It was cold in the canyon that morning with a crisp, blue sky and a strong breeze. Blowing golden leaves swirled through the air and splashed flashes of dancing shadows on the ancient cliff walls.

We shopped for jewelry and pottery at the lean-tos set up at the canyon's halfway point then plowed back through the sand to the visitors' center.

I paid the guide and said "Yah-te-he" (hell-o) to a weatherworn, wizened Navajo grandmother who was trying to sell her hand-woven rugs near the front door. I told her that her rugs and the turquoise jewelry that adorned her hands and neck were "na-zho-ni", meaning beautiful. She beamed from ear to ear while gesturing with her gnarled, worn hands and spoke with me in broken English that was interspersed with Navajo about her rugs.

By mid afternoon, billowy clouds began rolling in chased by a determined wind. We drove along the winding road that hugged the rim of the canyon, parked the car and walked down into the canyon on the only walking path available to non-Navajo.

I stopped numerous times to marvel at the richness of the sheer red cliffs and to watch the colors change on the cliff walls as a cloud danced by, painted its charcoal image on the wall, then erased itself. I held my breath and watched the shadows deepen as the sun slowly lowered itself deep within the canyon's folds.

That evening we gorged ourselves on Navajo fry bread that was laced with honey at the motel restaurant then returned to our room. I read for a while and went to sleep.

Sometime during the night Mother Nature sent us a gale-force snowstorm. On Sunday morning the flag on the pole outside in the courtyard was hanging on for dear life, its frayed tips snapping and bucking in the wind. The garbage that had been flattened and quivering against the fences the day before was tossed upward during an updraft and blown and tumbled to a new resting place.

The miniscule amount of snow the storm brought with it had turned the concrete and asphalt surfaces into skating rinks. The icing on the cake for the morning, or so I thought, was when the electricity blinked once, then twice and finally went out.

By eight o'clock, the motel room was getting cold. Because the power was out, the Motel restaurant was closed. I had a packet of nuts and ate a handful. I offered some to Pam but she declined. We were hungry for hot food, and Pam had yet to have her coffee.

We decided to head north toward home with hope that the next town would have its electricity on and a place to eat. When we went outside the sun was just peeking through the clouds and the wind was losing some of its bluster, but it was still bitterly cold.

Pam mentioned that she wondered if a stick or something had gotten stuck up above one of the tires while we were driving in the canyon because she had heard an odd noise the day before. She looked up under the right rear wheel well and decided it was too cold to look any further. She commented about how icy the parking lot was as she skidded her feet around to test the slickness.

We loaded our suitcases into the backseat of the car, took our coats off and put her dog in the back end of the vehicle.

Pam backed the car out of the space and headed for the street. I noticed an ambulance creeping along on the icy road toward the canyon, the opposite direction we were going to go. I mentioned the slowness to Pam and said the road must really be icy.

The car's tires spun as we pulled out of the driveway and turned left onto the road, drove to the stoplight and turned right. All of the business windows were dark and their doors firmly said, "Closed".

At the edge of town I saw a Highway Patrolman parked along the side of the road. I mentioned this to Pam who had a propensity for speeding and getting tickets. She asked me what the speed limit was. I told her it was fifty-five. She checked her speed.

I picked up my one-liter water bottle from the console between us, noticed I had only taken a couple drinks of it and set it back down next to her cell phone that she had found was useless on the reservation.

Out in the open country, the wind was whistling from the west. The buttes and spires, whose color resembled freshly washed blue jeans as the sun set behind them the day before, now looked a dull, filmy rose color. Crystals of icy snow, or perhaps it was sand swept up from the desert by the wind, swirled up and spattered the paint and the windshield of the car with a rat-a-tat-tat.

The road was obviously quite icy and glittered and twinkled where the peeking sun shined on it.

Driving north, I noticed that Pam was driving a lot faster than I thought she should have been. I thought about saying something to her, but I was sure she would inform me, as she had numerous times that weekend, that she used to be a professional driver and, "I know what I'm doing."

She was looking off to the west at something. I looked at the speedometer. From where I sat, it appeared that we were going between fifty-five and sixty miles per hour. Up ahead of us, I saw an old burgundy Chevy full of people rolling slowly down the road and wondered if we were going to go around them or run over the top of them.

The sun had just started to pierce through the skittering clouds and the wind was losing some of its bluster.

Pam was slowly accelerating the car while she still looked at the buttes.

We were slowly creeping toward the edge of the road. I was feeling agitated when—lo, and behold—I sensed my dog jump up on my lap, lean back against me and brace herself against the dash with her front paws. My dog died the week before our trip!—but there she was. I could see her clearly as could be.

Pam looked down at the speedometer and let off a little on the gas. I heard a clunk, like a tire flipping a rock up against the undercarriage, or of something jarred loose and falling from the bottom of the vehicle.

Suddenly, the car fishtailed clockwise, then counter-clockwise, and then back again while Pam frantically turned the wheel completely from one side to the other. We were sliding backwards with the front of the driver's side of the car closest to the ditch.

"Don't hit the brakes," I told her, thinking that she would lock up the wheels if she slammed on the brakes.

The front tire caught the edge of the road first, then the rear tire. We hurtled up into the air. She said, "We're gonna flip!"

I said, "Yep."

I grabbed onto the armrest with my right hand and braced the console with the other when I heard a voice from somewhere say, "Relax," and then, "Don't brace yourself, you'll get hurt worse." I relaxed myself like a rag doll.

We smashed down on the driver's side of the car with a thunderous explosion of bursting tires and crushing metal.

My head and body flew left and back between the seats. My left arm slammed down hard into the console. The seatbelt grabbed me and my head snapped back to the right like it had been slung out of a catapult.

"Don't disassociate," I kept telling myself. "Don't disassociate."

The next voice I sensed was saying, "Don't hit your head."

I tipped my head just as it hit the window so that the impact was blunt instead of sharp. My right leg smashed into the armrest. My head glanced off of the glass shooting to the left and slightly forward, then to the right where the right back of my head slammed into the post. Stars and a haze threatened to overtake me. Then I felt myself hurled out of my body....

I stood with one foot on the third step down and my right foot on the second step down of the three-tiered stairs. In the background were filmy-looking beings that looked like they were in absolute peace, calm, and serenity. A much larger angelic being came forward and spoke with me and then quite clearly said, "You have to go back now…your daughters still need you."

I jolted back into my body to catch it just as quickly as I had left it.

She's trying to kill me, I thought. I shot forward and then back against the seat with my head bouncing back and forth three times against the headrest. "No, no, no," I told myself. "Don't pass out. You might end up in a coma or wake up a vegetable." I blinked several times to clear my head.

When I stopped bouncing, I frantically braced myself with my left foot against the floor, my right foot against the wheel well, my left hand against the console and grabbed onto the above handhold with my right hand to keep from falling down to the left.

The vehicle continued to hurtle through the snow. I hung there, too stunned to believe what was happening. I saw and heard rocks and beer bottles and cans screech and scrape and rip and crease metal and chrome and plastic from along the side of the car. Dirt and snow flew up in a white and black cloud and boiled around us. Just when I thought we were done sliding, the car slid into a ditch, a hiccup of a ditch, pivoted in time lapsed motion and rolled onto its top.

The roof of the vehicle slowly caved in, crushing and splintering the windshield with its weight. I scrunched down lower and lower in my seat. I helplessly watched the windshield get smaller and smaller and cowered from the roof as it crept closer and closer.

Suddenly, it was quiet.

Smoke poured out from under the hood. I could smell the strong odor of hissing gasoline dripping from somewhere.

Momentarily panic-stricken, all I could think of was FIRE! I've got to get out of here! I thought. Oh, my God, I've got to get out of here!

I was held taut, hanging upside down in my seatbelt. I groped for the clasp and tried to release it. The weight of my body pulling against the straps held the clasp tight. I tried the door. It would not open.

I looked wide-eyed over at Pam, suspended by her seat belt, her legs bowed around the steering wheel, her hair hanging down as if in mid-scream, and I almost giggled.

I was about to tell her to turn off the engine

when she raised her hands like she was softening the voices of a choir and said quietly and calmly to herself, "Turn off the ignition." She reached down and turned the key to off. Pam searched for her cell phone to call for help, couldn't find it and remembered that there was no reception.

I heard two car doors slam then two men ran up to Pam's side of the smoking car yelling, "Are you okay? Is anyone hurt?"

They were frantically grasping at the handles on the driver's side doors, desperately trying to get them open. When the side doors wouldn't open, they tried the back door. One of them ran to my side of the car and tried to open those doors. None of them would open. The men had that deer in the headlights look and one man excitedly said to the other, "We have to get them out before the car catches on fire!"

Pam and I looked wide-eyed at each other. At almost the same time we asked, "Are you okay?"

She said she was okay. I told her I felt like my left arm and back were broken but I was okay, I wasn't dead. I wriggled my toes and I could them move around so I thought I was okay even though my toes felt "funny", as if they weren't really there. I hadn't lost control of my bladder or bowels and I thought that was also a good thing.

I braced my feet against the dash, gingerly hoisted myself up and let myself out of the seat belt. I tried to convince Pam to unhook her seatbelt, let herself down and get her feet up in the air so that she wouldn't go into shock. (Silly me—her feet were already up, up above her head!)

She refused. I tried again.

That sent her into a state. She started yelling at me and said we wouldn't be hanging upside down if she hadn't listened to me and had hit the brakes. I told her that I didn't want her to lock the wheels up then asked her if she had put her foot on the brake at all. She said she hadn't. I told her we would probably be dead if she had hit the brakes because the forward motion of the wheels helped slow the vehicle down since we were flying up the road backwards at sixty miles per hour. (I did not mention to her that she was over-correcting the steering wheel).

She wasn't buying it. She kept yelling at me that it was my fault we were hanging upside down in the ditch. In between yelling at me, she would turn back to the window and nicely tell the man who was still yanking on the door handle and pulling as hard as he could that we were okay.

It was like I was watching two people in one body operating!

I was feeling the absurdity of the situation by now and was waiting to wake up from the un-scheduled dream. The steamy fog floating around the car from the snow and anti-freeze and gas and oil sizzling on the still-hot engine did not help my reality at all.

I settled gingerly down against the ceiling with my feet up on the upside-down dash and lay there as if I were waiting for the movie at the drive-in to start rolling. Little did I know that the movie was going to be a reality horror film, and I was going to be the movie's star performer.

Pam suddenly remembered her dog. There was no sound from the back. "Where's the dog?"

We called her several times.

Finally we heard the jingling of tags as the dog got up and shook herself. She stumbled toward the front of the vehicle, hesitating, probably wondering if it was okay to come past the back seat, and wondering, where is the back seat and why am I walking on the ceiling? She was shaking like a leaf. Fortunately there was no blood.

"Pam, let yourself out of your seatbelt and get your feet up or you're going to go into shock," I told her again.

She argued and in a snotty voice said that she was "just fine."

After arguing back and forth several times, she finally relented. I helped her let herself down but she would only put one foot up. I shook my head.

The dog seemed to realize that someone was trying to break into her car. She started growling, which sounded funny considering she was shaking. I grabbed her collar and held onto her while we talked to her. She finally calmed down. I gasped as she sat her sixty pound butt down on my stomach.

The two guys were still yanking on the doors. I stupidly said, "Don't let them open the doors until help gets here or we'll freeze to death."

Pam told them what I had said even though the steam around the car was like the morning fog of the Oregon coast and the car could explode in flames at any second.

I was staying somewhat coherent and remembering what was happening. I was staying calm, but I was having trouble staying awake. From about lumbar region of my spine down everything felt "funny", especially on the left side. My mid back, left arm and right leg were throbbing, and I was sure that my arm and back were broken. My right shoulder felt like it had been torn out of its socket.

Within minutes, the fire truck arrived, a hose was strung and the firemen watered down the smoking engine.

Someone yelled through Pam's window, "Is the engine shut off?"

She told them that it was.

Watery, oily mud ran through the openings around the pedals and console into the vehicle and dripped down on us. Talk about adding insult to injury, I thought.

Jeez, my arm and back hurt.

The dog stayed perched on my stomach, still shaking and growling.

I heard pry bars rip into the metal around the doors. Someone told another person to get the Jaws of Life and then someone shouted, "Got it!"

The back door scraped open then my side door.

An EMT stuck his head in and asked if I was okay. The dog trembled deeper into my stomach. We kept talking to her like she was a baby. I wondered why people did that. She let someone take her.

I told the EMT about my back and arm. He asked if I could feel my toes and asked me to move them. I told him I could feel them, but I couldn't sense them. He did a quick physical exam and asked me if I could walk. I asked him if that was a good idea if my back was broken. He said, "They've found there is less damage if a person moves themselves." I thought back to my EMT training twenty years before and was surprised. It was a long time ago, and we handled people like eggs. What were these people thinking?

I drifted back into the moment. Startled, I realized that no one had taken my blood pressure. I blinked my eyes several times to clear my head.

What if I went into shock? People tend to do that after an accident, especially if they are up walking around....

The EMT was speaking to me. He asked me again if I could get out of the car on my own. I slowly rolled over and crawled out of the upside-down vehicle. He finished his exam, running his hands up and down my spine while I was standing up. I walked to the ambulance, turned and looked back at the crushed and mangled car lying in the ditch like an upside-down turtle. There was no doubt in my mind that it was totaled. I told the EMT that I needed to lie down. I climbed up the step into the ambulance and laid on the gurney.

...Sleep. I just wanted to go to sleep. I fought it. Fears careened around in my head. I didn't want to go to sleep and lapse into a coma. What if I never woke up?

Pam got into the ambulance through the side door and sat down on the bench facing me, even though she looked everywhere but at me. Someone else climbed in through the side door with the dog on the end of a strap from some ambulance equipment and sat down on the jump seat. I had never seen that dog so cowed.

The EMT wrapped a sensor around my finger, placed sandbags on both sides of my head, covered me with blankets and strapped me down.

I closed my eyes and tried to stay calm.

We made a U-turn and rolled slowly down the highway, back through town and turned right up the road that led to the hospital. During the ride I could hear chatter on the radio about another accident requesting an ambulance.

The ambulance pulled up to the emergency room doors, stopped, the doors opened, and they rolled me into the ER. A female doctor and a male nurse started poking and prodding me, checked my eyes and asked me the three questions. What day is it? ...Sunday. What year is it? I had to really think about it. Who's the President? I answered, "no one knows who the President is." They looked at me strangely. "...Unless the votes have been re-counted. Has a decision come in yet?"

Next came the x-rays—neck and mid-back only. I was okay.

Or, so they said—just bumps and bruises.

They left me alone in the curtained-off room. In came the teeth-shattering, bone-jarring shock. The male nurse brought in some warmed blankets and covered me up.

Time had warped. I had no concept of what time it was or how long I had been there. I sure wasn't going to tell anyone about the loss I was feeling—the feeling that something wasn't right, that I felt like I was a quarter of a turn off. I didn't want to be a burden.

Pam pulled back the edge of the curtain and

peeked into the room. "It's okay. You can come in," I told her. She stepped in beside the pulled-back curtain, folded her hands in front of her and stood staring at the floor.

She finally came and sat down next to me and said, "I'm so sorry I ruined our vacation."

I thought that was a strange comment. I told her, "I'll be okay."

She lowered the rail on the bed, took my hand and laid her forehead on my stomach.

I asked her if she was all right. I was quite uncomfortable that she had laid her head down on me. I really hardly knew this woman.

She told me they had x-rayed her neck, and she was fine. Quite proudly she told me that she had not gotten a ticket. She also said she didn't remember a thing after she said, "We're gonna flip."

How convenient.

The highway patrolman came in and told her that she was free to go and that no charges were going to be filed.

I couldn't believe it. She had obviously been going too fast for the road conditions. The question of whether she should have hit the brakes or not was a moot point because the speed we were going is what caused the accident, not the fact that she didn't hit the brakes. Besides, she had already lost control before my comment.

After the patrolman left, we talked about the accident. I told her that when I looked at the speedometer she was going somewhere between fifty-five and sixty miles per hour and that I heard something hit the bottom of the car just before we started to slide. She said she didn't hear anything and asked me to not tell anyone how fast we were going.

I shut up. She had already tried to kill me once. I didn't know what she was capable of.

The electricity came back on. Someone found us some food—hospital food, a carbohydrate lover's feast. The doctor informed us that we could leave. The doctor wanted to write us scripts for muscle relaxants. She said we'd really be hurting in a few days.

We both declined. I had already told the doctor that I had a history of substance abuse and had been clean and sober for seventeen years. Had no one taught this doctor to never give muscle relaxants or painkillers to people in recovery unless it was absolutely vital? I told the doctor that I no longer put chemicals in my body on purpose.

I asked her if we could get prescriptions for chiropractic and massage therapy. She acquiesced and wrote a script for both of us for chiropractic and massage for two months.

One million people are treated and released annually from hospital emergency rooms after sustaining a brain injury. There are approximately 300,000 hospital admissions annually for persons with mild or moderate traumatic brain injury and an additional unknown number of TBIs that are not diagnosed but may result in long-term disability. (See Bibliography, 1-2).

# Chapter Two
## We Shouldn't Be Alive

There are no taxis, buses or car rental companies in Chinle, Arizona.

Someone from the hospital staff found a Navajo man who would give us a ride back to the motel we had just checked out of a few hours earlier. We climbed into his blue GMC mini-van, dog in tow, and left the hospital.

We asked him to drive us to where they had towed the wrecked vehicle so we could get our suitcases, coats and the dog's food. He drove us to the fenced-in lot where he was sure they had towed the vehicle, but the gate was locked. He told us there had been fifteen rollovers on that stretch of road so far that morning and they were probably at another wreck. He said there were a lot of problems on the roads when it got icy because of the round-rock road surface they used.

We asked him why the road hadn't been sanded. He told us that the roads were never sanded because the ice always melted off by eleven o'clock. He said the people who lived in the area just drove slowly when it was icy because they knew the roads were untended.

He also informed us that a trailer being pulled down the road with several people in the trailer had been blown off the road about thirty miles north of Chinle and a baby had died. He said that was where the ambulance and fire truck were headed when they came upon our accident and that is why their response time was so quick.

He backed out onto the highway and drove us to the motel. I gave him some money, thanked him, and he left.

Pam said that she was paying for the motel room on her personal credit card since we wouldn't be back at the motel if we hadn't wrecked. I told the girl at the front desk what had happened.

I didn't really want to be in the same room with Pam because I wasn't sure I trusted her anymore, yet I didn't want to be alone. The adage "keep your friends close and your enemies closer" ran through my mind. I also didn't know how I was going to get back home if I didn't stay close to her.

We walked to the room we had been assigned to and Pam called her ex-husband and talked to her kids. She told her ex she thought all we needed was a new windshield and she would be able to drive the car home.

In the background I whispered, "Pam, the car is totaled."

I called my landlord who lived upstairs from me and asked him if he would go to the church where my daughter was attending services and give her the phone number where I could be reached. I told him about the car accident and said that we might need my daughter to come get us. I explained to him that we had been at the hospital and they said we were okay—just bumps and bruises.

There was no way I was getting into a rental car or any other type of car with that woman again.

When I returned to the room, Pam had the yellow pages of the phone book open and had started calling car rental companies. They would not deliver a car on an "Indian Reservation." Flagstaff, Arizona and Farmington, New Mexico, which were both several hours away, were the closest towns of any size to Chinle that had car rental companies. Neither could deliver a car to us on an Indian Reservation.

Pam called AAA National. They told her she would have to call her state AAA. The state AAA told her she had no AAA coverage on an Indian Reservation because it was considered a "Sovereign Nation".

Pam went ballistic and started yelling and, when that didn't work, converted to begging and whining at the agent at AAA.

The girl from the front desk knocked on the door and said there was a call from my daughter. As I walked to the office with the girl, I noticed that my left foot was dragging and not quite going where I wanted it to go. And my left arm and hand weren't hanging right. I chalked it up to "just part of the accident" and thought it would be better in a couple days.

My daughter was hysterical. My landlord had given the message to his sister who passed the message on to my daughter. Somehow the story had become something much worse than I had told him, or someone heard, told or had received the whole story enhanced.

I assured my daughter that we were okay and would be all right until the next day even though in the back of my mind I wasn't so sure. She wanted to leave immediately for the trip to Chinle. She said it was snowing where she lived. I didn't want her to start out in a storm and get in an accident, too. She calmed down finally and agreed to come in the morning.

I went back to the room. Pam was still on the phone. Now she was talking to someone at her insurance company and sweetly telling the person, "We couldn't have been going over forty or forty-five when we left the road."

And that was after fishtailing three times, then sliding backwards, I thought. I harrumphed to myself and shook my head.

She then added that she was sure all we'd need was a new windshield, and we'd be able to drive the car home. She told the person at the other end of the phone, "No, we didn't hit anything and nothing hit the car."

I whispered, "Pam, the car is totaled."

She still wasn't getting it. When she hung up I told her again that the car was totaled. She just asked, "Do you really think so? I don't think it's that bad."

I said I was sure. I told her again that she was going about sixty and I heard something, possibly a rock or a stick, hit the undercarriage of the car just before we started to fishtail. She said she didn't hear it.

Then she told me to not say anything to the insurance company about what I heard because they would consider the accident a collision instead of a comprehensive claim. She had already told the insurance person that we had hit nothing and nothing had hit us. She told me that she was afraid her insurance rates would go up, or that she would lose her insurance if they found out she had clipped something on the road or that something other than an Act of God had caused the accident.

While Pam made another phone call I limped over to the restaurant and got some food for us. Neither of us could eat more than a few bites.

When Pam finally finished her phone calls, she surveyed her body and found that she had numerous bumps and bruises, especially on her left side, that were just appearing. I did a Reiki treatment on her, and she said that it helped.

I lay down on my bed. Man, I was tired, but I

was too wired to sleep. I was freezing, my teeth chattered, my neck had started to hurt and my head felt like a melon ready to split. As soon as I lay down, I started coughing like crazy.

Pam called the towing yard several times and finally got someone on the phone who said he would deliver our suitcases and coats to us.

As I lay on my bed, I thought back to the months before the accident. I had had glimmers about being in a car wreck and had ignored the premonitions. Now I felt like my life had been shattered. I was upset at myself. I felt badly for Pam who was averting her eyes. I felt sorry for her and I was scared for me. As I lay there, tears welled up in my eyes.

A few hours later the driver and his wife brought the suitcases to us. Everything was covered with caked oily mud. A little later Pam and I walked across the street to the Laundromat rolling our suitcases behind us.

We were the only non-Native Americans in the Laundromat. Everyone stared at us. I had been on the reservation so many times that I thought little of the stares. Pam, however, was scared. I still couldn't understand prejudice.

We went to the restaurant and ate some dinner. After we went to bed for the night, I started coughing again. Not your average ordinary tickle-cough but a gagging, retching cough that tore me all the way to my toes. I tried covering my head with the pillow so I wouldn't wake Pam up. I figured out that if I didn't inhale I didn't choke.

When we got up the next morning Pam said she was surprised that my bed had not vibrated clear to the door because I was coughing so hard. I was exhausted. My head was pounding.

At eleven o'clock my daughter and her friend arrived. Tears filled my daughter's eyes as she quickly walked into the room and tightly hugged me and held on. She whispered, "I am so glad you're alive."

They had left from home on icy roads in the wee morning hours. Later on, my daughter would tell me that as soon as she saw me that I didn't "look right".

We loaded our suitcases and the dog into my daughter's car and headed for the tow yard where the SUV had been taken. The man at the desk checked Pam's license, had her sign some paperwork and led us into the yard where the remains of the SUV lay.

Now that the vehicle was upright, it was even worse than I had thought it was. It was a knee-shaker for Pam who thought all we'd need was "a new windshield".

Her illusion was shattered. The tires on the driver's side were shredded. The roof was squashed down flat—the crazed windshield was about half as big as it should have been. Pam said she was impressed, however, that the "moon" window on the roof had not broken.

The door on the passenger's side was held shut, kind of, by the seatbelt wrapped around the armrest. The door jutted up about four inches above the opening. The whole thing listed about thirty degrees to the left. I do not believe there was one straight piece of metal or piece of plastic that was reusable. Chunks of grass and dried mud hung off of what was left of the bent and twisted chrome and the bumpers.

The inside of the car was covered with oily dirt. The keys could not be pulled out of the steering column and that greatest of all inventions—the plastic container—had lost its lid and dog food was scattered all over the car.

Pam found that her newly purchased bottle of patchouli oil that had been lying on the console was thrown up into the map holder on the ceiling. She found her cell phone under the seat and my water bottle that we figured were the culprits in causing the large bumps on her head.

It was an impressive sight—impressive from the standpoint that we were still alive!

We looked around the wrecking yard at the other vehicles that had been squashed and mangled. I had told my daughter and her friend earlier about the death of the baby and there, but a few yards from the vehicle we had been in, lay the platform of the stripped carcass of the trailer where the baby's short life had ended.

My daughter's friend started to cry. My daughter and I choked back tears.

Suddenly our accident seemed miniscule next to those people's loss.

Pam continued to load her things into the trunk of my daughter's car.

We left the wrecking yard. I tried to convince my daughter to go to the store so that I could buy a camera and take pictures of the wrecked vehicle, just in case, I thought, just in case. Pam was adamant about hurrying home.

We stopped at a drive-thru and got something to eat, then headed north out of town. When we passed the sight of the accident, I asked my daughter to slow down so that I could memorize everything that I saw. What a benign spot in the road, I thought to myself. It was completely flat in the area with no reason other than neglect to have had an accident.

For many miles on the long ride north, it was deathly silent in the car. Each of us seemed lost in our private thought, each of us staring out of a window at the now desolate landscape realizing how, in a split second, our lives could be changed. Everyone's stomachs seemed to be turned by what they had seen and felt in the wrecking yard that day.

I was torn. I didn't want to leave Chinle…not yet. I was afraid of what awaited me when I got home and who I would be….

Brain injury claims more than 52,000 lives each year and leaves more than 80,000 individuals with lifelong disabilities each year. Four thousand people per day receive a traumatic brain injury. (See Bibliography, 2-1). These estimates, however, suffer from ascertainment bias since they are based exclusively on information about hospitalized patients and those who die before hospitalization. (See Bibliography, 2-2).

# Chapter Three
## The First Signs of Traumatic Brain Injury—
## I Think I'm Okay….

    During the long ride home, Pam questioned my daughter about insurance—comprehensive versus collision. We went over and over the accident. I kept telling her that she was going too fast for the road conditions and that something hit the car or fell off of it. She found every excuse in the book to excuse what had happened. After numerous denials and frustrating miles she admitted, "I guess I was just going too fast."

    Several times she asked me not to say anything to her insurance company about how fast she was going or that I had heard something hit the bottom of the car. By then, my daughter was totally disgusted with Pam and told her that if she didn't tell the truth she could be charged with insurance fraud.

    When we got home, I collapsed in bed and coughed my way through the second night. I had shooting pain down my legs, and my back and neck were in spasm.

    When I got up the next morning I couldn't get my hands to work correctly. My head was pounding. I tried to fix breakfast. I thought a hard-boiled egg would be easy. I put the pan on the stove, got in the shower and tried to wash my hair.

My hands just didn't work together. I kept dropping the bar of soap. I lost my balance several times and fell over. Then I couldn't remember if I had already washed my hair.

I got out of the shower and looked in the mirror—soapy hair stared back at me. When I went to check the egg, I discovered there was no water or egg in the pan—thankfully no heat either. I tried to get dressed and realized I couldn't button a button with my left hand. Tying my right shoe took numerous attempts.

When I got in my car I discovered that the clutch was now a foreign object. I just raised my eyebrows and thought that I had lost my marbles. Once I did get rolling, the rear end of cars was much closer than I had anticipated. I picked Pam and her son up at their house, dropped her son at school and delivered her to her workplace.

The day got worse. When I got to my job I couldn't remember what I was supposed to do. My sentences came out garbled. When I got up I tripped over my dragging left foot and fell into things. I kept trying to locate the smell of sewer gas, civet cat, decaying animal combination but couldn't find it.

My lunch tasted dangerously strange. My vision was blurry with dark "streamers" shooting past my right side. There were blank spots on printed pages.

Doing the deposit for the day was a nightmare. My math skills were missing, and I couldn't figure out what checks I had already put on the deposit slip and which ones I hadn't. When customers and agents called, I couldn't figure out who they were even though prior to the accident I spoke with many of them on a daily basis.

A claims adjustor from my insurance company called and told me what my policy allowed. He said they paid up to $50,000 medical and $50,000 rehab for up to ten years. Colorado at that time was a no-fault state. I had opted for a PPO shortly before the accident and that included one year of lost wages, or at least that was the way it had been presented to me by the agent who sold the policy to me. The adjustor asked me if I was still able to work full-time at my job, and I told him that I was able to work but I only worked twenty-seven hours anyway and had a part-time painting business on the side. I was in so much denial at that time that I did not tell him how much trouble I was having.

By two o'clock my insides hurt so much I had trouble breathing. By three o'clock I had to lie down on the floor. It helped my breathing and mid back, but then my lower back hurt.

Each day got worse. At night I was still choke coughing and would often choke during the day. When I was finally able to fall asleep I woke up with excruciating pain running down my legs—more so in the left leg. The pain was past moaning and made me angry. When I rolled over I was so dizzy that it felt like someone was trying to yank the bed out from underneath me. I had trouble swallowing my food and often choked on it or on what I was drinking.

Pam's insurance company told her they would only pay a ridiculously small amount for her totaled vehicle. She told them that the amount wouldn't pay off what she had left on her loan. They said that she hadn't given them a copy of her loan agreement so they were not obligated to pay a higher amount. Pam informed them that she had given them a copy of the loan agreement otherwise she would not have been able to get insurance. This argument went on for several days. Finally the insurance company acquiesced and paid her what they were supposed to plus she had some money left over after she paid off her loan. (See "Indicative or Contributory Signs of Bad Faith", pages 440, 441, numbers 21, 34, and 35).

The chiropractor I had seen about every other month before the accident was on a cruise so Pam took me to a chiropractor she knew. He told me I had some very serious injuries. It felt like I was being murdered when he worked on me.

The "silent epidemic" of brain injury, thus called because it is not physically visible, is illustrated best by a 1999 statistic from the Centers for Disease Control and Prevention (CDC)—there are currently at least 5.3 million Americans living with a disability as a result of brain injury, a little more than 2 percent of the population. (See Bibliography, 3-1).

By the weekend after the accident I was telling people to go f--- themselves. If Pam was with me, she just told the people that I had "bonked" my head too hard. On Tuesday I couldn't breathe I hurt so much. I had trouble deciding whether to go to Pam's birthday dinner or to the ER. I opted for the dinner because I knew the only help I would receive by going to the ER would be drugs.

When I remembered to, I slathered arnica Montana on my neck to help ease the pain and swelling. My face on the right side was squashed upward, my head tilted to the right. My right eyebrow resembled a lying down question mark. If I straightened my head I felt like I was going to vomit. If I looked right, left or up I fell over. My temper blew at the slightest thing.

I started having in-living-color nightmares that I later learned were probably hallucinations from the brain swelling (I pictured chewing someone's arm off leaving just a bloody stump dripping blood). My headaches just never went away. The left side of my face and head felt tingly.

Cooking a meal was out of the question. I couldn't figure out the sequence to cook. The problem was that if I put the egg in the pan I left out the water or simply didn't turn the stove on. Or I would put a bare pan on the stove, turn it on and just go away, having forgotten what it was I was going to do. My attention to this detail was usually tapped into when I heard a loud rattling noise when the pan began to dance around on the burner.

When I did eat, I was doubled over in pain within two hours. I finally tried to avoid the kitchen altogether because it terrified me, not only because of the stove part, but also because I couldn't figure out how to turn on the water at the sink. If I did turn it on I couldn't figure out why we had no hot water. To me, cold was hot at the spigot and hot was cold.

I had trouble grasping money with my left hand and would overshoot what I was aiming for. I dropped things and knocked things over. They just weren't where I thought they were. I pretended nothing was the matter with me when I was around others and even pretended nothing was the matter with me when I was by myself.

I got a letter from Pam's insurance company. They said she had an exclusion clause in her policy. Her policy only covered $1,000 in medical and had no PIP (personal injury protection) for out of state accidents involving non-family members. I had just started painting on my own, besides the part-time job, and now had to let those waiting paint jobs go. All I could do now was my temp job that I worked for only 24-27 hours per week. I thought that if I had to I could go back to working as a drug and alcohol counselor but couldn't figure out how I would remember what people told me or, even, who they were.

      My regular chiropractor, who I asked to be my primary care doctor, got back from his cruise. He told me he hadn't seen "that bad of a concussion on most professional football players" he had worked on over the years. "You look like someone hit you up the side of the head with a frying pan," he told me as he shook his head. He also said I had a double whiplash. On some days he adjusted my neck two or three times.

      A few weeks later, I started getting several calls from the chiropractor's billing department about the claims adjustor from my insurance company telling them something totally different than what he had told me. I thought, perhaps, that the chiropractor wanted me to pay up-front. When I called the claims adjustor, he robotically would state what he had said to the billing department personnel then said that he told them exactly that, as it is what the law states.

I found that very confusing. The claims adjustor said one thing and the chiropractor's office personnel told me another. I spoke with several people at the chiropractor's office who all said they had been told the same thing. They also told me that my particular insurance company was one of the worst ones to collect money from. (See "Indicative and Contributory Signs of Bad Faith", page 441, 442, numbers 34, 35, and 36).

I got copies of my x-rays from the Indian Health Center in Chinle—neck and mid-back only had been taken. The chiropractor looked at the x-rays and showed me where my head was off-center. "You shouldn't be able to walk," he told me. Then he exclaimed, "We can fix that!"

A traumatic brain injury occurs every 1.5 seconds. The cost of traumatic brain injury in the United States is estimated to be $48.3 billion annually. Hospitalization accounts for $31.7 billion and fatal brain injuries cost the nation $16.6 billion each year. (See Bibliography, 3-2). Estimates for average lifetime cost of care for a person with severe TBI range from $600,000 to $1,875,000. These estimates may grossly underestimate the economic burden of TBI to family and society. (See Bibliography, 3-3).

Several weeks went by. I was still having trouble finding words and still garbled my sentences. I was still saying inappropriate things. My left ear rang and buzzed and would be a major factor in not being able to sleep, besides the excruciating pain running down my legs. I missed appointments or had the wrong day or time. For the first time ever, I had to start writing things down. My friend Barb told me I used to have a mind like a steel trap. Now it was more like a steel sieve.

I was scared.

I couldn't sit through a movie or go anyplace where there were a lot of people, bright lights or shiny or patterned floors. My depth perception was so far off that I thought I needed to step up or down when I didn't need to. Stairs looked like sixteen-inch drop-offs instead of ten-inch steps.

When I turned my head to either side my eyes bounced up and down or rolled from side to side. My left eye was still doing a hard twitch. In general, both eyes just hurt.

My left leg felt like I was dragging a log when I walked. My left foot crossed over my right foot. I couldn't lift my left foot onto a step or pivot to the left. I could only walk short distances or at night the pain down my legs was worse.

At night when I turned on a light, my pupils didn't close down and I felt like I would have probably felt being interrogated with a klieg light.

I had trouble reading. I started at the left top of the page and my eyes just went to the bottom sentence on the right page. I blanked out and couldn't remember what I'd read when I did get through consecutive sentences. I saw two and sometimes three objects that vibrated sort of like in the 1950's TV show when Froggy twanged his magic twanger. Froggy sat on a spring. I could no longer look at a computer screen without becoming nauseous.

I went to an acupuncturist a few times whom I had gone to before. She was startled by my appearance. She noted that numerous muscles weren't working and had atrophied. She had me start taking digestive enzymes and bromelain to help me with my digestion problems as well as omega-3 oils, gingko biloba, Vitamin C and B's, Co-Q10 enzymes and chromium picolinate, all vitamins and herbs recommended for brain injuries. The insurance company only approved four sessions with the acupuncturist and wouldn't pay for the vitamins and herbs.

> Consequences of TBI (traumatic brain injury) can include: increased anxiety, depression and mood swings, impulsive behavior, more easily

agitated, egocentric behaviors; difficulty seeing how behaviors can affect others. (See Bibliography, 3-4).

On January 13, I woke up and started to cry. I remembered that someone told me once that no one ever cried to death. I wasn't so sure. No matter what I did or what anyone said I could not stop. The crying went on for hours and hours.

One of my therapists told me that these crying jags are called psychotic breaks and typical of head injury.

Vehicle crashes are the leading cause of brain injury. Falls are the second leading cause, and the leading cause of brain injury in the elderly. (See Bibliography, 3-5). In sports, a majority of head injuries occur in bicycle, skateboard and skating accidents. Children receive 21% of brain injuries, 800 bicyclists die each year, 2/3 of the deaths are from brain injury—45-88% could be prevented by wearing a helmet. It costs $81 million per year because no helmet is worn. The indirect cost of not wearing a helmet is $2.3 billion a year. (See Bibliography, 3-6). A helmet costs between $10 and $15. (See Bibliography, 3-7). About 21% of childhood injuries occur in sport-related accidents and 62% of injuries occur during practice. (See Bibliography, 3-8).

Cycling is the number one cause of TBI death in sports. (See Bibliography, 3-9).

# Chapter Four
## Optometric Testing—
## Is It All In My Head?

A few months after the accident, the chiropractor had me start doing Pilates and other exercises with his wife as the instructor. The exercises made my back and legs hurt worse. I was still so dizzy that it seemed I couldn't find the floor to fall down on. My head still hurt like crazy, but I was doing the exercises.

My daughter saw Pam and one of her friends at the Community Center. Pam's friend's daughter had just wrecked her car a few days earlier. Pam quite proudly told my daughter who worked for an insurance company that she was just telling her friend how surprised my daughter was when the insurance company comped (comprehensive) her claim instead of calling it collision. Pam then told my daughter, "I guess that just shows that you can get your own way if you whine hard enough." I just shook my head when I heard this. (If her claim had been called collision, she would have had to pay a deductible plus her rates probably would have gone way up and she could possibly have been dumped by her insurance company).

Usually it is difficult to predict the outcome of TBI during the first hours, days or weeks. In fact, the outcome may remain unknown for many months or years. (See Bibliography, 4-1).

As the months went by, I continued to go downhill. In Pilates I couldn't get my left side to obey commands. My body trembled from the exertion, tears ran down my face and my head wobbled from side-to-side just trying to lift my left arm or leg. I didn't think the instructor was "getting it" that there was maybe something more that was wrong with me.

The chiropractor just kept saying, "We've got to get you back to work [painting] or the insurance company is going to cut us off, or they're going to start questioning if I haven't released you to go back to work because we're friends." I was questioning my sanity by then and wondered what was wrong with me.

I couldn't figure out how I was going to get up on a ladder when I was still not sure where earth was and how I was going to paint because when I looked anywhere but straight ahead I fell over.

At my other job I kept forgetting to writing contracts and send them out. When my boss came in he would always ask me if anyone had called. I usually said, "No. It's been quiet all day." Later I would find a pile of messages I had taken dated that day.

Cognitive consequences of TBI can include: short-term memory loss, long-term memory loss; slowed ability to process information; trouble concentrating or paying attention for periods of time; difficulty keeping up with a conversation, other communications difficulties such as word finding problems; spatial disorientation; organizational problems and impaired judgment; unable to do more than one thing at a time; a lack of initiating activities, or once started, difficulty in completing tasks with reminders. (See Bibliography, 4-2).

My regular claims adjustor went on vacation. During the interim a nice lady took his spot. I told her that I could not paint because of my balance, visual and pain problems. She asked me if I was getting lost wages money for the painting. I told her it was the first I had heard that I could do that and had actually been told that I couldn't because my painting was only part time. (See "Indicative or Contributory Signs of Bad Faith", page 441 numbers 34 and 35).

I got together all of my paint invoices and sent them in. I started getting lost wages. The only problem was that I was making a lot more money painting than I could receive from insurance but, by law, I could only collect up to $400 per week in lost wages. Thank God I didn't have a house payment or car payment to make. I was only taking home $189 a week at my part-time job.

A massage therapist told me about a behavioral optometrist who worked with vision problems associated with auto accidents. I asked my chiropractor to write a script for me to go see her. He said, "Not yet."

I switched my Pilates instructor to one of the chiropractors in the office who was also Pilates trained. She started questioning if I had some motor neuron/brain stem problems. I couldn't do the dead bug exercise (you lift opposite arm and leg at the same time). It was torture for me to even attempt the exercises. She told me that I was getting worse. That was so confusing to me.

As time went by, my vision continued to deteriorate, or perhaps I was just becoming aware of it. I finally made an appointment and went to see the optometrist on my own without a referral from the doctor. I told her about the accident, and she gave me a head injury questionnaire. I was amazed that someone had put into a neat little package what I was experiencing. It was the first time I had contemplated that I, perhaps, had a brain injury. I was still too confused, however, to realize the impact this would have on my life.

The optometrist had me do hours of visual testing with one of her vision therapists. She had me try to walk on a balance beam. I could not lift my left foot onto the beam unless I started with my right foot. My left foot crossed over the right just as it had for months. She had me put on prism lenses with my glasses and, eureka! I could lift my foot a few inches and did not trip as badly as before. I could also hold my head straighter without falling over or throwing up. I was still nauseous but not nearly as badly.

I actually had 20/20 vision in both eyes when I went for the exam. The number did not take into consideration that the brain does not know how to process what the eyes are seeing or the depth of what a person is looking at.

The testing showed that my stereo acuity, which measures depth perception, was at 100 seconds of arc with 20 seconds of arc being normal. No wonder I didn't know where the floor was!

My ocular motility or eye movement efficiency was inadequate.

On the report, my doctor wrote that when I was asked to track an object in space, I did so "with full and restricted motilities, yet jerky and poorly controlled eye movement. This skill allows spatial orientation while moving, rapid and accurate shifting of the eyes along the lines of print in a book and sure tracking in sports."

The Jordan Left-Right Reversal Test "measures the ability to differentiate between correctly oriented numbers and letters and those that are reversed." I scored in the 64 percentile or 12.6 years of age in the developmental rank.

On the Test of Visual Perceptual Skills—Upper Level, which "is designed to determine visual perceptual strengths and weaknesses based on non-motor responses" I scored a whopping 25 on visual memory and a 1 on visual Sequential Memory. This was out of a possible 100.

The Beery Visual Motor Integration Test, a copy test form, was extremely difficult for me. In this test I was instructed to copy forms from a template onto a piece of paper. The difficulty level increased throughout the test. The problems I had in this area included: "completing paperwork in a timely fashion, poor or inconsistent handwriting and difficulty completing a motor task with visual input (such as painting.)" My age level: <14.0 years old. Percentile rank: 21st.

The Visagraph Integration Test "monitors the ability to move the eyes appropriately and as a team while doing visual skills tasks and while reading." This test showed that I did not move my eyes as a team and my visual skills showed a reading level of grade equivalent 10.4.

Ouch! There were many parts of the tests that I could not take because I could not look at the images without becoming ill. It took me much longer to take the part of the test that I could take than average people.

My optometrist sent the test results to the insurance company with a request for eighteen sessions of vision therapy and prism glasses. They wrote back and asked her how she was able to justify my vision problems being associated with the accident. She wrote back to them with detailed information. They denied the claim. (See "Indicative and 37, 441, 442, Signs of Bad Faith, pages 4numbers 3, 34, 35, 36, 39, 40).

I went back to my chiropractor and asked him to write a prescription for the glasses and for therapy. It made him mad, or at least I perceived that it did, because his face and ears turned red. He haughtily told me, "We don't usually send people to optometrists until the sixth month." I told him it had already been five and a half months and that I just couldn't see. That didn't help my case much. But he wrote the prescription.

He also wrote a prescription stating he was releasing me to go back to work painting that he didn't bother to tell me about. About a month later when I did not receive my check for lost wages is when I learned this.

> Vision system deficits affect more than half of all persons with traumatic brain injury treated in long term rehabilitation facilities (Garzia &

Harris, 1998). Unfortunately, many such persons "fall through the cracks" because they are not diagnosed or treated. Instead, these individuals may be inappropriately labeled as "agitated," "clumsy," "uncooperative during treatment," "cognitively impaired," "confused," "malingerers," "psychologically disturbed," or "performance impaired." Disruption of the visual pathways is of particular interest because the effects are so far reaching and can directly affect activities of daily living. (See Bibliography, 4-3).

    I had been having massages at the chiropractor's office also with two very good massage therapists. He decided to drop their wage to $20 per session even though he was charging the insurance company $118.40 per forty minute hour. They quit. I was now only allowed to go to the one massage therapist left who would agree to do auto claims work at $20 per hour. He had bony elbows that he dug into my back, bad breath and talked the whole time about his girlfriend.

    The next time I saw the chiropractor for an adjustment he said he was thinking of sending me to a clinic for positive thinking. I was startled. I told him I was thinking positively. I was just being realistic and knew there was something not right. Then I asked him why I was so dizzy and what was wrong with me. He tapped the side of his head with his index finger and said, "It's all up here." I did not see him again as a chiropractor, but when he wasn't there, I did continue to see the other two chiropractors in his office for a few months.

# Chapter Five
## Insurance—
## An Alternate Reality

The original Claims Adjustor I had was replaced by a woman who had never adjusted claims, sounded quite excited to start in her new position and hinted that the last guy had been fired from his position.

Everything that I ran past her, she would sweetly say, "If it is reasonable, necessary and related to the accident the insurance company will cover it." Then she told me that she would check with her supervisor and get back to me. Of course, when she got back to me there was always the excuse that I would have to prove my case. This was always followed by a resounding "no". I pictured this woman with large, unblinking eyes and with a head that was on a spring and could only move in the "no" direction. The insurance company had now shot down my request for acupuncture, vision therapy and prism glasses. (See "Indicative or Contributory Signs of Bad Faith", pages 437, 439, 440, 441, 443, 444, numbers 3, 14, 17, 22, 24, 35, 44, 48, and 54).

The insurance adjustor also told my caregivers that they had to get pre-approval for any type of care. When they asked for approval, the adjustor would tell them that they do not give pre-approval. That will pretty well cut out anyone doing work on a person unless the person pays upfront out of pocket. It is then up to the patient to collect from the insurance company. At that point in the process, the insurance company would deny my claims because they said I didn't get pre-approval from them to be treated. I kid you not. (See Indicative and Contributory Signs of Bad Faith, pages 437, 440, numbers 1, 2, and 24).

In late 2003, the managed healthcare industry announced operating profits for the first six month period in 2003 to have increased upwards of some 250% to $255B...and are planning for further double-digit increases in premiums for 2004. (See Bibliography, 5-1).

My insurance company switched from one managed care provider to another one. In the meantime, all requests would have to go through the new provider. Imagine the speed that this company could take with a sudden influx of thousands of claims. Not only that, but there were literally no doctors with the new managed care network within ninety miles of where I lived. I found out later that since there was no doctor within twenty-five miles of my home that I could have gone to whomever I wanted to and managed care would have had to pay for it, the detail of which was not relayed to me by the adjustor. Unfortunately, if that doctor did not become a member of the managed care and someone in the twenty-five mile radius did, I would then be required to switch doctors.

I found out that the managed care companies charged the doctor applying to the network $750 to become a member. Since most of the care providers in our area were with the previous managed care provider, many had to scurry and pay out the money and wait for several months so that they could treat people. The doctors also were paid a "re-priced" amount of money. The co-pay that people pay to the doctor is what the managed care keeps out of what they pay the doctor, and the managed care only pays the doctor what their schedule says the particular procedure being performed is worth. (Also, if a patient does not pay their co-pay, the doctor can lose his contract with the managed care company).

(Then again, in August, 2004, one of the major health insurance carriers in Colorado switched managed care providers leaving hundreds of insured patients without a doctor they were allowed to go to in their area and, once again, the doctors had to come up with money and fill out applications then wait for months to get approved by the new managed care company).

I spoke with one doctor who said the only way she could stay in business was to become a managed care provider since almost everyone now had opted for a managed care provider on their insurance policy in the belief that they would save money. This added an enormous amount of paperwork for the doctors and a lot of frustration because of the added time it took to get approval for any procedure or treatment.

One therapist I spoke with said she spent forty hours a week doing therapy and sixty hours a week doing letters and paperwork for the insurance companies. She said that many times she had to re-file the insurance papers four or five times. The insurance companies told her that they never received the paperwork or that it might have gotten misplaced. This game would often go on for months, even though by law, an insurance company has thirty days to reimburse a provider, therefore, the "lost" paperwork. Another doctor I spoke with said that she sent claims to some specific insurance companies certified-registered and to a specific claims adjustor so that they couldn't tell her they hadn't received the paperwork.

The risk of TBI is highest among adolescents, young adults and those older than 75. (See Bibliography, 5-2). Although 10% of all TBI's are from firearms, they account for 44% of TBI deaths. Nine out of ten of these victims die and are usually between 15 and 24 years of age. African-Americans have the highest incidence of death. (See Bibliography, 5-3).

I met with an attorney about filing a personal injury lawsuit. He had to call an attorney friend of his about every fifth question. It did not take me long to realize that this guy probably did not know what he was doing. I never went back to him. I left several messages with other personal injury attorneys in my area but did not hear from any of them except one several months later. Since it took him two months to get back to me I decided that he was probably not in my best interest.

My friend John and I went to Washington, D.C. to visit my daughter. I couldn't figure out where I was. The city where I had known the Metro system was now a terrifying mystery. John had to grab me several times to keep me from falling onto the Metro tracks or down steps. I couldn't walk on the marble and granite floors without developing terrifying nausea because I felt like I was falling.

I got in trouble and argued with a security person at the Phillips Museum for pointing too closely at a painting. She said I was closer than six inches to the painting. I kept telling her that I was more than 6" away when I pointed. My daughter told me that I was only a couple inches away. Of course, I argued with her about that.

I spent most of my time sleeping when we weren't moving. When I got back home to Colorado, I slept like the dead for days.

There was no improvement in my condition, which actually appeared to get worse.

> Individuals with severe brain injury typically face five to ten years of intensive rehabilitation with cumulative costs exceeding $35 billion annually. There are approximately 3,000 deaths yearly in 0-14 year olds. There are 29,000 hospital stays, 400,000 ER visits, and 300,000 sports related TBI's. (See Bibliography, 5-4). Of the sports-related injuries, 67,000 are from bicycle accidents. (See Bibliography, 5-5). One in 124,000 amusement park riders receive a significant injury that is detected. (See Bibliography, 5-6).

One day I was talking to a woman who, after a while, asked me if I had a brain injury. I told her that I was questioning that myself and asked her why she wondered. She said because she had a brain injury and recognized some of the problems I was having, such as finding words and mixing up words in my sentences.

She gave me the name of a doctor in Aspen who was her primary care doctor and said that this woman knew brain injury. She said she had been to a few doctors who told her that there was nothing wrong with her. She also told me about a therapist in Boulder who was a cognitive therapist. She gave me the phone numbers for these two women. I called and made appointments.

At least three times a week I had an argument with the claims adjustor. Fortunately I took notes of what she told me because the next time I talked to her she would change her story and say something totally different. She would become quite indignant and swear that she hadn't said what I told her she said. Then I would read back to her from my notes, and she would shut right up. I would then tell her that I didn't appreciate being lied to. At least she told me that the insurance company had admitted that I had a brain injury.

The chiropractor/Pilates instructor I was now seeing as a primary doctor wrote a prescription for six sessions of acupuncture. The insurance company approved the six sessions. What was very frustrating at this point was that each and every month I had to get a prescription from a doctor to collect my lost wages.

I called Pam's insurance company and asked for pictures of the vehicle to use in the therapy I knew I would need. The very rude claims adjustor I spoke to said I would have to ask Pam for the pictures. I wrote a note to Pam and asked her to contact her insurance company so they could send the pictures to me. (It is my understanding that she did call the insurance company. Her company's claims adjustor called my claims adjustor and told him that he would have to request the pictures. He requested the pictures, which is not the way it is supposed to be done in the first place. They denied him the pictures and said that Pam would have to receive them herself then give the pictures to me. Of course, that never happened.) (See "Indicative or Contributory Signs of Bad Faith, page 440, number 24).

I learned shortly after that that Pam's claims adjustor had been "let go."

# Chapter Six
## Cognitive Testing—
## I Should Have Passed Out

On June 7, 2002, my daughter and I drove to Boulder for a meeting with Dr. Mary Ann Keatley. Mary Ann would become my cognitive and speech therapist. She immediately recognized that I had a brain injury and wrote a letter to the insurance company and to my employer stating that I needed to quit my job because the number of therapy appointments I would need to attend would make it impossible for me to even work part-time. She wanted me to get to Boulder, a 400 mile round trip, at least once a week but preferred twice a week.

I started to cry. I felt ashamed, embarrassed that I was in a situation to have to ask for help. My self-confidence was shattered.

Mary Ann and I discussed my intense stomach pains, digestive problem, choking, and hoarseness. Mary Ann thought that I probably had damaged the vagus nerve. She also told me that people who are unconscious after an accident or in a coma for a short time have been found to actually get better faster than people who do not lose consciousness because it gives the brain (computer) time to reset itself.

Oh, great! Here I had fought to stay conscious.

Mary Ann explained to me that people who have a brain injury need to be in cognitive therapy within a few weeks of receiving an injury so that their brain doesn't lose more of what it had stored in it. It had been almost seven months since my injury so it sounded to me like I had an uphill battle. I guess the chiropractor's statement about waiting six months to find out how well a person will heal was erroneous….

By the time I had my first meeting with my cognitive therapist, my cognitive and physical symptoms had become even more apparent. When I remembered to, I wrote these symptoms down. Besides what I've already mentioned, these included: I dropped things, knocked things over, didn't recognize people I knew before the accident, forgot to go to appointments, couldn't remember what day of the week it was, had no sense of time, couldn't remember if I had eaten or not that day, drove to an appointment and kept going because I forgot where I was headed. I would turn around and head back once I remembered and would drive by the place again. It usually took three or four shots before I arrived at where I was headed. I got lost going to my daughter's house and couldn't recognize the neighborhood I was in. My temper blew up. I couldn't sit through a movie, not just because of pain, but I was over-loaded visually and mentally. Loud sound drove me nuts.

If over-stimulated, I got horrible headaches that left me with memory loss for that time period or I would become so nauseous or dizzy that I could not function. I had to talk my way through things that used to be automatic. Music other than light classical made me violently ill and disoriented for several hours. I could hear and see words in the back of my head (when I could find the word) but couldn't get them to my mouth.

I could no longer do my own banking. Just looking at the deposit slips made me physically ill and I could not do the math and got numbers backwards and out of sequence. It often took three or four attempts to spell a word correctly. I couldn't learn new information because I couldn't recall it. My attention was almost non-existent.

Grocery stores and all other stores made me dizzy and disoriented. I could not tell where I was stepping because of the shine on the floors and the dark/light patterns of the tiles and the dreaded fluorescent lights. I could not tell if the floor was actually going down like in a drop-off or if it was flat. All floors looked lower than they were and appeared to be slanting downward. I had to hang on for dear life going down steps because I could not judge their depth.

I avoided crossing streets where there were crosswalks because the white patterns on the black asphalt felt as if they were leaping up to swallow me. I often had to slam myself up against a wall or pillar if I stepped into a place with pillow-top tile. The sidewalk at my optometrist's office was false-brick concrete. By the time I got to her office, I was ready to ask for a bucket. Finally, my vision therapist started meeting me in the parking lot. I closed my eyes and she led me into the building.

Words were still coming out mixed up, as were sentences. Something as simple as "please pass the potatoes" came out "una matta potato". It was still difficult for me to organize a routine and to begin or finish a task.

I started having vivid dreams about when I was a child, complete with family members and people I had known but hadn't seen for forty to fifty years. In these dreams, I even saw the people decked out with their "tailfin" eyeglasses.

My roommate told me that I would be in the middle of a conversation and just start staring. I would later learn that this was probably a catatonic state. Oftentimes I would find myself someplace and not remember how I got there. I put garbage in the refrigerator and things in the oven that were supposed to go in the freezer.

My face still twisted up on the right when I got tired. My eyesight was better with the prism glasses, for which the insurance company still had not reimbursed me, but it was far from normal. The optometrist still had not been reimbursed for the exam and testing.

Mary Ann asked me if I was getting essential services. I had no idea what she was talking about. She explained to me that essential services provided money, usually for up to twenty-seven hours a week, to help take care of someone who has been injured. I told her that I was doing just fine and could take care of myself. She could tell that I was not just fine and urged me to reconsider my stance.

Mary Ann had me take the Woodcock-Johnson Psycho-Educational Battery test. I scored in the 82 percentile for someone who had finished high school. (I actually have five college degrees and certifications. I was doing painting and part-time work because I wanted a change of pace in my life….). The lowest scores were in the reasoning area (58%) or at a grade percentile of 20%, visual perceptual speed area (58%) with a grade percentile of 19%, and memory at the 68 percentile with a grade percentile of 75%.

Mary Ann stated in her report that "the reasoning cluster consists of a combination of analysis-synthesis, concept formation, analogies, and antonyms and synonyms. Her difficulties with reasoning were readily apparent on the concept formation subtest when the patient was unable to utilize strategies to solve problems that she had performed correctly on previous items. She became very overloaded and missed eight items in the middle of this subtest and could not seem to understand the concept in solving the problems." The analogies subtest was also difficult and she stated that 'I don't understand what you're looking for,' when trying to find the relationship between word concepts." The perceptual speed subtests are timed tests which require the individual to visually match numbers as well as spatially relate shapes. In order to compensate for her visual difficulties she was very slow and methodical on the number matching task, as well as when matching shapes."

"The memory cluster requires an individual to repeat back sentences of increasing length and syntactical complexity. The WJPEB measures only immediate and not short-term memory. It was more difficult for her to repeat back numbers in reverse order and she revealed delays and perseverations on this task. When repeating back sentences of increasing length and complexity, her performance was slow but primarily accurate. She reports that sometimes she forgets what people tell her as well as what she has read and sometimes forgets significant information like where she has parked her car."

"Specific examples of word finding difficulties revealed an extremely slow processing time as well as paraphasic word errors. This may affect her ability to communicate in her functional home environment as well as her job."

"Difficulties in functional memory may affect the patient's ability to meet appointments and recall what individuals have told her. This may affect her ability to perform her job as a secretary as this requires good multi-track thinking skills as well as memory skills."

Her recommendations:
1. Use an organizational notebook and be counseled regarding the need to perform only one task at a time, routinize daily activities and document all significant information.
2. Language treatment is recommended in order to improve word retrieval skills through sentence completions, antonyms, synonyms, analogies and categories.
3. Work in the area of executive functions is recommended in order to increase awareness related to cognitive and language deficits as well as improve self-initiation, goal setting, self-correction skills and strategic behaviors.

4. Attention process training is recommended in order to increase sustained and divided attention in quiet as well as noise.
5. Functional memory strategies should be provided in order to help compensate during these initial phases following her accident. This may include an organizational notebook.
6. Remediative memory strategies should also be worked on in the treatment program.
7. Work in the area of speed and capacity of information processing and multi-track thinking should also be addressed at this time to help improve her word retrieval skills.
8. She should obtain a visual-perceptual evaluation by a behavioral optometrist to determine her visual functioning and whether this is contributing to her dizziness.
9. The patient may want to obtain a psychological evaluation in order to determine the presence of post-traumatic stress disorder as well as learn coping strategies to deal with the trauma of the accident.
10. A complete neuropsychological evaluation is scheduled in the near future, and this will better define areas where she is experiencing difficulties. It will also provide additional information on higher-level cognitive functions, such as speed and capacity of

information processing, multitrack thinking and short-term memory.

I was told that if I was a man with the same brain injuries, because of where the injuries were in my brain, I would probably be incapacitated and in a wheelchair. (Men are left-hemisphere dominant and women are more right-brain dominant but tend to use both sides of the brain.)

There are two types of traumatic brain injury: "closed head injury (CHI) and "open head injury" (OHI). CHI is usually caused by a rapid acceleration and deceleration of the head during which the brain is whipped back and forth, thus bouncing off the inside of the skull. The stress of this rapid movement pulls apart nerve fibers and causes damage to the activated system of neuro-fibers which send out messages to all parts of the body. (See Bibliography, 6-1).

I spoke with my Claims Adjustor and told her that the cognitive therapist confirmed that I had a brain injury. She sounded very excited. She told me that she had just been to a seminar about head injury and they listed the symptoms that I had told her about. Her exact words were, "Oh, wow! I just went to a seminar on head injury!"

A few days after this conversation, I was talking to my daughter who lived in D. C. While looking out the window I spotted a huge plume of smoke that just kept creeping around the mountain. My younger daughter lived north of me around the mountain and in the west part of town. Finally I told my older daughter that I had to go because I believed that my younger daughter's hill was on fire. What I did next is just an example of the stupid things I would do because of my head injury.

I got in my car and headed for my daughter's house. I noticed that the sky was orange. As I went over the bridge and headed west, there was a huge wall of fire about a mile away coming toward me. The fire had split. One side jumped the railroad tracks, the river, and four lanes of interstate highway and was burning toward her house. The other split continued on its way toward my house.

I continued on, driving against the parking lot of cars filled with horrified drivers trying to get away from the flames. When I got to my daughter's house I found a ladder and crawled through a window to get inside. (Her roommate had panicked, left all the lights on, the windows open and locked the door).

I was a woman driven.

My daughter had been working on a manual for her work and was almost done with it. She had been working from home and I couldn't see those months of hard work go up in flames. Ironically, she was a regional trainer for an insurance company.

Once inside, I couldn't see from one end of the house to the other because the smoke was so thick. I threw a bunch of clothes into suitcases (not her favorite clothes I found out later—her favorite ones were in the dryer), wheeled the suitcase to the car and left the house. I started back down the hill and remembered her computer. The cops were swarming through the streets shouting on their PA's for everyone to drop everything and evacuate NOW! I turned the car around, went back up the hill to her house, grabbed her laptop and stumbled back outside through the smoke-thickened air.

I started back down the hill and got about twenty yards and that was pretty much the end of the road. I was now a member of the bumper-to-bumper parking lot club.

I could hear explosions from gas and propane tanks. Cinders and ash were floating through the car. The temperature had to be at least 140 degrees. There was no way I could have the windows up because I dared not turn the air conditioner on. I had a painter's mask in the back of the car and put that on. The smoke was so thick by now that I could only see about three cars ahead of me. People were leaving their cars, running back to their houses and coming back with wet washcloths to put over their mouths. Trees were bent in half from the gusting, fire-driven wind. The roar from the fire was like a train coming at us. I wondered if I should just abandon the car and run.

Oh, yea, I couldn't run.

The line of cars crawled forward inches at a time.

Finally we started moving.

It took me an hour and forty-five minutes to drive the four miles to and from her house. I got back to my house and started packing my important "stuff". I stood and watched out the window at the flames creeping closer and closer. The mountainside where my daughter's house stood was now a ball of flames. I could not imagine that her house was still standing.

My daughter arrived with her boyfriend of the time. She said, "We're leaving now." They loaded my important "stuff" in my car. I looked around the brand new condominium built up against the side of the mountain that I had just moved into two months prior to that and wondered why I had all that "stuff". The important "stuff" didn't fill my car and half of it was optional "important".

We were evacuated from our homes for five days. Some friends of my daughters managed a motel in a nearby town. They let us stay there free of charge.

And, miracle of miracles, when we were allowed back home, my daughter's house was still standing.

Mine was, too.

And, of course, the training manual for my daughter's work was forwarded every day to the main server.

# Chapter Seven
## "Dr. Dapper" and the Broken String

    I was supposed to start vision therapy on June 12, 2002. The day before my appointment, the receptionist at the optometrist's office called and said they couldn't start the therapy because the insurance company wouldn't approve it. She also said that they still had not been paid for the testing that had been done in April. I still had not been reimbursed for the money I had paid out for the prism glasses even though it was past the thirty-day limit.

    I called the claims adjustor who, like a broken doll, just kept repeating in her high-pitched, syrupy-sweet voice, "...if it's reasonable, necessary, and related to the accident." I kept telling her that I didn't have the problem before the accident. I actually wondered if she had a string with a little plastic loop at the end of it hanging out of her back because I could swear I heard little plastic gears meshing together as they rotated around.

Physical consequences of brain injury can include: seizures of all types, muscle spasticity, double vision or low vision, even blindness, loss of smell or taste, speech impairments such as slow or slurred speech, headaches or migraines, fatigue, increased need for sleep and balance problems; and paralysis on either or both sides. (See Bibliography, 7-1). Non-neurological complications include, but are certainly not limited to, pulmonary, metabolic, nutritional, gastrointestinal, musculoskeletal, and dermatologic problems. (See Bibliography, 7-2).

    I made an appointment with a semi-retired neurosurgeon so that an MRI could be ordered to rule out brain lesions and hematomas. He, quite frankly, probably should have gone ahead and retired. He was a relatively sweet old man, very structured and quite dapper in his turtleneck shirt that he wore under his white lab coat that had his name stitched over the left pocket.

    It did not seem that he knew much about the American Brain Injury Association's definition of brain injury. He just said they sometimes see symptoms get worse several months after an accident. He told me the symptoms would go away. He also said that swelling in the brain is gone within five days, an old school thought. (Numerous doctors and therapists have told me that the brain swelling does not go away within five days but often takes months as substantiated by numerous articles by medical personnel).

    He asked me about my accident and what I had been experiencing since the accident. I had taken my notes with me because I had such a terrible time remembering more than one or two items of anything. I tried to give him a copy of my notes. He declined the notes and asked me to tell him the symptoms in my own words.

I told him that I had gotten lost driving to the hospital where his office was located, which is quite difficult to do since it was six blocks from where I lived in a town with a width of six streets and a length of twenty-eight streets. I told him I couldn't remember things, kept falling down, kept getting lost, couldn't remember things and kept falling down. These were pretty much the three things I kept repeating, but he still didn't want me to look at my notes even after telling him the same things over and over. I think I changed the order occasionally.

I was able to tell him more of my physical symptoms since they were with me almost all of the time. I told him I had double vision. He jumped to the conclusion that I was referring to the double vision (astigmatism) I had since I was young. I kept trying to tell him that this double vision was different. This was the kind of double vision where I would actually see two or three people or objects that were separate and vibrating, like a camera double or triple exposure. He never did understand what I was trying to explain to him. It seemed that his demeanor wouldn't have allowed room for the "twang your magic twanger, Froggy" comparison.

He had me do several exercises. I couldn't find the tip of my nose with my finger, especially with my left hand. When directed to walk toe-to-toe, I had to hang onto him because I couldn't drag my left foot in front of my right foot without falling over. He had me close my eyes and tip my head back. I fell backwards into his exam table.

After the physical exam, we discussed what treatment I needed to do. I took notes. He said I needed to do cognitive therapy, visual therapy, cranial sacral, chiropractic, and see an ear specialist for my dizziness. He said I had what is known as post-concussive syndrome, (also known as traumatic brain injury).

A few days later I got a copy of his written report. His report was so far off base with information that I questioned if he was confusing me with someone else. He had me in the wrong vehicle, stated that I took over-the-counter drugs on a daily basis. (I didn't even own aspirin!) He stated that my x-rays were unremarkable even though he hadn't seen them and had no reports to support his statement. He said my leg pain at night was "cramping, like you get from sports".

The important aspects of his report state that he was "not able to appreciate her extraocular muscle weakness, though her diplopia (double vision) gets worse on downward gaze to the right. Her cranial nerves otherwise appear unremarkable though she describes some mild decrease sensation to touch in the left side of the face compared to the right. There is no facial asymmetry. Her weber does not lateralize. Air conduction is better than bone conduction bilaterally. Motor, sensory, and cerebellar functions appear okay, with the exception that she has difficulty with rapid alternating movements with either upper extremity. Reflexes are 1+ in the upper and lower extremities with down-going Babinskies"—(a brain injury symptom.) Romberg and tandem gait are performed satisfactorily."

He further states that she "is a very complicated case with a lot of symptoms that are of concern, though I am not sure that I can relate a number of them to her automobile accident. Her fourth nerve palsy is of some concern, as are some of her other symptoms, though her exam appears somewhat better than the symptoms that she described."

After he received the MRI report, which showed no hematomas or lesions of the brain, he wrote, "I suspect that many of her headache complaints and other symptoms are due to the psychological component of her accident, and she may need some counseling for those complaints."

His impression was that I have "a headache, fourth nerve palsy, rule out structural lesions."

I knew I had a headache…!

There are several reasons why a vision deficit may go undiagnosed. Health professionals may be unaware that a vision deficit can actually be a source of a person's poor performance or poor behavior. (See Bibliography, 7-3).

A week later I had an appointment with Dr. Scannell.

Dr. Scannell immediately recognized the problems I had and flatly stated that I had a brain injury. I told her that I had seen Dr. Cecil, the optometrist, and that she had prescribed prism lenses and eighteen sessions of vision therapy. I told her about my meeting with Mary Ann, the cognitive therapist, and she agreed that I needed the cognitive therapy and the other therapies that Mary Ann recommended.

Then I told Dr. Scannell about the neurosurgeon and what he had said. She got quite upset and said she was writing a hand-written letter to the insurance company so they would get it right away. She stated that I had frontal, occipital, left Broca's and left parietal lobe injuries. She further stated that I had severe disabilities involving my vision for which I required special glasses; motor and verbal dysfunction requiring extensive occupational and physical therapy; massage; acupuncture; chiropractic; speech therapy. She wrote that "these measures are essential to her recovery" and that "her disabilities stem directly from the car accident—there is no question that she will need these therapies."

Dr. Scannell further told me that she wanted me to get approval to get treatment in the hyperbaric chamber and have a PT scan.

The letter was sent to the insurance company.

The insurance company said they wouldn't approve anything because they understood that I had gone to a neurosurgeon and were waiting for the report from him. They also said it was because Dr. Scannell was not part of their managed care.

In the meantime, my daughter and I fired off a letter to the neurosurgeon asking him if maybe he got me mixed up with another patient. We listed all the incorrect information. I spoke to his secretary about the absurdity of his letter, all of the mistakes and asked that she not send the report until the errors were fixed and I could read it. She promised me that she would call me to read the report before she sent it. A few weeks later I found out that the report was sent anyway.

Okay! By now I was ready to have a nervous breakdown. I was still arguing with my claims adjustor several times a week. The insurance company denied me any treatment because of the neurosurgeon's letter including psychological treatment even though that is what he said I needed. I was sleeping restlessly only a few hours a night, if at all. I was absolutely rigid from worry that I was never going to get the help that I needed. (See "Indicative and Contributory Signs of Bad Faith, page 441, 442, numbers 34, 35 and 36).

Then my claims adjustor informed me that I was to be scheduled for four IME's, Independent Medical Exams, with a chiropractor, an optometrist, a neuro-psychologist and a rehabilitation doctor. Since I was with a managed care, the word independent should have been deleted from the equation. I did not receive a list of five doctors from the state, which is usually what happens if you are not with a PPO. In a PPO scenario, of the five names received, the patient crosses off two names, the insurance company crosses off two names and the patient goes to the doctor that has not been crossed out. With a managed care you go to the doctor they tell you to go to. Loving managed care more and more…. (See "Indicative and Contributory Signs of Bad Faith", pages 441, 442, numbers 27 and 41).

My claims adjustor told me about the IME's on July 5, 2002. The only synonym I am able to comprehend at this point in my brain-injured vocabulary is auto insurance/alternate reality.

I went to see my insurance agent and told him how badly the insurance company was treating me. He said he would talk to the claims adjustor and get back to me. When I returned to his office he told me he had told the adjustor that he knew me before the accident, that I was fun and funny and quite active. He said he told her that he didn't recognize the person I was now—that my speech was slow and fouled up, that I could hardly walk. He said the comparison was "like Jekyll and Hyde". He then told me that my adjustor was pretty new and that she was denying my medical and therapy requests because she was, and I quote, "covering her ass."

I called and met with a personal injury attorney in Boulder who was ranked one of the best personal injury attorneys in Colorado in Who's Who. He wasn't surprised at all by the way the insurance company treated me when I told him what company it was and said that it was one of the worst and that I needed to change carriers as soon as possible.

He explained how complicated my case was going to be. First of all, the accident happened out of state. Secondly, the accident happened on an

Indian Reservation, a.k.a. Sovereign Nation, which is considered not a part of the United States. Third, my ex friend had a terrible insurance policy. He questioned if her policy was even legal because there was only $1,000 in PIP coverage and had the exclusion clause for out-of-state accidents involving non-family members. (I later checked my policy and discovered that I had the same exclusion clause).

The attorney said we might have to file the lawsuit in Arizona where the statute of limitations is two years. There was a possibility that they would bounce it to Federal Court.

He checked the statutes and said we could start out filing in the county where we both lived (the law is that a suit must be filed in the county where the defendant lives), but he was pretty sure they would bounce it to Federal Court anyway. Also, the driver's insurance policy was legal. He couldn't believe any agent would sell someone a policy with such shady exclusions or that anyone would purchase such a policy. He asked me if the policy was a part of her business insurance. I told him that it was and he said he sees bad policies a lot in businesses because it is cheaper for the owner but not better.

The attorney further advised me to see a doctor who specialized in balance and dizziness problems. He said that someone from his office would call me within the next week to interview me about the accident. He told me not to talk to the insurance company because he was going to call them and see what was going on. He also told me that, no matter what my financial status, to not sign with an attorney who said they would get me a "quick settlement" as head injury symptoms generally take a long time to manifest and a long time to know if they are going to go away.

I left his office with a tremendous load taken off of my shoulders.

I started getting price quotes from insurance companies to replace my insurance carrier. I was now listed in the computer as someone who had been in an accident within the past two years and too high of a risk to sign with unless I was willing to pay almost triple rates. Even though I argued that I was a passenger, not the driver, I was told that it did not matter in a state with no-fault insurance because the computer showed that I had been in an accident

> ...According to the rules and regulations of the industry, if the insurer is not happy or satisfied with the [first] reporting agency's report and rating, it has the option to suppress its publications and go elsewhere to have a second financial rating agency report and rating done. In addition, it has been alleged that there is one agency that financially rates

insurers that is not paid by insurers, that is Weiss Ratings, out of a total of approximately four or five widely used financial rating agencies that are paid by insurers to rate them, which include A.M. Best, Fitch, Moodys and S&P. A 1995 study by the GAO indicated that Weiss and Moody's assigned insurers fewer top ratings out of the five agencies providing the service. (See Bibliography, 7-4).

# Chapter Eight
## Guided Introspection Brain Injury Inventory— Is Someone Reading My Mind?

"Saccades" is a term used to describe rapid scanning eye movements used when we are looking to quickly focus our visual attention on something. Because the eye movements are so quick during saccades, not all of the images we "see" with our eyes are processed by the brain. Some images must be left out for us to perceive a clear image of what we are focusing on. (Burr, Morrone & Ross, 1994; Ross, Burr, & Morrone, 1994). This exclusion of certain motion images is called suppression. For instance, in a functioning visual system, the eyes move rapidly across a page while reading, but a blur of letters is not seen—only the words that are being focused on, because of suppression. Another example of suppression is when we search for our car in a parking lot. The unnecessary visual motion signals are suppressed as our eyes move quickly to find the car. We perceive a stationary environment, the parking lot. If the extra motion signals were not suppressed, the parking lot would appear to be spinning as our eyes moved quickly while looking for the car, and we might experience a sense of dizziness.

(See Bibliography, 8-1). (Remember I said that I often could not find my car in a parking lot).

I made an appointment to see the Dizzy Doctor in Denver. She was tightly booked so I would not be able to get an appointment with her for several weeks.

In the meantime, I started seeing a different massage therapist who told me about another chiropractor who he claimed was excellent. I went for the final time to "the chiropractors" and their massage therapists. I told the chiropractor who worked on me that last day that my lower back was just killing me still. He adjusted me and told me that skeletally I was fine. I knew this couldn't be right. No one had done x-rays or an MRI yet of my lower back.

I met with a psychologist about the emotional/psychological aspects of the accident. He gave me a questionnaire and asked me numerous questions. He gave me an eighteen-page "Guided Introspection Brain Injury Inventory" that I took home and answered. The questionnaire took me days to fill out. I learned from the inventory that I was able to answer something to almost every question. The following is what I found:

Yes, I had a lot of trouble with days, time, where I was going, where I was and why. I had trouble staying awake during the daytime and had to nap. I felt that strange things were happening to me that I could not explain, such as being somewhere and not recalling how I got there. I had not started having seizures yet, or so I thought. I had blank-outs and fadeouts. I sometimes fell asleep for a moment at any time of the day.

I got lost easier. Before the accident I never got lost. I felt like I was in a capsule or a cloud where things seemed unreal. I lost awareness for periods of time—sometimes for days. My body did not seem real, especially at the beginning before the pain set in. My body now seemed foreign and my mind and body didn't seem attached. I felt like I had a hangover most of the time with headaches or fuzziness.

I had very little sense of time. I was unsure if an interview took one hour or three hours. It used to feel like a day took forever. Now I felt surprised when the day was over. Often it would be late in the day and I would wonder if I had eaten lunch. I would be shocked to look at the clock and see that it was four or five o'clock. Usually I would still be sitting in the same place I had been when I sat down early in the day.

I would all of a sudden get very confused. I was drowsy more frequently and fluctuated between drowsiness and agitation. I could not keep track of dates, times, places. More often than not, I felt over-whelmed and over-stimulated. Cars, people, most external things seemed to be going in fast motion. Movements and conversations distracted me. I startled easily. I could not concentrate in noisy environments. I had trouble recognizing things, pictures and faces. When I got lost, I couldn't recognize where I was. My thinking sometimes seemed to move too fast and felt out of control.

My sensory experience produced feelings of dizziness, loss of balance. My sense of smell was reduced and food tasted bland. The smells I did smell were foul. Noise was very intense and annoying. My left ear had a ringing or a buzz in it all the time. Noises sounded different—almost like in an Alfred Hitchcock movie with the shrieking violin background music. Noises seemed loud and distorted. I had trouble recognizing things by their sound. For instance, I couldn't tell if it was my phone ringing, my roommate's phone ringing or a phone on the TV ringing. There was a change in my ability to tell where the sounds were coming from when moving and I often heard a phone ringing when there wasn't one ringing. I locked onto sounds more often and would focus my attention on the sound, causing me to be quite annoyed. My attention jumped from sound to sound making my eyes bounce around.

I had a change in sensitivity to touch. I was very sensitive when people touched me and was often afraid the touch would hurt or would knock me down. Most things were different and unfamiliar.

My sensitivity to light was profound. If I turned a light on at night, my eyes could not adjust to the brightness. I absolutely could not go outside during the daytime without sunglasses without getting a blinding headache. I had difficulty seeing at night. New asphalt on the road or newly tarred seams in the road practically blinded me. (I learned later on to close my right eye to get rid of the glare). Things looked different and distorted. Sometimes people looked too tall, too short, etc. Sometimes they looked like they were shaped like flat, round-faced Gumbies or similar to a carnival mirror reflection. I had a definite change in my ability to see details. I was a perfectionist before the accident. Now I had trouble even seeing errors. I had dark flashes out of the corner of my eye and spots.

My vision, as I've already mentioned, was blurred with double vision. I had trouble with colors and couldn't tell if things matched. I had trouble seeing things in certain places, especially on my left side. People could sneak up on me. When my head really hurt, I had the sense that I was looking through a tunnel. I had a lot of trouble spotting a familiar face in a crowd. I could not focus on objects, buildings, or people with my eyes when walking or driving without feeling sick. The ground felt like it was moving. I could not watch cars driving along while I was waiting at a stoplight. In the morning, especially, my vision seemed cloudy or blocked out. I now stared for lengthy periods of time. When trying to lock focus onto something, my eyes jumped from object to object. Flowers, however, looked better—almost like they were in animation.

I was then asked about headaches and pain. I wrote that my head hurt, especially on the left front and the top of my head, with the rest of my head hurting, also. My neck had sharp pain a lot and always ached. My chest hurt mostly on the left side. My right shoulder hurt worse than my left. My jaw ached and I could only open my mouth a little bit. My teeth didn't fit together anymore, making it hard to chew. My back hurt so much sometimes that it hurt to breathe. My lower back was in pain constantly and, of course, my legs were in constant pain with the pain worse at night when I was lying down.

My muscles seemed stiff and were always achy. My left side was weaker than my right. I still tripped a lot. When I stood up I had to stand still for a bit before I walked or I lost my balance and fell to the right and backwards. If I walked without looking down, I listed to the left.

My skin felt like pins and needles, especially when I was agitated. I had spasms, shakiness and jerks in my legs and arms but mostly in the right leg. The left leg felt like a log when it wasn't in pain. My left hand occasionally would spasm and would almost knock me in the chin.

I got tired fast, was fatigued in the morning as if I hadn't slept, which I usually hadn't. My reflexes were slow. I was almost constantly nauseous and felt like vomiting. My appetite was very increased. My bowel habits changed dramatically and I could not sense when I needed to go to the bathroom but as soon as I lay down I had to urinate. This usually occurred five or six times a night. They asked several questions about changes in sexual function and thought process. Since sex was the furthest thing from my mind at that time, my answers were blanks, but they asked if there was a change in sexual desire/sexual tension, level of sexual excitability able to reach, change in experience of orgasm, frequency of erection/size (morning erection), desire to masturbate or if there was a change in sexual orientation.

I often talked very slowly, then very fast. I gained about 15 pounds the first year after my head injury. I often felt like my heart was racing or pounding as a result of emotions or exercise. I was much more dizzy standing up than sitting down and was dizzy when I moved my head. I did not have hair loss. My body temperature was out of whack. I felt hot all the time, but not sweaty hot.

My emotional life was like a roller coaster. I felt very irritable in situations that used to not faze me. Where I was very patient before the accident, I was now easily angered. I had a quick temper, my feelings were hurt easily and I had moments where I was quite euphoric or very sad. I was anxious and nervous all the time. I was quite confused by certain people or situations. I got tense and edgy more easily. I had not thought about suicide but many head-injured people I talked to do. I felt like my emotions were flatter in the sense that I did not enjoy much. I never felt like the television was communicating to me personally. Sometimes I felt like the insurance adjustor was out to get me, which I am pretty sure even now that she was....

I was less obsessive than I was before the accident. My feelings and emotions often got out of control and then I would crash. I worried almost constantly. I started crying in about June of the year after the accident over strange things like homeless people and children playing in the park. I became suspicious of minorities.

My daughter commented about my behavior being inappropriate many times. People seemed weird to me and I would become frightened if someone was in a bad mood. The only strange things I saw that were not really there were the flashes out of the corner of my eye. I was angrier with people. I lost interest in previous hobbies and activities.

Intellectually I was not interested in things I had seen or heard. I went through a period where I thought of lots of things to invent, then no thoughts. I could not plan things out like fixing a meal, going to the grocery store, filling out a deposit slip at the bank. It took tremendous energy to do simple things that were routine before. I got exhausted just thinking about how to think.

I could not get motivated to start a new project because I knew I would forget in the middle of it why I was doing it. (I could no longer do crafts like cross-stitch because I couldn't get the pattern to focus and would lose track of where I was). Challenging things were out of the question. My mind went from being blank to being so busy that I couldn't catch a thought. I could no longer multi-task and had trouble finding even one way of doing things. It was very difficult and taxing to express myself. My intuition became sharper, however.

There was a definite change in my ability to find the right word when trying to describe or explain something. The words got lost. I could sometimes hear the words in the back of my head but couldn't get them to my mouth. There was a definite change in my ability to put thoughts into sentences and have the sentences make sense. I made mistakes often, was more easily distracted and found it hard to stay interested in things. I would get too focused or stuck on thoughts and ideas so that it was hard to move onto other things. My thinking often felt hyperactive making it difficult for me to concentrate. I didn't understand jokes at all. My sense of humor was slower.

    I lost interest in the news reports and found sitcoms just too overbearing to bother with. (Actually, I couldn't stand to watch and listen to TV at the same time so did just one or the other). If I tried to read something, I had to read it over and over and still would get lost somewhere in the middle of it and not know a thing that I read. I was mathematically fast before the accident. I refused to use a calculator ever because I did not want to lose my math skills. Smacking your head like I did will take care of math skills. I was a spelling queen before but now had trouble remembering how to spell even simple words. I wanted to do more artistic and creative things but I had trouble getting around to doing them.

    My ability to figure out what other people were thinking or feeling became keener. I could not hold different thoughts in my head at the same time. They seemed to go by too fast and I would often lose them. I could not combine or juggle thoughts. My abstraction was pretty much nil, for example, I could not solve complex problems that required imagining certain factors and what role they may have played. It was just too hard to understand.

I was asked if there was a change in my ability to analyze or think critically about things, for example, finding shortcomings or faults in other persons, beliefs or ability to evaluate whether someone else's argument was right or wrong...I didn't really care what they thought.

When writing, my sentences were fouled up. Now, what was strange during this period of time was that words I hadn't used or thought of in years were flashing through my brain—like lugubrious—so when I got to the memory part I was still in words and their definitions mode. That quickly left me, however. After that stint, I couldn't figure out the opposite of up. (I actually had to picture going up a ladder then down to get the word down, then, of course, I couldn't get the word out of my mouth).

The statements in this part which I have already mentioned the answers to were: change in ability to remember definitions of words, change in memory for faces of people known for a while, change in ability to remember faces when I met new people, change in memory for names used to know quite well and change in ability for memories of names of new people introduced to.

They asked if there was a change in my ability to remember a second language, to remember picture or scenes, layouts of buildings/locations or stores in malls/locations of items on shelves. I couldn't go into a store to buy a toothbrush without becoming ill because of visual over-stimulation, or I would fall into things. (After that I would go into a blackout and lose most of my memory for a period of time.) The heightened part of my memory was for old things I used to know pretty well, such as the fact that Arlington Cemetery consists of 319 acres and that rats produce up to 2,500 offspring a year (cockroaches produce up to 350,000 offspring a year). Who cares! My daughter told me I was an encyclopedia of useless information many times before the accident.

I could retain very little of things I had just learned. I could not remember the lyrics to songs, which really annoyed me because before the accident I was like a jukebox of old songs and their words. Actually I could not sing anymore let alone remember the words to the songs. I could maybe name a few questions I was asked after I walked out of the room. I could no longer remember dance steps or play sports because my body just didn't get the cues.

My personal life history was much sharper, especially since I was having nightly visits back to my childhood and the people there. I just couldn't remember new people and things. Thoughts and ideas faded away faster and, I could not fully develop or mentally work through these thoughts because I lost them.

When asked if there was a change in my ability to remember new conversations, I realized that I didn't care about what was being said unless it was something worth remembering. A few hours later I didn't remember it anyway. I was definitely more absent-minded. My biggest fear during this time period was that I had Alzheimer's or Pre-Senile Dementia. My dreams were not hard to remember because they were so bizarre. At the same time, I couldn't tell you at the end of the day what I had done that day.

In the self-regulation section I learned the following: I had to silently talk to myself to control or regulate thoughts or actions. I did things impulsively and had disasters to deal with later. Since I didn't know whom to trust, I became more guarded and careful with whom I shared information. I had to start making notes or nothing would get done because I would simply forget what I was supposed to do. It was hard to stop some activity/thought/fantasy once I started focusing on it. The thoughts would just go on and on. I was aware enough to not fantasize because I had become quite aware through my life experiences that when a situation actually did manifest the reality was always disappointing if I had created a grand fantasy out of it. I had trouble finishing most things that I started. Although I never told jokes, my comments and actions were often inappropriate. I did not have a problem controlling sexual impulses since I didn't have any.

    I was less bold and confident around people, more shy and careful because I knew that my sentences and thoughts would come out jumbled or I would trip and fall down or simply fall over thus embarrassing me and other people. I was quite careful about making mistakes because I knew that I screwed things up a lot. I had trouble realizing if I did make a mistake.

    My thinking/emotions/mental imagery was often sluggish or slower. I tended to continue with something or get locked into it even if it seemed wrong, especially when I was still working. When I was still working, my boss would explain something to me, I would tell him I understood what he was saying, then do it wrong. This would happen several times, and I never would get what he was saying. I just kept doing it incorrectly the same way over and over.

    I never had quick flashes or impulses about killing people or doing strange things that were scary. There was no change in the amount of drugs or alcohol I used since I never used either, and I never took prescription drugs, which really baffled and annoyed many doctors I saw. (Almost every doctor who I went to tried to get me to take anti-depressants and sleeping pills. I would just say, "Do you know what those things do to your body?" [Research shows that anti-depressants actually cause brain damage]). I don't think I developed any nervous habits. I couldn't chew my fingernails because my teeth were so out of alignment now and had to kind of grind or gum my food instead of chew it.

My experience of self changed dramatically. To the comment "change in degree feel in touch with past or personal history," I easily answered, "I was someone else then." I knew that I was different than the person I had been all my life. My edges/flair was hazy now. My mind/thinking was more tense sometimes and hazy other times. I was very affected by noises and loud sounds.

I did not have more cruel urges or fantasies. It was much more difficult to put myself in someone else's shoes. It took too much energy to feel for others when they felt sad. I really didn't care about things as much as I used to. I felt that my personality was reduced or simplified. I really didn't care much about what other people thought of me. I felt that my mind was partially dead or broken.

I got excited less, generally lost interest in things. The amount of pleasure I got out of things had smoothed-off edges. It was not so much that I felt more or less optimistic about my personal future but felt that it was confusing, exciting, and scary because I didn't know how dopey I would be. My life's meaning didn't really change. I already felt that it had meaning. My ability to love others stayed about the same, but I was less tolerant. In some ways I was happier—as long as I didn't leave the house. The outside world was now a very frightening, intimidating place. I was more of a loner than before.

I didn't know if my personality was warmer than before because I wasn't sure I had one now. It was not so much that I had strange thoughts as confused thoughts. I was definitely less playful than before because of my balance problems. I had no change in religiosity. My feelings were dulled. I felt less bonded or attached to people/pets. I felt less strongly about how much I cared about things. I'm not sure that I had a change in my passion for political matters. I was still incensed about crooked politicians, elections and media manipulation.

I felt that I looked differently in the mirror and was more preoccupied with myself and focused in more on myself. I had trouble understanding when people said they were sad or angry. I felt that life is good and should be rejoiced in. Now I just had to figure out how to rejoice.

Other people did comment that my personality had changed. I was much less tolerant of people's behavior and patterns. There was definitely no change in my concern or fear of dying since I am not afraid of dying. I had a problem with my ability to feel connected with other people/activities because I lost interest.

The psycho-social, behavioral-emotional impairments due to TBI might include: fatigue, mood swings, denial, self-centeredness, anxiety, depression, lowered self-esteem, sexual dysfunction, restlessness, lack of motivation, inability to self-monitor, difficulty with emotional control, inability to cope, agitation, excessive laughing or crying and difficulty in relating to others. (See Bibliography, 8-2). These also include increased risk of suicide, divorce, chronic unemployment, economic strain, and substance abuse. These consequences are tragic to individuals and families and place additional burdens on social service agencies, law enforcement, and courts. (See Bibliography, 8-3).

The next area was about Post Traumatic Stress Disorder. I thought about the accident and replayed it in my mind for quite awhile. Then I got to a point where I was more concerned about insurance and wondering if my brain/body would ever get it together. I was anxious and fearful around things that reminded me of the accident, such as, if I saw Pam, a white SUV or a car like the one Pam replaced her wrecked vehicle with—she might be in it! I had developed new fears/phobias since the accident, and I felt sometimes like something was crawling on my skin. I startled quite easily and became more watchful with my eyes. I did not have nightmares after the accident so much as bizarre dreams. I avoided things that reminded me of the accident—like the driver. I did not flash back to the accident but could easily go back there if asked about it.

My sleep depth changed dramatically. I tossed and turned at night and seldom slept for more than 2-3 hours before I woke and was distressed most of the night. Usually I dropped like a rock into sleep but couldn't seem to stay there. I now woke myself up talking and I almost think I was sleep walking because I often felt as if I wasn't totally awake when I was walking around at night. I don't know if I had any unusual movement during sleep, such as punching, since my injury. My dreams seemed more real and the anger/fear in my dreams was more intense, especially the anger. My dreams were very colorful, more often and recurring. There was a change in how imaginative my dreams were—they were more bizarre. I'm not sure that there was a change in the amount of symbolic meaning in my dreams as I think they were pretty self-evident.

And finally, the area of practical activities completed the questionnaire. There was a definite change in using a bank/banking machine. I simply could not fill out a deposit or withdrawal slip. I couldn't do the math, nor could I fill in the boxes. I had to have someone at the bank do this for me. My driving skills were not as keen as they were before the accident and I could not drive at night. My distance vision was quite different than before the accident. I could not use or look at a computer because it was too stimulating visually. If I looked at the screen, I became physically ill and would lose track of time for hours. And I could not remember how to type.

I didn't play games anymore. It was too frustrating to try to remember what we were doing. Shopping was a nightmare. I could do one store a day and pick up only one or two items or my brain would just collapse. I had to quit my job because I couldn't do the banking, remember to do contracts, who called and why they called. I didn't care very much if I cleaned house, but kept everything obsessively orderly because I knew I wouldn't be able to find what I was looking for if I didn't.

I was not very interested in being a parent nor was not as invested in what my daughters were doing. When I was talking to them, I changed the subject a lot, as I did with other people.

It was difficult for me to find places because I couldn't remember where I was going. One day I found myself in downtown Denver and couldn't figure out why it didn't look like Boulder.

I did not have trouble keeping myself clean. Even though I usually couldn't remember if I had bathed, brushed my teeth or changed my clothes on any given day, I must have because I sure had a lot of laundry.

My daughter now had to take care of my finances and pay my bills because I couldn't quite figure out how to do it. I was now not sure if my clothes matched so I am sure there was a change in the way I dressed. I had no change in marital status. I know that the quality of my handwriting changed. At first, even I couldn't read it.

They then asked if there was any change in the way my thinking works or in the way my emotions work. That seems pretty self-explanatory.

Once again I was amazed that someone knew what I was going through. Were they mind-readers or was this scientific research? Why did medical doctors not "get it" that a person had a brain injury if they displayed these changes after having their head played ping pong with?

On that same day I met again with Mary Ann, my cognitive therapist, who gave me word tests. I was unable to find the words in my head and in a short period of time I was unable to function mentally at all. She gave me take-home work that consisted mostly of synonym fill-in-the blanks that I worked on every morning.

> Persons with suppression impairment can experience: an inability to suppress the extra motion images while visual scanning; a disturbing sense of motion, such as that of a jerky camera motion; interference with the perceived timing of motion which can effect reaction times; impaired execution of planned body movements, which can affect the performance of all daily living activities; and reading difficulties. (See Bibliography, 8-4).

# Chapter Nine
## Neurological Testing—
## Denial!

I went to Boulder on July 24 and July 25 to do testing with Jan, the neuropsychologist. The testing was pretty much exhausting. We had to stop numerous times because my brain would just "blow out". There were many of the tests that I could not take because I could not look at the forms or pictures. At that time it seemed that I was still running on adrenaline from the accident so had the illusion that nothing was really wrong with me except for "a few kinks". This is also known in big red letters as "DENIAL"! (With many head injured people I have talked to, they invariably believe that they are "all right" or "fine").

It is routine for Jan to not give a copy of her report to the patient because it can be quite depressing. I did, however, receive a copy of the report several weeks later from the insurance company. It was like getting a bucket of ice water in the face. Somehow I now had to accept that I had a brain injury. Up until this point I had been pretty secure in my denial.

The test results were quite astonishing to me. They ranged from above average to severely-impaired. Jan did not administer tests that required prolonged visual processing due to my visual impairments. We did, however, complete the Picture Completion Subtest, but it took quite a long time with frequent breaks. A full scale IQ was not determined since Jan was not able to administer three of the performance subtests due to my fatigue and visual disturbances. My "prorated verbal IQ was 111, in the below average range." I remember that I answered that water boiled at 112 degrees and on that particular day the temperature outside was well over 100 degrees when, in reality, it was about 70.

    Jan wrote that my "poorest performance was on the Digit Symbol test, a test of divided attention, psychomotor speed and visual-motor coordination. This test was severely fatiguing for her because of the visual processing that it required. This test is only administered for ninety seconds. Her performance was in the severely impaired range. She scored in the below average range on the Picture Completion subtest, a test that required her to perceive missing visual detail. She scored in the moderately impaired range on the Digit Symbol subtest, a test of auditory attention/concentration. Average performances were found for Comprehension, Similarities and Information subtests. She scored in the above average range on the Arithmetic subtest. On the WAIS-R, slowed processing and word finding problems were evident on the Information, Picture Completion,

Comprehension and Similarities subtests. Very slow processing occurred on the Digit Span subtest. She required repetition of information on the Arithmetic subtest because of difficulty holding two or more pieces of information in mind at once. On the Comprehension subset, she had trouble putting her thoughts into words. Slowed processing was evident on the Similarities test, and in the middle of the test she forgot what it was she was supposed to be doing. During the Digit Symbol subtest, she experienced tugging and aching in her head and she felt nauseous. She reported during the Digit Symbol subtest, 'My brain knows what I need to do, I just can't get that information to my hand.' On the WAIS-III, Letter Number Sequencing subtest, a test of working memory and organization, she scored at the 16th percentile."

"On a strength of grip test (Hand Dynamometer), she scored in the moderately impaired range for both dominant and non-dominant hands. However, there was a statistically significant difference between dominant and non-dominant hands, suggesting lateralizing significance because of the moderate impairment in her non-dominant hand. The same lateralizing was seen on the Finger Oscillation test.

On the Finger Oscillation Test, a test of motor speed, she scored in the severely impaired range for both dominant and non-dominant hands. On a test of fine motor coordination, (Grooved Pegboard), her performance was severely impaired for the right hand or dominant hand and moderately to severely impaired for the left or non-dominant hand." I was quite startled when I performed these tests to realize that I could not easily do them.

The report continued, "Slow processing was quite evident during the Sensory Perceptual evaluation. It is important to note that she evidenced faster processing speed when I applied stimulation to her left hand or left cheek. While her processing was extremely slow, she was accurate in terms of being error free. On the Reitan-Klove Tactile Form Recognition Test she was moderately to severely impaired for the dominant hand and severely impaired for the non-dominant hand. Again, there was lateralizing significance such that she was significantly more impaired in the non-dominant hand than the dominant hand."

"I attempted to administer the Letter Cancellation of C's and E's, a multitrack visual processing task to [the patient]. We couldn't even get through the first line because it was too disturbing, visually, to her. As noted earlier, her auditory attention was moderately impaired, (Digit Span subtest of the WAIS-R). On the Seashore Rhythm test, a test of auditory discrimination of non-verbal material her performance was in the mildly to moderately impaired range. She scored in the bottom of the average range on the Speech Sounds Perception test, a test of Auditory Discrimination of verbal material. On the Paced Auditory Serial Addition Test, her performances were approximately one standard deviation below the mean on all four trials. She was behind on her productions on trials two through four."

"On the Rey Auditory Verbal Learning Test, a test requiring her to learn a list of 15 words over five trials, her performance was impaired for new learning, as well as evidencing an abnormal amount of shrinkage from the fifth learning trial to the first recall trial. She was able to learn 41 words across five learning trials, where the mean for someone her age and sex is 48.5 words. She lost four words from the fifth learning trial to the first recall trial. Her 30-minute delayed recall trial was impaired as well. Her recognition memory was within normal limits. Memory for information presented in paragraph form was severely impaired. On the immediate memory portion of the Logical Memory (Wechsler Memory Scale-Revised), she scored in the 10th percentile. On a 30-minute delayed recall trial, she scored at the 14th percentile. She uses visualization to try and remember things. During her report of what she could remember on the Wechsler Memory Scale, 30-minute delayed recall trial, she gave one word replies."

"On the Trailmaking Test, Part A, a test of simple sequencing, [the patient] scored in the severely impaired range. Because of the difficulty she evidenced on this test, Part B was not administered. On the Hayling Sentence Completion Test, a test of basic response initiation and suppression ability, her performance was poor for basic response initiation and abnormal for suppression ability. This test measures the ability to suppress a habitual response in favor of a novel one. On the Brixton Spatial Anticipation Test, a test of rule detection and rule following, her performance was abnormal as well. During this test, she would get stuck on an approach to decipher the pattern and even though she was given feedback that her performances were in error, she was unable to switch to a new strategy. Her cognitive flexibility is greatly lessened. On the Behavioral Dyscontrol Scale, a test of motor programming to evaluate executive functioning, she evidenced slow and effortful performances, particularly on the left and quite a bit of confusion. [The patient] completed a Dysexecutive Questionnaire, rating her executive functioning in everyday life. Very often she has problems understanding what other people mean unless they keep things simple and straightforward. She also has difficulty realizing the extent of her problems. She tends to be restless and has difficulty sitting still for any length of time, and she finds it difficult to keep her mind on something and is easily distracted. Fairly often she has trouble making decisions or deciding what to do. She also finds it difficult to stop herself from doing something even though she knows she shouldn't."

"She is lethargic or unenthusiastic about things and alternately gets overexcited about things. She has difficulty thinking ahead or planning for the future. Sometimes she loses her temper at the slightest thing, and at other times she has difficulty showing emotion. She is unconcerned about how she should behave in certain situations, and she finds it hard to stop repeating, saying or doing something once she is started. She is unaware of or unconcerned about how others feel about her behavior since the motor vehicle accident. She gets events mixed up with each other and gets confused about the correct order of events. She does or says embarrassing things at times when in the company of others."

"On the Controlled Oral Word Association test, her performance was seriously deficient. She scored at less than the 1st percentile."

"On the Hooper Visual Organization Test, a test of the ability to conceptually re-arrange pictures that have been disarranged, her performance was approximately one half a standard deviation below the mean."

"She was administered two tests to measure effort/motivation. She was administered the 21 Item Test and the Rey 15 Item Test. On the Rey 15 Item Test, she correctly identified 15 out of 15 figures. On the 21 Item Test, her score was 18 correct. The mean is 17.9. These scores indicate that [the patient] was using adequate effort-motivation and was not trying to appear impaired."

"The Personality Assessment Inventory was administered as part of this neuropsychological assessment. Her validity indices indicate that the number of completed items was within acceptable limits. She attended appropriately to item content and responded consistently to similar items. She responded in a reasonably forthright manner and didn't attempt to present an unrealistic or inaccurate impression. Clinically, there were significant elevations on scales having to do with thinking and concentration as well as concern about physical functioning. Her thought processes are marked by confusion, difficulty concentrating, distractibility, and having the experience of her thinking being disrupted or blocked. She reports numerous and varied physical problems. Her self-concept is a generally positive one. She tends to be an optimistic person with a good sense of humor and maintains resiliency in the face of her significant injuries. Her interpersonal style is best described as being independent and pragmatic."

She goes on to say that I am "experiencing real organically-based cognitive impairments that significantly affect her everyday life. Impairments were documented for verbal fluency, auditory attention/concentration, visual processing, attention and tracking, divided attention, psychomotor speed and visual motor coordination. Impairments were also found in grip strength, motor speed and fine motor coordination. Auditory discrimination of nonverbal material is impaired. Sequencing ability is impaired. Speed of processing is impaired. She evidences short-term verbal memory impairments. Executive dysfunction indicators include motor programming deficits, basic response initiation deficits, suppression ability deficits and impairments in rule detection and rule following. There was no attempt at distortion, nor any gross psychopathology."

"It is important that she continue in formal cognitive rehabilitation as well as functional organizational therapy. She needs quite a bit of help with executive functioning deficits that impact her everyday life. Attention focus training, attention process training, language treatment and memory remediation will be important. At some point in time when she is able to tolerate it, EEG biofeedback or neurofeedback will be valuable to improve cognitive stamina and increase overall cognitive efficiency. It is important that she continue in her work with Dr. Cecil because she does evidence severe visual tracking, attention and visual processing deficits. Since the motor vehicle accident, [the patient] has experienced anxiety, hyperarousal and an altered nervous system excitability. It will be important for her to begin in trauma release work with a trauma release therapist. Her healthcare practitioners in her home area, if they have not already done so, may want to evaluate her for adrenal insufficiency as well as any hormonal changes that may have occurred following the motor vehicle accident. Persons who have experienced traumatic brain injury as well as being in significant pain often experience adrenal insufficiency.

A repeat neuropsychological re-evaluation is recommended in approximately one year."

(One doctor I know believes that diabetes is triggered by a head trauma).

I read and re-read the report daily for a couple weeks. I thought I had performed fairly normally so I was astonished that I appeared, in my mind now, as a real mess. Of the tests I had taken so far, the results of this one stunned me the most. I was pretty mad now at Pam, the "professional driver". Sometimes I wanted to laugh—one of those hard laughs a person does when amazed. At other times I wanted to cry.

Once again, vision therapy based on the neuropsych evaluation was requested from the insurance company. Once again, it was denied. My request for an adrenal insufficiency test was also denied.

**Illusions.** Researchers hypothesize that the brain uses information from the visual pathways to construct 3-D depictions of the environment (Rogers, Diane, & Ramachandran, 1997). If the visual pathways are disrupted, illusions can occur instead of accurate 3-D images of the person's surroundings. (Rogers, Diane & Ramachandran, 1997). When a disruption to the visual pathways occurs, the timing of the visual pathways may be out of sync (Steinman, Steinman, & Lehmkuhle, 1997). Therefore, the damaged visual pathways may be unable to determine which visual information to process and which to filter out—thus, creating an altered image, an illusion. Furthermore, changes in visual processing speeds, the inability to compensate for when the object we are focusing on moves, and the failure to keep our eyes on a something as it moves can create an illusion of motion or action (Bassi &

Lehmkuhle, 1990; Steinman, Steinmanm, & Lehmkuhle, 1997). (See Bibliography, 9-1).

I sent a letter to the State Insurance Commissioner and complained about the problems I was having with the insurance company. The Commissioner's office sent a letter to my insurance company giving them twenty days to send in detail the "basis for non-authorization of the treatments needed for [the patient] to recover from her accident. Be specific as to what treatments have not been authorized and provide the specific basis for each non-authorization. Provide copies of the specific doctors' reports and consult reviews used to deny each treatment authorization." The letter further demanded a detailed explanation as to why bills were not paid within thirty days. For any bills partially paid they also demanded an explanation why the full amount was not paid.

The letter from the insurance company gave the following excuse: "As you know, we have requested a PPO exam be conducted to help determine the best course of treatment for your injuries. Please rest assured that once the PPO exam is completed, we will proceed accordingly in a prompt manner. It is not our position that you cannot seek further treatment, should you and your medical providers determine additional treatment is necessary. However, we cannot guarantee payment for your treatment until the PPO exam is completed. This includes your request for payment for additional acupuncture and prism glasses." This is all that an insurance company has to tell the Department of Insurance to be excused from further investigation and any further legal responsibilities.

The letter from the insurance company further states that they do not reimburse for mileage until the corresponding, approved bills are received from the medical provider. In other words, if a provider does go ahead and treats before approval, you will not be reimbursed for mileage or lodging until, possibly, months later and only if the PPO exam says you needed the treatment. Furthermore, in my policy, long distance phone calls were not covered nor were meals even when I was sent to Denver for an IME, or what the insurance company's letter called a PPO exam. Financially I was getting deeper and deeper in debt. (See "Indicative and Contributory Signs of Bad Faith", pages 437, 441, numbers 1, 4, 27, 33, 34, and 41).

That was the last that I heard on the subject, and I never heard another word from the Insurance Commissioner's office.

Generally, the state DOI (Department of Insurance) Department is way understaffed...they may get to investigate 10-13% of claimants' complaints which usually, at best, involves a phone call from the state examiner to the insurer asking a question about the case or claim. The insurer responds, the DOI gives the benefit of any doubt to the insurer over the claimant and takes the word of the insurer generally resulting in making a note in the file which usually settles and satisfies the examiner's inquiry of most any question and in one minute or less closes the file. (See Bibliography, 9-2).

Interestingly, several therapists told me that the Insurance Commissioner at the time my situation occurred was insurance-oriented. Within a few months of the complaint that I filed, the Insurance Commissioner was replaced by someone who was not "working" for the insurance companies.

# Chapter Ten
## The "Dizzy Doctor" and How Diligence Pays Off

Cognitive therapy was finally approved. I was still getting a big "no" on the vision therapy. I still had not heard from the attorney's investigator. The messages I was leaving now with the attorney were being unanswered.

I started seeing a new chiropractor. Anna was a lifesaver for me. The old chiropractors had only worked on my spine, hips and neck.

Anna started out by hooking me up to a machine called an EAV, or electro acupuncture according to Voll's. Anna had one of the older models that use formulas rather than just electrical current. Within a few sessions, my severe dizziness and disorientation became more tolerable as did my intense headaches.

She worked inside of my mouth, on the fissures on my head and adjusted all of my organs. My digestion started to improve. I was able to go through most days without being doubled over on the floor by mid-afternoon from stomach pain.

Later on in the therapy she started breaking up lesions on my head, neck, shoulders, back, hips, legs, arms and abdomen. Although tearing the lesions lose was painful, my muscles started to relax more and my skin could actually move. She did numerous tests and found that the upper motor neuron loop was not connecting to the lower motor neuron loop to the arms and legs.

> Symptoms are related to the type of affected nerve and may be seen over a period of days, weeks, or years. Muscle weakness is the most common symptom of motor nerve damage. Other symptoms may include painful cramps and fasciculations (uncontrolled muscle twitching visible under the skin), muscle loss, bone degeneration, and changes in the skin, hair, and nails. These more degenerative changes also can result from sensory or autonomic nerve fiber loss.... Physical injury (trauma) is the most common cause of injury to a nerve. Injury or sudden trauma, such as from automobile accidents, falls, and sports-related activities, can cause nerves to be partially or completely detached from the spinal cord. Less dramatic traumas also can cause serious nerve damage. Broken or dislocated bones can exert damaging pressure on neighboring nerves, and slipped discs between vertebrae can compress nerve fibers where they emerge from the spinal cord. (See Bibliography, 10-1).

I was approved for six sessions of acupuncture. This time the acupuncturist put needles in my head that felt like 16-penny spikes, hooked me up to electrical stimulation then turned on the juice. Sweet Jesus! I thought I was going to die! A few days after the treatments I noticed a lessening of the stuffiness in my head. She only worked on the brain point three times and stopped because it was so painful for me and worked on my neck and my back the last three times.

On August 5, I was fitted for ear filters to help alleviate some of the tinnitus and external noise. What I found amazing was how noisy the road sounds in a car were for me. When I took out the ear filters, however, sounds seemed extremely loud.

I started doing EMDR trauma release work with a psychologist. I found that the little buzzers that you hold in each hand were so annoying to me that I simply could not tolerate holding them. We did the work without them. I went step by step through the accident and positioned myself where I was thrown to and began to understand what the trauma had done to my body and why my brain was such a mushy mess. I saw that during the thrusting of my head, my brain had collapsed in on itself, kind of like if you trip carrying a tray of jell-o and it slams into the wall.

I went for my exam with the "Dizzy Doctor" in Denver. She scheduled me for tests, some of which I can only describe as painful and disorienting. These tests were for hearing and balance issues. They ran the usual hearing tests with tones then put a mini-hose down my left ear, shutting off all external sound. The tester spoke words into my right ear that I was supposed to repeat while holding my eyes still. The pressure was so great that I simply could not hold my eyes still. They rolled up into my head. When I was finally able to say the word, it came out slow and slurred as if I had had a stroke, which was not far from the truth as a head injury is also known as a mechanical stroke. The plug in the other ear was not as bad but was still very uncomfortable with the words coming out quicker and less slurred.

When the doctor did her exam, one of the things she had me do was stand up and rotate my head from side to side. I was only able to do this at a very slow speed. She became quite perturbed with me and wanted me to turn my head quicker. I tried, but I could not. She told me again to turn it faster, that I would not fall. It just didn't happen. Although she didn't seem to realize it at the time or just didn't state it, later on this would be diagnosed as apraxia.

The doctor diagnosed me with a concussion in my inner ear and some hearing loss from the accident, which she said would most likely be permanent. She had me go down the hall to a physical therapist for vestibular therapy to teach me how to find my balance.

The physical therapist sent a foam pad home with me that I was to stand on in a corner each day. This particular exercise was quite hard to do since standing upright and still on a solid floor was iffy. When I walked, I tilted my head to the right and straight down. I was also supposed to walk up and down stairs without looking at them. This was not possible for me at this point because I had absolutely no sense whatsoever where the steps were.

After several weeks of doing these exercises, I was finally able to walk up and down stairs by not quite looking at the stairs directly as long as I was holding onto a rail. I could now stand upright on the foam pad for several seconds without falling over. I still fell over constantly during the day, however, whether just standing still or walking. I could usually only walk 8-16 steps before falling over. I got very good at catching myself and was not getting nearly as many bruises.

The foam pad exercises advanced to attempting to close my eyes while standing on the pad. I never did get that one.

On the third visit, the physical therapist had me stand on a pad that was hooked to a computer.

By shifting my weight, I was supposed to follow a shape into another quadrant. I had a great deal of trouble understanding how I was supposed to shift my body. I kept bending over at the waist instead of staying upright and shifting my weight onto my feet. After several attempts, I was finally able to figure out how to do this. Until that point, I did not understand how to move my upper body in relationship to my lower body.

On the fourth visit, the therapist told me that I had balance all figured out and that she would release me from therapy but first wanted me to have a follow-up visit with the "Dizzy Doctor". I couldn't figure out how she was going to release me from vestibular therapy when I was still falling over and not understanding my surroundings.

I made a dual appointment with the doctor and the therapist but would, of course, have to wait weeks for the appointment time.

> Persons with visual illusions can experience: impaired reaction times; disrupted perceptions of speed and direction; impaired recognition or auto-recognition of patterns, shapes, letters, colors, numbers, and symbols. Recognition is necessary for higher cognitive skills for learning and memory; the order of letters in a word can be perceived as being mixed up, superimposed, or only partially seen

when reading; the perception of words appearing to move or float on the page; impaired visual attention; overstimulation, frustration, and/or agitation when in crowds, such as school hallways, classrooms, supermarkets, or other environments with movement; and distractibility. (See Bibliography, 10-2).

I went back for another appointment with Dr. Scannell. She wrote a prescription for me to have a PT scan done to find the exact spots in the brain where there were "holes". She pointed to her head and said, "You'll have holes here, here, here, here and here." She pointed to both sides of the front of the head, the side of the head above the ear on the left and both sides of the neck (occipital) area. She also wrote a prescription for cognitive therapy. I sent these prescriptions to the insurance company then started to find where I could get the scan done.

The closest place to Colorado for the scan was the University Hospital in Salt Lake City or at the University Hospital in Irvine, California. My therapists told me that they have had excellent, thorough results from the lab in California. I set up an appointment for two months down the road but would have to pay cash up front for the testing because they said they have trouble collecting money from the insurance carriers as a rule. PT scans are recognized as a diagnostic tool. I approached the insurance company about an advance payment. They, of course, said they would not pay for the PT scan until it was completed. Since I was now flat broke, there was no way I could come up with $1,600 and pay my way to California and back.

On August 9, 2002, I filed for disability with Social Security Disability. I later received pages of questions that were focused on head injury and physical limitations.

On August 13, I called the managed care and asked for the person who was, I was told back on July 3, supposed to schedule my PPO exams. I figured six weeks was long enough and could not understand why I had not heard from them about my appointment schedule, especially since the claims adjustor had told me that my appointments would be within two weeks. The man I talked to said that he had just received the paperwork the day before. I told him that I had been told that the paperwork was sent to him on July 3. He said the paperwork he had in his hand was stamped "received August 12".

At any rate, he said the paperwork requested exams with a neuropsychologist and a physiatrist, or rehab doctor. He said he had no request for an optometrist for my vision problems or a chiropractor like the claims adjustor had told me. I told the man what I had been told and how frustrated I was because the insurance company was withholding approvals and reimbursements until the IME's were done. He promised that he would call me at the end of the week with my appointment schedule. (See "Indicative or Contributory Signs of Bad Faith", pages 437, 441, 442, 444 numbers 1, 27, 30, 34, 36, 41, and 54).

    The "end of the week for my appointment schedule" did not come until August 29 for my schedule with one doctor and until September 9 for the second doctor and that was after I called the scheduler back again. Of course by this time, the original scheduler had been replaced, and I had to spend time trying to locate the new person. When I sent in my monthly mileage, I wrote on the bottom of my letter to the claims adjustor what she had told me versus what actually happened and that "I do not appreciate being lied to."

    I was finally reimbursed for motel expenses that I had accrued since June. I had to prove that I could not drive six hours in one day after attending three sessions of therapy.

    I remembered that someone once said that his glass wasn't half empty, the damn thing was broken. As soon as the thought shot through my head I realized that my glass wasn't half empty, it was full. I just had to decide to drink from the glass.

# Chapter Eleven
## Bio-feedback and Climbing Rocks with a Wedgie

Brain injuries can cause epilepsy. (See Bibliography, 11-1).

I awoke one night and found my left hand and head jerking spasmodically like a seizure. I didn't think it was a seizure because just the hand and head were involved. I had memory loss for a period of time after the seizure stopped.

I started seeing Jackie for biofeedback. She hooked me up to the biofeedback computer, and I could see for the first time just how sluggish my brain actually was—more like asleep.

My theta waves, which Jackie described as a pre-sleep indicator or cells indicating a slow, non-productive frequency, were fluctuating between 16 and 24mv and often shot above the graph. Normal theta waves are less than 4 mv.

Jackie explained that alpha waves measure a waking, restful state, helps reduce fatigue and stabilize mood. Eyes open, fluctuates according to task. Eyes closed, should rise above theta amplitude. Mine averaged 9.5 mv and never rose above the theta waves.

Low Beta measures sensory motor rhythm. They are found in the sensory motor cortex only.

They produce hyperactivity and improve focus. They are used to train seizure reduction. Normal is 2-3 mv. My low beta averaged 5.2mv but would often be as high as 9.6mv.

Beta is the fast frequency used for sustained, intense focus. Beta indicates good concentration when higher than theta. My beta averaged 5.42mv, way below the theta.

High beta is the very fast frequency used by the brain in fight or flight reactions and high muscle tension states and should be less than 8 mv. Mine were nowhere near that.

When my brain relaxed, a clicking sound on the computer occurred. The object was to get 1,000 clicks per session. I was only able to get about 50 clicks during the first session. I was told that biofeedback is also very successful in treating patients who have had strokes, in children who have ADHD, and it is often used in treating people in drug and alcohol rehabilitation centers. Biofeedback helps to teach a person how to refocus their brain activity to complete tasks. I was told by Dr. Harry that doctors do not recognize biofeedback as a viable treatment tool. Odd, hypnotherapists use a type of biofeedback to place their patient in the low-frequency delta and theta so that they are more suggestible.

We also worked on raising my peripheral temperature. The first time my peripheral temperature was checked it was only 80 degrees. With visualization and relaxation techniques I could get my temperature up to 86.4 degrees. Normal peripheral temperature is between 90 and 94 degrees. My therapist explained to me that my peripheral temperature was low because in trauma episodes the heart, stomach, kidneys, and other organs steal the heat from the external to feed the muscles and tissue around the organs that need to be protected. In a trauma case, the muscles and tissue don't get the message that the initial trauma is over with.

The new massage therapist I had been seeing started out fairly gently with me. Evidently the guy had some serious anger issues because each time I went, the massages became more painful. He did skin scraping and cupping, and I left bruised and in pain. I looked like I had been to a hickey festival. Somehow or other, I had let him convince me that his massaging, I'm sure, clear to my bones was the best way for me to get better. It took me several months to figure out that he was not in my best interest.

Visual neglect can result from brain injury to the right cerebral hemisphere of the brain (Spinelli, Angelelli, & Burr, 1996). It causes a decreased or absent visual perception of the left half of a person's viewing range. Persons with visual neglect will disregard the left side of their bodies and objects from their midline to the left of them. Not only can a visual neglect impair safety, but also activities of daily living performance. (See Bibliography, 11-2).

In September I went to an Outward Bound School for people with head injuries. The experience was bittersweet. I was able to be with other women with head injuries. That was the best part.

One woman's injuries were younger than mine so I was able to see what I probably looked like at that stage—she was still startled by even the slightest sound or movement, tired extremely easily and was still quite disoriented. There were also women attending the school whose injuries occurred several years earlier and some women who had sustained numerous head injuries. Each one of them shared that at least three doctors had told them that there was nothing wrong them—they just needed a psychiatrist….

The Outward Bound School in Colorado is in the mountains above Leadville. It is quiet, peaceful and serene. Since it was late in the summer, nights were sprinkled with frost, the middle of the day was hot and sunny—except for the first day when it rained all day which is the arch nemesis of people with head injuries because the barometric pressure drops and puts more pressure on the brain.

I was still pretty arrogant at the time about non-medicinal recovery and was finally able to understand that some people simply could not exist without their medications. Most of the women had seizures, which I thought I was free of so far, and I wasn't about to tell anyone about the seizure-like things I was experiencing. I wasn't aware of seizures other than grand or petit mal at the time.

The other ladies experienced depression or sleep disorders from their head injuries that stemmed from all sorts of accidents from oxygen deprivation during surgery, falling down steps, crashing their bikes, auto accidents to falling off of a horse and some had a combination of these injuries that had occurred over their lifetime. During this School I was able to understand how head injuries affect everyone a little differently. Many of us had similar after-effects from our injuries but, for the most part, each of us portrayed our symptoms differently than anyone else in the group.

Some did the ropes course and we learned to use a compass to find landmarks. (I couldn't do the ropes course do to my extreme visual disturbance). We ate together, slept in bunk beds in a dorm and played games designed to make our brains work. We did an exercise with a partner who was to guide their partner who was blindfolded. When I was blindfolded, I lost most of my ability to use my left side. One of the therapists told me that my left hand and leg went "decorticate". I had to figure out a way to get through the course trusting my brain-injured partner to guide me while dragging my left side. This was a totally new phenomenon for me. I was always so independent. I felt humiliated and finally realized how seriously physically impaired I was. Tears leaked from under my blindfold.

On the day before we left the School, we went to Camp Hale to rock climb where, during World War II, the 10$^{th}$ Mountain Division went to train. I had never climbed rocks before with equipment so felt relatively safe since I was not afraid of heights and was used to climbing ladders—and there was a team of four people below holding the ropes, albeit head-injured people.

In the equipment I felt trussed up like a hog and had a serious wedgie. The only glitch for me was that my left arm and leg didn't work very well and if I tipped my head right, left or up my eyes went into nystagmus and I fell over. I had to lift my left foot onto the next rock opening or out-cropping with my hands and without turning my head upward to see where I wanted to go. Many times I just pulled myself up with my hands so that I didn't have to contend with lifting my left leg up to the next step.

I was somewhat amazed at myself that when I got to an area where there were no more handholds I had the wherewithal to stop and say that was the end of the road. Before my head injury, I would have backtracked and started over, determined to finish the climb whatever the cost. For the first time ever, I realized that I was actually taking care of myself instead of doggedly thinking I was a failure for not completing the task—or at least my concept of completing the task. Not completing the climb to the very top (I was 6' from the top) was probably my best accomplishment. I was finally able to understand that it truly is the journey that counts.

On the last night we had the option of sleeping under a tarp on the rock-laced, hard, frozen ground or staying in our uncomfortable, but warm, beds until 5:00 a.m. at which time we were awakened and went outside to climb under the tarp we had set up for ourselves the night before. It was very cold. A deep frost had set in during the night and the now-crackling tarp was about six inches too short to cover both head and feet. I watched the stars move slowly across the sky and, as twilight broke, listened to the animal sounds of the forest.

Our assignment was to write a letter to ourselves that would be mailed back to us in six months so that we could see our progress and remember what we had experienced during our stay at the School. I had trouble writing anything and didn't want someone else to get hold of the letter. And worst of all, I didn't want me to see the letter.

Until now I had not really thought about the school. It seems like lifetimes away, but in reality was really only a short time ago. And I realize that I gained so much….

> Repeated TBI can result in cumulative neurological and cognitive deficits of time can be catastrophic or fatal. (See Bibliography, 11-3). After one brain injury, the risk for a second injury is three times greater; after the second injury, the risk for a third injury is eight times greater. (See Bibliography, 11-4).

# Chapter Twelve
## Independent Medical Exams—
## Prescription Drugs to Fix the Problem

Social Security sent me for a physical exam by one of their doctors for my disability claim. The doctor they sent me to see was so nice that I had trouble believing it. She had me do the same neurological tests that Dr. Dapper did but with a different finding.

In her report, she stated that I had "slowed speech, cranial nerve abnormalities including a right deviating tongue, weak left orbicularis, occuli, right facial droop, left arm and leg weakness with 3/5 strength in her left thigh flexor, left knee extensor, left foot dorsiflexor, left arm abductor. Her finger-nose-finger was slightly impaired on the left side. She had slowed speech with probable word finding difficulty, but a fairly good ability to communicate otherwise. She had a slow, but normal, gait." She also found that my Romberg test was positive and was actually now higher than Dr. Dapper's finding.

In her functional assessment/medical source statement, she states, "The claimant is severely impaired. She is not necessarily unable to stand or sit for long periods of time. However, I do not believe that she would easily be able to lift more than 10 pounds secondary to right upper extremity weakness. She also has significant environmental limitations, including visual, communicative, cognitive, and environmental (inability to look at computer screen secondary to severe episodes of vertigo)."

"She has manipulative limitations such as complex motor function."

"Although there is no evidence on MRI of intracranial damage, this can be seen in the case of closed head injury. I think that given the claimant's exam and history, as dictated above, there is no doubt that she suffers from severe neurologic damage as a result of this accident, which limits her ability to function in the workplace."

I sent a copy of this report to my insurance company.

The next week I got a phone call from the IME neuropsychologist's office wanting to postpone my appointment. I pretty much pitched a fit and told the girl that I had been waiting three months already for the exam so that I could be approved for my therapies. She called a truce and agreed to let me come in at my appointed time.

I am not sure that that was a good idea because the neuropsychologist, who received no reports written by my doctors or therapists from the insurance company, was on super speed mode to get the interview over. Fortunately, I had all of my reports with me and gave him copies of them.

(See "Indicative and Contributory Signs of Bad Faith", pages 441, 442, numbers 27, 40 and 41). I was at his office for over two hours before he offered me a glass of water and a bathroom break. One of the things about head injury is that an injured person just cannot keep up with fast dialogue. By then I had pretty much shut down and gone into stare mode.

After about two and a half hours he prodded me back into the now and told me that he was going to recommend that I see an optometrist for my vision problems as he believed that I would experience a "concomitant improvement in many other areas of her functioning." He agreed with Jan's neuropsychological report that I should see an endocrinologist to make sure my adrenal glands and thyroid were functioning adequately and that I was not suffering from depression. Strangely, he told me that he was going to recommend that I wait for three to six months before doing any more psychotherapy. This seemed to me quite contrary to a diagnosis of head injury that completely changes your whole life. He said it was because I was already doing so many other therapies. He asked me if I would agree to that. I didn't really feel that I had a choice, or he would write in his report that I was uncooperative, and I just wanted to get out of there.

The neuropsychologist further stated in his report that I should continue cognitive therapy and six sessions of biofeedback. He wanted me to start taking anti-depressants and sleeping pills, which was quite confusing considering he said I didn't need any psychotherapy. He made me repeat what he had just told me several times and I was unceremoniously excused from his office.

Although these medication may be essential for TBI (medications for anxiety, depression and/or agitation), they may not help at all with cognitive functioning and—in some cases—actually may cause and contribute to cognitive dysfunction. Despite dramatic improvements in care of brain injury, there still does not appear to be a commonly used medication or medication regiment that can be used to alleviate or improve cognitive impairments. Though there is substantive research suggesting that some medications may improve cognitive functioning in individuals with cerebral dysfunction, findings are mixed and can be confusing. (See Bibliography, 12-1). (I was told by my vision therapist that anti-depressants cause the pupils of the eyes to dilate, causing blurring).

It states in the report that the IME neuropsychologist sent to the insurance company that "the patient is experiencing significant sleep difficulties at this time and should be prescribed some sedating antidepressant medication. I would recommend she undergo a trial of Trazodone at night and Zoloft in the morning. This combination has been found to be quite successful with patients having experienced similar injuries. It is imperative that her sleep condition be improved." That is why I was doing trauma release/psychological work that he said was unnecessary! And once again, did he read my medical history for substance abuse issues?

In the report, which didn't get done until November 8, he limited my biofeedback to ten sessions but said I should "continue to receive ongoing cognitive rehabilitation treatment." He left out the endocrinologist part and said that I had no depression. He also wrote that psychological treatment should be suspended at this time but did not write that it should be started again in 3-6 months. He did, however, refer me to an optometrist for a vision evaluation. The insurance company denied my visits to the psychologist. I kept going anyway.

He also stated in his report, "it does not appear the patient is capable of working at this time and she should be considered temporarily totally disabled."

The insurance company finally agreed to schedule me for an optometric IME. This, of course, would not happen for another two months.

I wrote a letter to the IME neuropsychologist after receiving a copy of the report and told him that he had told me that I should continue with psychological treatment in 3-6 months, not stop it completely and forever and that I should see an endocrinologist.

After the IME neuropsych evaluation, I tried to reach the attorney who I thought was going to represent me. Several weeks later he finally returned my call and said he just couldn't take my case. It would have been nice if he had told me that long before he did. He referred me to an attorney close to where I live and I went to see him. He pawned the case off on a young man who was one of his partners and, I thought, way too nice for my case. I continued lawyer shopping.

I received $500 from the Brain Trust to help me with my expenses.

# Chapter Thirteen
"Dr. Satan" and
"Insurance Whores"

I think that the fact that this is Chapter Thirteen is apropos with my IME with the physiatrist. I swear to God when she entered the exam room a faint odor of sulfur followed her. This woman, as far as I could see, had no pupils in her black, reflection-free eyes, wore strangling support hose that looked like ace bandages and was about seven months pregnant. For the life of me, I could not get past staring at her belly and sending sympathy to the child about to be born to this woman. I thought about Rosemary's baby and even pictured a bifurcated tail, cloven hooves and horns on the little waif as it came out.

Maybe I was having another hallucination. Perhaps she was a mind reader because I felt that she took an instant dislike to me. Perhaps it was because I wore a slight grin on one side of my face from the vision I was having.

I was not in the oven hot room, which I thought was appropriate under the circumstances, for five minutes, which she complained about for the first minute, when she referred to the neurosurgeon's report. This was the only report, I might add, the insurance company had sent to her. She mentioned "Dr. Dapper", the neurosurgeon with the turtleneck and white smock's name, and I made a snorting noise.

Her hackles went up, she glared at me and said, "What? You have a problem with Dr. 'Dapper's' report?"

I told her that I did because he had the report all screwed up and I had questioned if he had me mixed up with someone else. Well, I didn't think it possible that a doctor could treat another human— or rather, a human being—that way, but I was wrong. She said, "Well! He seems to think you have psychological problems and I tend to agree with him."

I knew then and there that she had already made up her mind and my visit there was a folly. (By now I'm thinking about sending a sympathy card to her baby when it is born).

I asked her if she had reports from anyone else. There was one letter from my cognitive therapist that was written on the first day I went to therapy stating that I needed to quit work because I would have to attend so many therapy sessions. There were no reports from any chiropractors, massage therapists, physical therapists (Pilates and vestibular), acupuncturists, ear doctor, neuropsychologist, cognitive therapy notes, biofeedback therapist, medical doctor, optometrist or psychologist. The doctor was tainted. (See "Indicative and Contributory Signs of Bad Faith, pages 439, 440, 441, 442, numbers 17, 24, 27, 30, 33, 36, and 41).

    I wisely had taken my big fat 3-ring binder with some of the doctor's reports with me and pulled out reports from the Dizzy Doctor, Dr. Scannell, my neuropsychologist and behavioral optometrist. She read part of Dr. Scannell's letter and demanded, "What kind of doctor is he? What qualifications does he have to diagnose this?"

    I explained that **she** had worked in the trauma unit at Jackson Memorial (Miami) for eight years before moving to Colorado and is a surgeon. She disgustedly threw the report on the exam table and said Dr. Scannell was not qualified to diagnose head injury since she was "just a surgeon", and she could hardly read her writing. I could easily read her writing and so could everyone else who read the report.

    I then gave her a copy of my neuropsychological evaluation, which she didn't read, but wanted to know what his diagnosis was and started ranting about not finding the heading where it said specifically <u>Diagnosis</u>. I told her that I thought that **she** had put the diagnosis in the last paragraph. Because there was nothing with a heading that said <u>Diagnosis</u> she said she wouldn't even consider reading the report because there was no exclusive diagnosis heading.

I told her that I didn't have copies of the physical therapists' report or the cognitive therapist's report, but I was sure that the insurance company did.

She then started arguing with me that Mary Ann was my speech therapist, not my cognitive therapist. I told her that Mary Ann was my cognitive therapist and my speech therapist and had also shown me some exercises for my tongue and the left side of my face, which are weak. I told her that when I stuck my tongue out it curves to the right, and I have trouble putting it in the roof my mouth and clicking it. She made a "tuh" sound, made a face and shook her head.

She asked me if I had any other reports. I told her what the "Dizzy Doctor" had found about my hearing and that I was going to vestibular therapy to help me with my balance. She made a huffing sound and looked back down at her notes.

I told her that the doctors in Boulder wanted me to have a cineoesophagram because of my choking problem and a PT scan because of the pain in my legs and lower back, mid back and neck muscle spasms and because my left arm and leg go decorticate.

Her head snapped up and she asked me in a tone that you would use on a six year old, "Who told you **that** word?" I said, "Well, for one thing I worked ambulance for eight years in the eighties and also because one of my therapists called it that." She made a "puh" sound, got the "I just sucked a lemon" look on her face and shook her head.

We moved on to my past history. She kept asking me if I was depressed, if I was on any medication. I told her no, that I was not depressed and was not on any medication. I told her that I just couldn't sleep more than three hours at a time—sometimes because of stomach pain, sometimes because of leg or back or head pain.

She wanted to know why, actually demanded to know why, I wasn't on any medication for sleep and depression. I simply told her because I wasn't depressed. She wanted to know how I would know if I was depressed. I told her because I'd been depressed fourteen years ago and knew what it looked and felt like so if it came up now I would know what it looked like and how to stop it.

Then she got hooked on depression and hammered away on that and said if I went to a "real" psychiatrist he would find that I was depressed. I told her that I had had an IME neuropsychological evaluation and the IME doctor said I had no depression. She asked if I had a copy of his report. (I guess an IME neuropsychological report carried more weight for her than a regular neuropsychological report). I told her that I hadn't received a copy of the report yet. She asked me what his diagnosis was. I told her he said I had a brain injury, needed to continue with my therapies and see an endocrinologist and an optometrist. She actually softened a bit about this report. She asked when the exam had been done. I told her five weeks ago.

I told her that I had taken several tests for depression and they didn't show that I had full-blown depression. She asked me if I wanted to kill myself. I restrained from saying, "not until I met you," but instead told her no. Her whole query was like an interrogation. I was waiting for her to tip the light bulb and start the water dripping.

Dr. "Satan", which is what I decided to call her because I was sure she was at least Satan's sister, asked me if I had any other IME's. (One of the only jokes I remember from my whole life was about the guy sitting peacefully in a church praying when all of a sudden with a deafening roar a bolt of lightning split the church in half. The man didn't even flinch. Satan appeared to the guy and asked, "Didn't that scare you?" The man answered, "Why should it? I'm married to your sister").

I told her that I had an exam done for Social Security Disability and that the doctor who did the report was shocked that the insurance company was giving me trouble. I told her that the doctor said I definitely had a head injury but had no depression. She wanted to know if I had that report. I told her "not yet".

I also told her that the SSI doctor did some tests for balance and vision and said my vision and balance were so "messed up" that she was afraid I would hurt myself so she stopped doing the tests. I also told her that the SSI doctor said that I needed vision therapy and to continue with the doctors and therapy I'm doing.

She asked me about specific pain areas. I told her again about leg, low back, mid back and neck pain. I told her my head ached pretty much all the time but was worse when my vision got over-stimulated. I told her my leg pain was mostly when I lay down and was worse after lying down for several hours. I told her my mid back ached toward the afternoon when I was tired—usually after 2 p.m. She asked if I was in pain all the time. I could have sworn I had just explained that to her. She questioned me like she thought I was lying to her.

Next came the physical exam. She did not check my pupils—my chiropractor found that the left one is slower. She did her hammer on joints test. I told her my reflexes had been okay but, as Dr. Anna had found, the nerve loop in the arm and leg were okay, it was the message loop from the brain to the arm and leg that didn't work.

She snorted and asked me what qualifications Anna had to diagnose that. I explained what Anna did (muscle testing). She said Anna wasn't qualified to know that. (An exam done by the IME rehab doctor would later confirm Anna's finding).

She put the tuning fork to the top of my head. I could only feel it on one side. She said, "Good!"

She told me to stand up, close my eyes and tip my head back. I walked over to the wall because I knew I would fall over backwards—that's why I was in the vestibular rehab. I tipped my head back, closed my eyes and fell into the wall. She disgustedly told me to do it again only move out away from the wall. I did and fell over backwards against the wall and ended up on my butt. She turned away and said, "Good!" (After this, the pain in my lower back increased dramatically).

She had me walk back over by the exam table and told me to stand on my tiptoes. I tried to think how to do that and said, "I can't remember how."

She snarled, "Don't think about it! Just do it!"

After awhile, with one hand on the exam table and one on the floor I got somewhat on my tiptoes, bent over at the waist and with my knees bent. She then told me to walk. I took two steps and fell over. She said, "Good!"

Next she had me walk toe to toe. And, of course, I couldn't drag my left foot in front of my right foot without hanging onto the table. She said, "Good!"

She then did eye exams. She told me to follow her finger. As soon as she moved her finger, my eyes closed. When I opened them, I had trouble finding where her finger went. "Good!" she shouted!

This was followed by more motor exams.

She then happily announced that there was nothing wrong with me physically, that all of my problems were psychological. I said, "So what about all of my other care-givers? Are you saying that none of them know what they're talking about?"

She angrily answered with a foreign accent so this sounded really funny, "That's exxaaactly what I'm saying. You don't have a head injury. I know head injury and you doooon't have one. I graduated from Haaavard and the Mayo Clinic. I know head injury. In my report I'm saying you don't have a head injury. You need a psychiatrist and someone to take your case who knows what they're doing. I would do it, but I'm closing my practice next month so you'll have to find someone else."

...I thought there was nothing wrong with me.

I then asked her about my cognitive problems. She snappishly said, "I could care less about your cognitive problems!"

She then picked up the reports that I had given to her, threw them across the exam table and as they fluttered about the table and onto the floor yelled, "These are useless! I'm not even going to consider them. You can get dressed now and leave." She gathered up the reports, banged them against the table to coordinate them and flounced out of the room to make copies.

Even though I had just spent an hour being abused, I was somehow able to blink, breathe, move again, get dressed and leave. I went to my primary care doctor's office and fell apart. The two doctors who were there that day were aghast when I told them what happened. They shook their heads and said, "She's the one who doesn't know what head injury is! She sounds like she was paid off by the insurance company." (They seemed to have forgotten that it was their fellow doctor who pointed his finger at his head and said, "it's all up here" when I asked him what was wrong with me).

The next day I saw one of my friends who is an acupuncturist and told her who had done my IME. She was appalled and said, "I heard that woman is a witch and mean." I concurred.

She then told me that Dr. Satan had referred a patient to her who told her of this doctor's abuse and unprofessional behavior, sued her and won. She said the doctor never referred anyone to her again. "Gee, I wonder why," she said. "She really had that guy screwed up."

Several months later I started working with another therapist who told me pretty much the same story about someone Dr. "Satan" had referred to her who was so loaded up on drugs he couldn't function. Dr. "Satan" had prescribed the drugs.

At about the same time, I started hearing stories about "Dr. Dapper" misdiagnosing people and putting them on drugs that were wrong for them. When confronted by other doctors I was told that he would literally lie.

I have learned to ask questions of many people before I go to any doctor. Some people will rave about the doctor simply because they don't know any better because they haven't gotten another opinion or two or three. The best source for information is another caregiver. I learned to "sniff out" doctors and clinics that have "rolled over" or become "Corporate Patient Factories". For example, I know of one clinic that sends people with head injuries to six sessions of counseling. They then tell the people that they are fine and send them on their way. Once the person has tried to commit suicide or starts having numerous seizures, the hospital they are sent to sends them to therapists, finally, who haven't "rolled over". Make sure you find hospitals and rehab centers that are not—somewhere down the ownership line—owned by an insurance company. (See "Indicative or Contributory Signs of Bad Faith" pages 449, 441, 442, number 24, 27, 34, and 41).

I learned to take meticulous notes after all doctor's appointments so that I would not forget what was said versus what got written in the report.

In 1944, The U.S. Supreme Court (in opposition to the insurance industry) found and established that insurance was interstate commerce and therefore within the jurisdiction of federal government regulation. This sent a shockwave through the insurance industry which realized that the Federal Government and Federal Trade Commission would be there to oversee and regulate their industry, disturbing the long-standing close and cozy relationship established by insurance companies with each state insurance department commissioner. So the insurance industry went to work to have the U.S. Supreme Court decision overruled. The insurance industry put all their lobbying might and resources together and in less than a year had the U.S. Congress in 1945 pass the McCarran-Ferguson Act which overturned the findings of The U.S. Supreme Court and exempted the insurance industry from federal regulation and returned oversight authority of the industry back to each state. The McCarran-Ferguson Act also in effect also exempted the insurance industry from federal antitrust laws making the industry non-competitive. Being exempt from federal anti-trust laws, the insurance industry and insurance companies are free to collect and share information and documents amongst themselves which are not available to policyholders, claimants, and/or their attorney. Because insurance companies are much less regulated, they are free to collude and charge as much as much as they want. (See Bibliography, 13-1).

Several weeks later I received "Dr. Satan's" report. I can only say that the report was one of the most bizarre things I have read in my life. For a doctor who ascribes to having graduated from Haaarvard and the Mayo Clinic, it is obvious in her report that she really did not know about head injuries. She said, basically, that I had no loss of consciousness and my MRI appeared normal so there was nothing wrong with me other than psychological problems. Neither of these is criteria for a head injury.

In her objective findings she states, "The patient is very slow in answering questions about her age but can pick out some of the letters that she wants me to read rather fast, and identifies them easily among a stack in a binder." (Of course, I practically lived on a daily basis with the reports and had tabs from whom each report was written and those two tasks come from a different part of the brain). "There are a lot of gyrating motions when I ask her to walk on her toes, and this actually demonstrates excellent balance. She has again gyrating types of motions on Romberg testing, reaching with the arm towards the wall behind her to prevent a fall but she actually never falls or has a significant sway that is dangerous." Later on she again states, "at no time did the patient fall while in my office" and that, "there are indeed, as Dr. [Dapper] has stated, an abundance (Dr. Dapper never used the word abundance) of psychological factors involved in the patient's current presentation, but I do not believe that an adequate work-up has been done to sort out how much of the presentation is due to psychological factors and how much may indeed be due to true post-concussive symptoms." (Psychological problems are a part of post-concussive syndrome).

In another paragraph she wrote numerous sentences describing symptoms of apraxia but at no time in the report does the word apraxia appear.

The insurance company wrote a follow-up questionnaire to Dr. "Satan" asking what injuries were causally related to the accident. She answered in part, "She likely has post-concussive symptoms (also known as traumatic brain injury) based on the injury mechanism, but how significant these are as opposed to a contribution from psychological factors and an element of symptom magnification is unclear without further work up."

Another question was about her current diagnosis and prognosis. She, once again, stated that she felt that I was "clearly affected by psychological factors that needed to be more closely examined in order to render appropriate medical care. Until this is accomplished, her prognosis is guarded."

Dr. Satan recommended that all of my treatments be put on hold until a complete medical evaluation was performed—"including formal testing by a psychiatrist." Throughout the original report and the follow-up answers, she made reference to a psychiatrist or that I needed psychological counseling eleven times. And at one point she stated that my left hand was "decorticate"....hmmm, but there was nothing wrong with my brain?

A few months after that, one of my attorneys and I had a conference call with my nurse caseworker at the managed care. I told the nurse what had happened in Dr. "Satan's" office and how I had been treated. I also told her what I had heard "around town" from other caregivers about this abusive doctor and the lawsuits filed against her. She made appropriate noises and clicks and apologies but three weeks later I was told by my attorney that the case manager told him that if Dr. "Satan" had not closed her business that they would have sent me to her for my rehab.

Unbelievable...!

No wonder they call these doctors "insurance whores".

> Persons with visual neglect can experience: reduced visual scanning of the environment; they may only or primarily demonstrate awareness of objects from their midline and to the right; a disregard or ignorance for the left side of their bodies and limbs; for instance, a person sitting in a wheelchair may be unaware that his/her arm is dangling on the wheel instead of the armrest; another example is that a person may only shave the right side of his face and not the left; difficulty maneuvering or mobilizing without running into things; difficulty reading—a person may see half of a word or set of words and experience difficulty comprehending what he/she is reading; difficulty locating objects, for example, a person may only eat the food on the right side of the plate and leave the

food on the left of the plate; decreased safety awareness; impaired independence with all activities of daily living. (See Bibliography, 13-2).

# Chapter Fourteen
Doctors Who "Do Work for the Insurance Company"

On November 15, 2002, I had a videoesophagram performed with speech therapy completed at the Boulder Hospital. For this test, I sat in front of an x-ray machine. The picture could be seen on a monitor while I was given crackers, bread, fruit nectar-thick liquids and honey-thick liquids. It would have been a great snack for the mid afternoon when I took the test but for the barium smeared on the food and mixed into the drink. After putting said items in my mouth, I was told when to chew and swallow.

The results of the test showed that I had "significant oral dysphagia which required oral motor treatment". This particular problem was a safety issue since I was choking when drinking thin liquids or eating mechanical soft or solid foods. The oral peripheral examination revealed that my tongue deviated significantly to the right side. I was unable to retract the tongue and pull it up in order to move substances back into the oral area.

"Diagnosis: oral apraxic dysphagia, apraxic verbal disorder. Oral stage of swallow deficits place patient at risk on mixed consistencies and regular consistencies as well as the inconsistent oral patterns of deficit. Recommendation: Referral to outpatient speech therapy for apraxia of swallow disorder (dysphagia)."

The problem of my throat deviation was becoming more apparent as part of the choking problem. Dr. Anna worked on adjusting my hyoid bone and relaxing the muscles around my throat. My diaphragm was still going into spasm.

I met with three different attorneys. One would only take slam-dunk cases where he basically told the defendant and the insurance company what they would pay. He didn't want to take my case until he got the report from "Dr. Satan". I met with another attorney who just wanted to sign me up that day. The third attorney was the one I chose to sign with.

He was upfront with what my case was worth at that time and seemed to love what he does. He talked about his family, his surgeries, his shortcomings, and was able to laugh at himself for those shortcomings. In other words, he appeared to be a kind human and had a good reputation as an attorney. I would have to wait and see if my impression was correct.

Suddenly things started happening with the insurance company once I got an attorney. They still had not approved vision therapy. I was still waiting for the IME exam, but everything else started to fall into place. I was able to sleep better at night and not wake up in a panic attack worrying about being "cut off" by the insurance company. I also started using Bach Rescue Remedy and Star of Bethlehem at bedtime that helped me sleep.

I got a letter from Social Security stating that they were denying my claim. I went to our local Congressman to ask for his aid. The Congressman's Aide sent a form letter to Social Security asking for a reason for the denial. SSI simply said that I did not qualify because I worked after the accident for six months—they did not take into consideration that I had to cut my hours back to four days a week, then two days a week because I had so much trouble functioning.

> Ronald Regan letters: As you know, the Social Security System is teetering on the edge of bankruptcy. ...Finally, we must eliminate all abuses in the system that can rob the elderly of their rightful legacy. The same situation prevails with regard to disability payments. No one will deny our obligation to those with legitimate claims, but there's widespread abuse of the system which should not be allowed to continue. (See Bibliography, 14-1). (Thanks to Ronald Reagan, we must now jump through unjustifiable hoops to collect money that we paid into the system. Do the words

"teetering on the edge of bankruptcy sound familiar?)

I filed an appeal and started asking about Social Security attorneys. The one who was recommended to me was a no-nonsense woman who I was told usually only had to go through one appeal versus those attorneys who have to go through two or more appeals. This woman, Judy, was like a pit-bull and sent two-page letters to my caregivers with detailed questions asking for detailed information.

My lost wages money ran out. I filed for food stamps and discovered that I was also eligible for a whopping $277 in welfare. One perk was that the telephone company was only going to charge me $14.99 base for my phone service because I was on welfare. I also applied for Medicaid. I tried to imagine what I would do with the leftover money after I paid my half of the $950 rent, electricity, and telephone. Right…. My daughter moved in with me to help with my expenses.

The insurance company sent a letter to the IME neuropsychologist asking how many cognitive sessions it would take "for the claimant to reach MTV" or the maximum I would ever be able to function. He answered that "the rehabilitation sessions should inherently be limited to assisting her in the development of the necessary compensatory and limit-setting strategies required for her to function effectively in her everyday life. As such, it would be expected that most of those interventions would have already been initiated. She should receive some ongoing direction toward learning cognitive exercises to improve her functioning but the value of these interventions are inherently limited by the fact that she is not working and has no specific outlet toward which to direct her rehabilitation." (I thought my outlet was learning how to boil an egg).

He then states, "should [the patient} continue to receive cognitive rehabilitation services these should continue over the next six months on a limited basis. Assuming she has learned all of the skills necessary to cope with her everyday life, given her current brain dysfunction it is reasonable to conclude that one visit every month for the next six months would be appropriate."

Next came the shocker. "If she does return to gainful employment an increase in her rehabilitation sessions would be reasonable."

My cognitive therapist almost fell over when she read the recommendation. She wrote a letter to the insurance company and stated, "I am not sure how she can return to gainful employment without the ability to think or use cognitive skills. The commonly understood concept in physical medicine and rehabilitation is that people with brain injuries are rehabilitated in order to return to gainful employment, not that they spontaneously recover and then go back to work and then after that get rehabilitation."

My therapist then called the IME neuropsychologist and asked him what in the world he was thinking. He told her "I shouldn't even be talking to you. I do work for the insurance company." Well! There you have it in a nutshell….

My cognitive therapist also requested in her letter at least another 16-20 additional treatment sessions for my oral dysphagia since "choking is a life-threatening situation". She then stated that cognitive therapy could be addressed at a later time. The insurance company approved 20 sessions for the oral dysphagia and said that the cognitive treatment should be done at the same time as the oral dysphagia sessions. This would be pretty tricky to do in a one-hour session with all the breaks I had to take so that my brain could rest and the fact that it sometimes took several minutes just to stick my tongue out because of the apraxia.

Mary Ann wanted me to be in either a treatment facility so that I could be worked with everyday or to at least see her twice a week. My daughter and I discussed my moving to Boulder. It would not feasible for me because I could not pay rent or live on my own. At that time there was a two-year wait in Boulder County for housing under HUD (Section 8).

I started physical therapy with Marianna and Cass. I started to learn another set of terminology. During the first two sessions Marianna noted that I had ataxic movements and the three outer fingers on my left hand were curled up in spasm, my hand turned outward and down and my arm was bent at the elbow and was hypertonic. The same held true for my left leg and foot.

I had difficulty crossing the midline of my brain. For example, we did some Brain Gym exercises. When I tried to draw a figure eight, the left side flowed smoothly and the right side of the circle took several minutes and was jerky (co-contraction). With my left hand, the figure eight was just the opposite—flowing smoothly on the right side and jerky and slow on the left side. The same held true when I tried to walk in a figure eight.

When I attempted the exercises my head was shaky, and it took a great deal of effort to do the task because my muscles were fighting each other. I had great difficulty marching, crawling backwards and cross crawling—lying on back, raising left arm and right leg then right arm and left leg. After these sessions, my quads seized up for days. Age wise, my motor skills were at pre-school level.

My therapists contacted Craig Rehabilitation Center in Denver to see if I could be admitted for therapy. Marianna told me that since I was not in a wheelchair, I was not a candidate for their program. Marianna called numerous people about my apraxia and went to a seminar in San Francisco about apraxia. She had many questions that no one seemed to have an answer for except to say that apraxia sometimes took years to treat and that treatment for apraxia was not always successful.

I flew to my dad's house at Christmas with my two daughters. My older daughter drove from the airport to my dad's house even though I tried to tell her that riding in a car would make me sick. By the time we got to my dad's house, I sat down in the chair and had a strange "seizure-like thing" but was conscious of those around me. I couldn't stop the jerks and couldn't talk or respond to anyone for a couple of minutes. I could hear my stepmother ask my daughter, "Is your mom okay?" My daughter said, "Yea, she's okay."

Obviously my daughter was still in denial. For the next few days I was "out of it" and slept 12-14 hours each day. I wasn't sure if the sleeping was from the change in altitude, the exhaustion from flying, over-stimulation or from the seizure.

I kept hitting my head on things—trying to get into the car, on the door of the dryer, leaning over and misjudging where objects were. Each time I hit my head, my speech and vocabulary would go down the toilet for about a week to two weeks and my dizziness and falling would increase. My "spatial awareness" was missing. This is similar to a small child stooping under a table, raising up and hitting their head. Because they lack spatial awareness, they will continue to do this until trained not to or they learn not to.

In my third physical therapy session, Marianna did an evaluation for apraxic tendencies. She noted that my right quad had a high tone spasm. She had me try to rock while lying on my back and holding my legs then try doing movements while sitting on the exercise ball using midline crossing and reciprocal movements.

My lower body worked in the opposite direction of my upper body instead of together. I could only initiate bouncing on the ball with my arms crossed at shoulder level.

I tried walking by counting. We used two poles, one in each hand, with Marianna holding onto the poles also while walking behind me. It was the first time I realized that I didn't really understand how to walk. I wondered if that is why I fell over all the time.

I was also doing cranial sacral work and myo-facial release work with Cass. The cranial sacral work left me bewildered at first because I was not used to the fluids moving in my brain and spine. The myo-facial release work was like heaven when my muscle spasms released. The muscles still were not familiar with being relaxed so they did not stay relaxed for very long.

A lady from the state Medicaid office came to my place for a home visit. She asked me questions pertaining to my injuries. She experienced my inability to walk very far without falling over, the slowness of my writing, my slurred words and the difficulty I had initiating answers to her questions.

Her questionnaire was made up of questions that pigeon holed people and were inaccurate for diagnosing brain injury. For example, did you lose consciousness, did you hit your head—neither of which is pertinent to receiving a brain injury. She frankly told me that even though she had seen me and that I was obviously messed up, my request for Medicaid would probably be denied as that is standard procedure the first time around for claims and because they use the numbers total on the questionnaire with loss of consciousness and hitting the head having a high number of points. My, I thought, how efficient from a financial standpoint…. Not only that, they didn't even know the pre-requisites for a brain injury.

A person with suppression impairment, illusions, and visual neglect from a visual system impairment following traumatic brain injury can <u>appear</u> to present: disorientation, impaired judgment, impaired safety awareness, impaired balance, impaired reaction time, poor attention span, behavior problems, impaired task performance, decreased independence performing activities of daily living, agitation, confusion, and uncooperative behavior. (See Bibliography, 14-2).

I had a dream one night that eight people were standing around me while I lay on a table. One of the people said, "She's hurt." Another one said, "We need to heal her."

I was still driving to Boulder every week for therapy unless it was snowing too hard. The weather still didn't seem to be much of a factor for me since I really didn't have the brains God gave a goose and, therefore, didn't comprehend the danger.

My cognitive therapy was moving along at a snail's pace because of my vision deficits. I could find words faster now but still had trouble getting them out of my mouth. I could literally see the words in the back of my head but couldn't get them to move forward. I found that if I picked up an object or clicked a pen I could move the word faster. My therapist said that is because the language and motor part of the brain are next to each other in the brain and when the motor part is triggered, it triggers the language part. I could only do a few series of word exercises because of brain fatigue.

The biofeedback showed that most of my brain was still mostly asleep, especially on the left side. I could not do any logic work on the computer. The visual stimulation made me nauseous and the noise and changes on the screen startled me.

On January 7, 2002, I met with a holistic neurologist who had been recommended to me by the first attorney, my cognitive therapist and neuropsychologist and the Dizzy Doctor.

Her diagnosis was that my case was high complexity. She stated that I had concussion without loss of consciousness, apraxia, post-traumatic brain syndrome, a head injury, vestibular dysfunction, and muscle contraction. She also questioned if I was having complex partial seizures because of the spasms, the losing track of conversations, loss of time and the many falls or near falls.

Her recommendations were to continue the current treatment I was doing addressing apraxia, to obtain plain films of the lumbosacral spine with flexion and extension views to rule out spondylolisthesia because of my severe lower back and leg pain. She said I needed to have urodynamic studies and a GU evaluation to determine if my bowel and bladder problems were due to an upper motor neuron, lower motor neuron or apraxic problem. The results of these tests would be the basis on which a decision about further studies might be necessary including MR imaging of the lumbosacral spine.

She further recommended that I consider institution of B vitamins for decreasing nerve pain. We discussed a B-100 complex as well as sublingual B12 at 1000 mcg a day. For spasms and possible seizure, it was recommended that I take magnesium chelate at 400 to 500 mg a day and would be best taken at night to promote sleep. I was to discontinue any other magnesium supplements.

The doctor said to use arnica Montana on inflamed areas. We discussed stress management techniques to reduce muscle spasms. She recommended that I become aware of my posture while performing activities during the day and focus on relaxing my muscles. She said that stretches to the cervical area could also be helpful. It was most importance that I prevent further falls. It was recommended that I keep a diary. She said that if my falls at this rate persisted, she would recommend that I wear a helmet (my cognitive therapist also recommended that I wear a helmet).

She further stated that, "In reviewing the patient's history in order to determine if her falls are related to cataplexy, she has had vivid dreams. She does not have sleep paralysis and does not give a history to suggest episodes of falling asleep with excessive daytime sleepiness. This is something we will keep in the back of our minds and evaluate should nothing else pan out as the cause of her falls."

I was to do a sleep deprived EEG in order to determine if I had seizures. I was instructed to document my episodes of losing track to determine if these were secondary to poor focus or lack of attention or if these were due to loss of consciousness.

The neurologist also stated that she thought that my hypothalamus had been damaged and that is why I broke into sweats when I took any supplements, meds or ate, especially, sugary foods or carbohydrates.

The doctor provided me with a handout on good sleep hygiene so that I could optimize my sleep. I was instructed to sleep on my back. B vitamins were suggested to help in decreasing my pain. We also discussed the benefits of guided imagery. Rapid thinking often affected my ability to sleep. We reviewed blocking techniques with redirection.

We talked about the basics of a diet appropriate following head injury, many of which I had already instituted. I was told to not eat processed foods or foods with additives or preservatives and to limit compounds such as MSG and aspartame as well as caffeine and simple sugars. I was provided with a handout regarding this information as well as one that outlines foods that have natural antioxidant properties.

I was to start taking a combination of essential fatty acids paired with Vitamin E 400 IU a day and to increase my ester Vitamin C to 1000 mg a day. It was recommended that I institute a multivitamin with minerals and micronutrients without iron. Finally, I was told that alpha-lipoic acid can be an excellent antioxidant taken at 50 to 100 mg a day and slowly increased as necessary and as tolerated to 200 to 300 mg bid. We reviewed the side effects of alpha-lipoic acid, which include an increase in bleeding time as well as potential drops in blood sugar.

"I also recommend treatment for her visual abnormalities as this is a significant contributor to her dysfunction."

I was to return to her in six to eight weeks for a follow-up exam. The insurance company said they would pay for this one visit, but because she was not with my managed care, they would not pay for the follow-up visit.

I was already taking many of the vitamins that the doctor prescribed. I never ate anything with refined sugar or aspartame anyway so that was certainly no hardship to stay away from. I had not had anything with caffeine in it for over three years, including chocolate. Juice is too high in sugar content. I also never ate processed foods or foods with additives or preservatives. Basically the only thing I added to what I was already taking was more B vitamins and water-soluble magnesium (CALM). I actually started sleeping better at night, my pain was less and the muscle spasms and seizures lightened up.

I hoped with this additional report that the insurance company would finally approve my vision therapy. I was denied again.

On Thursday of that week, and after requesting vision therapy for nine months, I finally had my appointment with the IME optometrist. He seemed nice. I told him about my double vision—the Froggy definition. He said, "Just a minute. I need to go look this up. I never can remember the word for it." And he left the room. When he came back he said I have what is called oscillopsia and explained that it was when the eye sends an image to the brain, the brain doesn't know what to do with it so sends back a message for the muscles to twitch—trying to get an image that the brain recognizes. Finally, a name!

He told me that I should have 18-24 sessions of vision therapy and that the prism glasses were appropriate. He said I needed to switch my progressive lens to a traditional flat bifocal lens. I told him that I tried a flat top before, and could not wear them. He would not listen to that and in his report stated that I needed the flat top lens as the progressive lens "is known to exacerbate dizziness and imbalance situations triggered by visual stimulation."

In his report he also stated that I would need 12 vision sessions, not the 18-24 that he told me.

The following week I met with the "Dizzy Doctor", the IME optometrist, the vestibular therapist (the one who was going to release me from therapy after four sessions), another physical therapist and a neurologist. The physical therapist who I had never seen before had me do several exercises. After these exercises, the physical therapist realized that I had apraxia and pointed it out to the doctors. They all agreed that I had apraxia and should continue with balance therapy. The original vestibular therapist looked rather sheepish and disappeared quickly.

> Vision is the most far reaching of the five senses and an important part for performance

of activities of daily living (Scheiman, 1997). The overall treatment goals for a person with visual pathway disruption are to normalize visual input as much as possible and enable residual vision for activities of daily living by incorporating as few adaptations as necessary. This can be achieved in therapy by: neuromuscular re-education; therapeutic activities, self-care and home management, home safety evaluations, use of adaptive devices, community and work reintegration, education and solicitation of input for goal setting from the person with brain injury and his or her family and supporters. (See Bibliography, 14-3).

The next day I met for the first time with my new orthodontist Mark to be fitted for a mouth splint, or an Intraoral Orthopedic Mandibular Repositioning Splint. Mark was not with my managed care but the managed care did not have any dentists that specialized in neurological problems so I was allowed to continue going to him. The insurance company paid him their "re-priced" amount and I had to pay hundreds of dollars out-of-pocket to cover the difference.

We met in Mark's conference room where he explained everything that he was going to do and patiently answered any questions that I had. His assistant took panoramic x-rays then Mark did a very thorough exam of my face, neck and head. He touched spots on my head that I had no idea were so sore. Because of the apraxia, I had trouble opening my mouth on command and my mouth could only open 33 mm at the time. The soreness in my head and neck muscles was caused because I was clenching and grinding my teeth.

The signs and symptoms I had were "TM (temporal mandibular) joint sounds (my jaw cracked when I opened my mouth), joint pain, joint dysfunction, masticatory muscle spasm, other muscle spasm, pain of head, neck and shoulders, frequent headaches, pain associated with ears, bruxing/clenching and dizziness."

Mark admitted that he did not specialize in what I needed to have done to my jaw. I mistakenly told him to go ahead and do what he knew to do since he at least knew something. Other orthodontists said something silly like, "Your teeth are straight..." Well, the problem wasn't with the teeth. It was with the jaw.

Mark's assistant filled my teeth area with a nasty-tasting, clay-like substance to make a mold of my teeth.

Mark's diagnosis was that I had a traumatic joint injury with extrinsic injury and Temporomandibular Pain-dysfunction Syndrome. I was instructed to not eat anything hard or chewy because that would exacerbate my symptoms.

I returned two weeks later for my splint. That night I slept for twelve straight hours. The pressure was taken off of the muscles in my head and neck and jaw, and I felt when I woke up that I had stepped into a new dimension.

## Chapter Fifteen
### Grab a Gas Mask and Put on a Helmet

One Sunday afternoon before my trip to Boulder, my muscles were extremely tight. I could not imagine making the trip the way I felt. My chiropractor referred me to a woman who was a massage therapist and an acupuncturist. She did a massage that day and told me that because I was in such bad shape she would do acupuncture on me without concern about whether the insurance company would reimburse her. (It was also quite snowy that week which I found exacerbated my pain, stiffness and head stuffiness).

That week the acupuncturist called the managed care nurse. I was approved for 16 sessions of acupuncture because the acupuncturist told the nurse that even Harvard (Haaarvard) Medical School said it took at least 10 sessions of acupuncture before a person knows if the acupuncture is going to work. She started by specifically going after the pain in my spine and working on the dizziness. Within four sessions, my back pain and dizziness eased somewhat.

After a few months, however, I was getting very annoyed with her sessions. She was often late for my appointments—sometimes not showing up at all. Oftentimes she would have me on the table for two to three hours by the time she did the massage and the acupuncture. She would massage for about forty-five minutes then start putting in the needles. By the time she got done putting the last needle in a half hour had elapsed, then she would leave me there for another half hour to an hour. I learned later that acupuncture needles should only be left in for twenty-five minutes as that is how long it takes Chi to make a revolution. I started having more seizures, and she admitted that she was probably causing them because she was pushing my body too hard.

She was not very good at massage (it was more like Lotion Application 101). On the last day I went to her I asked her to not do massage before the acupuncture session because my back actually hurt worse from the lengthy time I was on the table. She did the massage anyway, stating that I "really need it and I won't charge for it." I also found out later how much she was charging for these sessions, up to $300, and how creative she was at finding things to bill for. I also learned that she was tutoring my chiropractor on how to bill more for individual therapies she was doing.

I quit going to her.

I found an acupuncturist in Boulder who had done a lot of work on head injury cases. I knew that I had to be very careful about how much the caregivers charged because I would run out of money if the caregivers charged inflated prices. I had signed a paper at the new acupuncturist's office stating that my treatments were to be $72 per visit. I was quite pleased with the price he was charging and figured out that I could do several sessions with him without using up so much of my insurance money.

A few months later, I found out that the acupuncturist was charging the insurance company $225 per visit. The Catch-22 was the fine print that said they would charge an extra fee for billing the insurance company. (If you do the math, it would have cost $720 if I paid out of pocket and got reimbursed by the insurance company versus the $2,225 the insurance company paid because the acupuncturist did the billing. The extra $1,505 would have paid for almost twenty-two more sessions).

My biofeedback therapist recommended that I start using Pine Needle, Basil, Eucalyptus and Jojoba essential oils in my bathwater for pain. I found that these oils worked much better for me than Epsom salts.

The managed care sent a list of names to my attorney of rehab doctors that I could choose to see. There was actually a name on the list that my attorney knew and wanted me to go to in Boulder. My first scheduled appointment was a mess. Most of the staff had gone home that day with the flu.

The doctor I was supposed to see also went home because her child had the flu.

I saw a different doctor who immediately recognized that I had apraxia and ataxia. He had me do a few of the exercises others had me do and said I wouldn't need to do any more as the apraxia was "obvious".

Fourteen months after the accident, Dr. Betsy, my new rehab doctor, ordered lumbar spine x-rays. I had spondylolisthesis of L4, which means basically that the pars part of the vertebrae had been fractured and the vertebrae had shifted forward causing nerve pain. The discs above and below L4 were bulging outward. When I leaned over, L4 popped right out of position.

> In the spine, L (lumbar) 3 controls the sex organs, uterus, bladder, knee, prostate and large intestine. L4 controls the prostate gland, muscles of the lower back and sciatic nerve. L5 controls the lower legs, ankles, feet and prostate. (This information can be found at any chiropractor's office or online). (See Bibliography, 15-1).

A few weeks later I saw the physician's assistant for the doctor I had been referred to but still had not seen. In the report that she wrote to the insurance company she recommended injections into my spine. I balked immediately at that and said that I preferred to try the holistic route first.

The insurance company grabbed the word injection like a rabid dog grabbing onto a pant leg and worried it to death stating that they were cutting off all of my other therapies and that I could do injections only. (See "Indicative and Contributory Signs of Bad Faith", pages 440, 444, numbers 26, 44, and 52).

A few months later the insurance company wrote a letter to all of my caregivers stating that they were not paying for any of the treatments I had had from the date of the physician's assistant's examination on—because she had written the word "injection" in her report. This, of course, threw everyone into a panic because they had been treating me for almost two months with no compensation and with no compensation in sight since I had no income.

Finally on March 4, I met with the doctor I had been assigned to. She said that she felt that injections were too invasive and painful and would rather try other therapies first. She wrote scripts for acupuncture, massage, chiropractic, and physical therapy. The insurance company shot themselves in the foot by letting me go to one of the doctors in their network who obviously didn't "work for them" or hadn't "rolled over" and wasn't an "insurance whore".

It took a lot of phone calls and maneuvering by my attorneys to get the insurance company to honor the doctor's prescriptions instead of forcing me to do the injections. My attorneys spent a lot of time convincing the insurance company to pay the back money owed to the caregivers. Each and every month that my caregivers sent a bill to the insurance company, a battle ensued with my insurance carrier as to whether or not they were going to pay for the therapies and appointment. (See "Indicative and Contributory Signs of Bad Faith, page 441, 442, numbers 34, 35, and 36).

I had the MRI done on my lower spine. It supported what the x-rays had shown. My rehab doctor said I would need to have surgery on my lower back and neck to keep them in alignment. In the meantime, I was still waiting for the approval to start my vision therapy.

I checked into the hospital in my hometown and had adrenal and thyroid tests done.

A letter from the welfare office arrived stating that my financial benefits were being dropped to $134 a month from $270 per month due to budget cuts. Whoo! Wee! I was thinking about going on a shopping spree.... I started hearing then about other people with head injuries who were now homeless because they couldn't even rent a room for $134 a month. (Less than a year later the governor of Colorado would go on TV and brag about how the state was now financially stable. The following session, a bill was passed allocating $3.4m toward advertising for tourism).

On March 7, I received a letter from LaVonne Mercure of the state Medicaid Benefits office.

In the letter the Medicaid worker stated that I was not eligible for benefits because I: "did not lose consciousness, you worked until June after the accident, your brain MRI is normal, although you complain of balance problems and visual disturbances, your recent neurological exam showed that you had normal strength and sensation."

It then, unbelievably, states, "although you complain of memory problems, a neuropsychological evaluation showed your cognition was normal". (I have just stepped into another alternate reality!) She says also "your overall medical conditions limit you to work not requiring more than 20 pounds of lifting occasionally and 10 pounds frequently. You should avoid working around hazards and unprotected heights due to your complaints of balance problems. Because of your report of memory problems you are limited to work that doesn't require extreme attention to detail or require frequent interaction with the general public.

Although some kinds of work are not possible, your condition does allow other less demanding work. This conclusion takes into consideration your age and education."

Amazing, considering she had reports from both neuropsychologists, the cognitive therapist, biofeedback therapist, chiropractors, physical therapists, and the social security doctor. Much of what was written was verbatim from the Social Security Doctor's report. I know for a fact that they did not have a report from Dr. Satan or Dr. Dapper as a letter sent to me from Medicaid showed that those reports were requested but never sent. Nowhere in any report that had been sent to them was it stated that my cognition was normal.

I, of course, appealed the finding.

When my cognitive therapist and neuropsychologist read the letter from Medicaid they were almost dumbstruck. For months now on an almost weekly basis notes were written about my severe cognitive problems, my apraxia, pain problems, physical, visual and balance problems, reports of which the Medicaid lady had. To top it off, it was quite obvious that the Medicaid worker did not know much about brain injuries.

My therapists wrote a joint letter stating: "The definition of mild traumatic head injury according to the Mild Traumatic Brain Injury Commission of the Head Injury Interdisciplinary

Special Interest Group of the American Congress of Rehabilitation Medicine (1993), reads 'This definition includes instances in which TBI (traumatic brain injury) is produced when the head is struck, or during a whiplash injury in which the head is not hit. Cerebral CT scans or MRI's may be read as normal.' This is an outrageous statement." They go on to write six pages about my cognitive and physical problems as outlined in the neuropsychological evaluation and therapy notes that Medicaid already had.

A few months later I received a letter from Medicaid saying that they were scheduling a hearing.

During that time period, I had been having a lot of problems communicating with my psychologist. She was bound and determined to have me do the EMDR therapy (Eye Movement Desensitization Reprocessing) even though I kept telling her that the buzzers made my brain go goofy. (I understand that this method is very well received by many people with head injuries and Post Traumatic Stress Syndrome so please don't discard this therapy because of my experience. However, I heard from another therapist that EMDR sometimes brings up issues that the EMDR technique does not address).

On the last day that I saw the therapist, I was holding the EMDR buzzers in my hands. She, of course, wanted me to sit there with my eyes closed. For some odd reason, I kept sneaking peeks at her. Each time I peeked I saw that she had her head laid back on her chair and her eyes were closed. I wanted to ask her if she was too tired to be there working with me but kept my mouth shut.

She started choke coughing, tried to gag it down and then the most unbelievable thing happened. All of a sudden a choke came her way and she let the most tremendous, awe-inspiring fart I have ever heard in my whole life and then started coughing.

Well....

Now, how do you continue to: a) keep a straight face, b) take this person seriously, or, c) continue in the same room with her ever again with any modicum of respect? I was saved from this mind-boggling conundrum when I learned a couple of weeks later that she moved out of state. We had no closure and I often wonder if she ran away in embarrassment, humiliation, or simply realized that she was an idiot.

I put together a little set of rules for your visit to a therapist:

1. Do not go to a therapist who does not listen to you.
2. Do not go to a therapist who lays their head back with their eyes closed and pretends to be listening.
3. If they start to choke-cough, ask them to leave the room or, if you do not want to be so bold, put on a helmet and a gas mask.
4. Get up and leave the room before you start giggling uncontrollably. TM

After this awe-inspiring therapy session, I went to my cognitive therapy, to my biofeedback, then to my physical therapy. For some dumb reason, every time I thought about what had happened, I got the giggles so hard I could not control my thoughts or the tears running down my face. My therapists had the giggles, too.

It was a few weeks later that I got really angry over this and realized that I had not been honored—not just because of the enormous fart but because she moved without talking to me so we had no closure. Several months later, I learned that no one had heard from her.

# Chapter Sixteen
## Miss-Managed Care—
## Hillary, What Were You Thinking?

I went ahead and did my follow-up visit with the holistic neurologist and paid for it out of my pocket because I felt that it was worth it to continue with a doctor who "had a clue". The insurance company had sent a list of neurologists to me who I could go see who were with the managed care network. I did some research on the names on the list and each one was crossed off by other people with head injuries or caregivers I knew who said these doctors were not in my best interest. The most frequent response was that the person was "mean" to the patients or that they were so arrogant that they did not listen to the patient.

By this time I had my x-rays and MRI of my lower back. In the follow-up exam, the neurologist added more items to her diagnosis. She added Degenerative Disc Disease, Vestibular Dysfunction, and Episodic Tremors.

> The visual pathways are nerve tracts that extend off the back of the eyeball. The visual pathways carry neurological messages from the eyes throughout the brain. For visual processing to take place, the visual pathways

and brain lobes must be intact. (Scheiman, 1997). Damage to a brain lobe that the visual pathway passes through or a direct insult to the pathways may cause impairment. Following traumatic brain injury, any, all, or a combination of systems may be disrupted (Scheiman, 1997). Some the most common visual impairments include: suppression, illusions, and visual field neglect. (See Bibliography, 16-1).

Finally! I started my vision therapy on March 20, 2003, one year and almost four months after the accident and ten weeks after I saw the IME vision doctor.

The optometrist I was going to had to follow the insurance company's guidelines that said I had to have flat-line bifocals. She prescribed them with a whole new frame since I could not see without my glasses and the lenses needed to be factory fit to the frame since they had a prism in them with a strong correction for astigmatism and it would take almost a week to get the new glasses. The insurance company, of course, balked at the new frame stating that they had already paid for one frame. Through many phone calls, letters and maneuvering by the optometrist and my attorney, they ended up paying for the full set of glasses. I was finally reimbursed for what I had paid out of pocket a year prior, as was the optometrist but at a "re-priced" managed care rate from what she had charged. Fortunately all but two of my previous caregivers had agreed to treat me at the "re-priced" rate or I would have been thousands of dollars in debt by now.

The first week of vision therapy was quite torturous. I had no idea that my eyes were so wacky. By this time, my right eye was deviated to the right and up like a misaligned headlight. I kept my head turned to the right and slightly tipped when I walked. It was found that my eyes were not working together, or teaming. One eye would occasionally shut off, or suppress, completely (suppression impairment). That eye would turn back on then the other eye would turn off.

No wonder I ran into walls and doorways and fell down all the time. You will notice that if you close one eye, it appears that objects shift to the side. Because I was not actually closing my eye, I didn't realize the shift was going on. I just knew that objects were not where I thought they should be.

When I tried to follow an object my eyes jerked back and forth (nystagmus). Something as simple as moving my eyes caused pain in the muscles above my eyes. Within five minutes of starting the therapy, I started yawning and wanted to fall asleep. When I got home from the therapy I slept for three hours.

Many of the visual problems I was now experiencing had not been evident when I had my testing done the year before. I wondered how many of the new problems would not exist if the insurance company had allowed me to start vision therapy when it was requested.

Each day I spent about twenty to thirty minutes doing eye exercises. I spent the rest of the day exhausted if I did the exercises in the morning. I finally realized that it worked best if I did the exercises before I went to bed.

It was immediately clear to me that the flattop bifocals did not work. I literally could not walk across the room without falling down and I had an urge to go into a rage. (Perhaps if you are head injured or someone you know is, the rages they might be experiencing are simply caused by incorrect glasses or the need for glasses). My optometrist ordered a pair of progressives with the new prescription and told the insurance company that I absolutely could not wear the flattops.

After I got the progressive lenses with the new prescription and had done a couple of sessions of vision therapy, I started to understand my surroundings and my place in those surroundings a little better. Before that, I truly did not understand time and space. My posture improved, my headaches started to lessen, and I could actually read from side to side and comprehend some of what I read.

The first take-home eye exercise I was given to do seemed simple enough. I closed my left eye, held a pencil out in front of my right eye, pulled it slowly toward my eye, held my gaze for five seconds, then moved it slowly to the right, holding my gaze for five seconds, then to the left, up, down holding each for five seconds. I then repeated this exercise with the left eye. This was quite painful to the muscles above my eye. When I looked to the left I got a blinding headache and my eyes jumped from side to side

Several weeks after starting the vision therapy, my cognitive therapy and physical therapy started to accelerate. I was finally able to look at pictures and graphs without becoming as nauseous, albeit for only a short time before my brain overloaded, but at least I was able to look.

In my biofeedback, my theta waves still shot way up and my beta waves dropped when I opened my eyes. My eyes were still taking most of the brain juice I had accumulated.

In my cognitive therapy I was still having trouble retrieving words. Sometimes I couldn't say the word, but I could write it even though I sometimes lost track of my hand control while trying to write. I had learned to help initiate words by rubbing my fingers together, or by picking up an object.

It took me three to four hours to do logic matrix problems that should have taken twenty minutes to do. My tongue still deviated to the right. My speech was still slurred and I still drooled and lost food out of my mouth—not the perfect date.

Within months of starting the vision therapy, my biofeedback sessions improved. My theta waves were becoming more controllable and not flying off the top of the graph as much. My beta waves were coming up, but it still showed that only the right side of my brain was working part-time. The other half was still asleep. I tried sniffing sweet orange essential oil and my beta waves went up even more. Spearmint essential oil also worked for me.

In physical therapy I was learning to roll over and open doors. If I had a door open part of the way and someone took the door from me, my muscles just continued to pull the door even though the door was no longer there. I still had to have touch to be able to turn my muscles off or on. Once the door was gone, I just fell forward, which really seemed to disturb the person who took the door from me.

With any activity that I did, my head tilted to the right to initiate the action. When I did the activity I listed to the right as if there was a hurricane wind coming my way. I still could not initiate many actions on command without hanging on to someone's hands. The memory of how to do the action wasn't there. Someone had to show me how to do the action, and then it was a crapshoot if the action actually happened. I found that the toes on my left foot, when stimulated, would help my left foot or left leg work. But as long as I was flat-footed, nothing happened.

    I advanced to trying to walk my feet from side to side while sitting on an exercise ball. My feet would not move until I crossed my arms. I could not walk backward unless I crossed my hands above my head. We became more creative on how to get my brain to send messages to the muscles. We tried tap dancing. That didn't work very well. I couldn't get my left leg to move at all. We asked the receptionist to come into the room and hold my hands since I had no balance while I tried to get the tap shoe on the left to make any noise. Occasionally I could get a scuff, scuff sound. The receptionist had taken tap dance lessons as a child and went nuts and became her own minstrel show. I'm sure that in the back of her mind, she could hear the strains of "Way down upon the Suwannee River"….

    At least we had fun. One must laugh at one's self or go nuts. I chose laughter.

Closed head injury as a result of motor vehicle accidents places extreme stress on the brain stem—which connects the large areas of the brain to the spinal cord. A large number of functions are packed tightly in the brain stem, e.g. regulation of consciousness, breathing, heartbeat, eye movements, pupil reactions, swallowing and facial movements. All sensations going to the brain, as well as signals from the brain to the rest of the body, must pass through the brain stem. (See Bibliography, 16-2).

Each week in my biofeedback I was better able to lower my theta waves and raise the beta waves. We started doing word retrieval to measure brain function. My brain, for the most part, was still pretty much asleep. Jackie described my brain cells to a forest that had been clear-cut with sprouts growing out of the stumps. I was still like a baby. My brain could only be awake for short periods of time before it went back to sleep. I realized that the medical profession is trying to teach us with brain injuries to sleep totally incorrectly. If they allowed us to establish a sleep pattern like a baby does, since our brain cells are growing like a baby's brain cells do, I wonder if we would get better faster and wouldn't have to use sleeping pills that interrupt our healing process. (I spoke with a friend of mine who was twelve years into her brain injury and said that it was six years before her sleep patterns regulated and that was with sleeping pills).

I got a notice that I had a Medicaid hearing scheduled for March 16, 2003. I didn't think much about it because I thought it was for social security. I assumed that my social security attorney was preparing for this. When I didn't hear from her a week before the scheduled hearing date I finally called her. She, of course, had heard nothing from Medicaid because the key word in the equation was "Medicaid" not "Social Security". She told me that she would take care of it pro bono and asked Medicaid for a postponement and told me that she had never done a Medicaid hearing before. She said that usually the Social Security hearing precedes the Medicaid hearing and Medicaid automatically goes into effect once the social security benefits are approved.

The hearing was rescheduled for June 16.

I finally had my appointment with the endocrinologist. He told me that my adrenal and thyroid levels were low but within accepted limits. After looking at the chart he showed me, it appeared that the only way the levels could be lower would be if they were non-existent or if the glands were completely missing. I actually wondered if someone had cut off the bottom of the paper.

I asked him why head injuries caused adrenal and thyroid problems. He said because the pituitary gland sends the needed information and chemicals to the thyroid and adrenals and, since the pituitary gland is in the head, it is common for the gland to malfunction when the head is hit. I told him that I had spoken to no medical doctor who knew about this. He said he was not surprised as there was really no information published about it that he knew of. I asked him why and he told me that it's simply because no one has done it. This doctor was semi-retired. I asked him why he didn't write a report on it. He looked sheepishly down and said, "It would take a lot of work."

> From a chiropractic point of view, C-1 (cervical-1), or the atlas, controls the pituitary gland, the blood supply to the head, scalp, bones of the face, brain, inner and middle ear, sympathetic nervous system, eyes and ears. (See Bibliography, 16-3). (A friend of mine compares the atlas to a finger trying to hold up a bowling ball). The neurotransmitter dopamine is somewhat more prevalent in the left hemisphere of various species. The neuromodulator norepinephrine is more prevalent in the right hemisphere.

Neurohormonal estrogen receptors are more prevalent in the right hemisphere than the left hemisphere. (See Bibliography, 16-4).

My physical therapist bought a video camera, and we started videotaping some of my sessions. I wish we had done that at the beginning of the therapy because there were some things I could do now that I could not do at the beginning of the therapy.

My cognitive and biofeedback therapists joined us in physical therapy sometimes to come up with ideas about how to initiate function. We tried dancing to fifties music—the stroll. I did fairly okay going to the right but going to the left was out of the question. I figured that since the room we used had a door on one side and another door on the other side I could just keep going to the right and come back through the other door. That wouldn't work, of course, as it would take too long, it would be lonely out there in the hallway and my therapists would wonder where I went.

We tried saying nursery rhymes to integrate speech, rhythm, rhyme and music to help with my balance. I just could not get the words of the rhyme out of my mouth.

By this time, however, I could do eight to sixteen repetitive physical movements before becoming over-loaded and falling over.

We realized that my hyoid bone was shifting due to my weak neck muscles and causing a lot of the choking problems. On top of that, when I got fatigued, my diaphragm would go into spasm. I sounded like a little mouse squeaking when I tried to breathe.

One night my diaphragm went into spasm and I could only inhale or exhale in miniature gasps for almost an hour. I was bent over at the waist and had to crawl an inch at a time toward my daughter's bedroom since I couldn't get in enough air to call her name and I was in so much pain I could barely move at all. She finally noticed me lying on the floor and came out of her room. She kept asking me what she could do for me. I lay curled up for quite some time. I was about to cave in and say let's go to the emergency room, but I couldn't figure out how we would get there since I absolutely could not straighten up enough to do anything but rock back and forth, let alone crawl down the hall to the elevator then out to a car. My daughter started rubbing my back and after awhile the spasm started to subside. (Later on, my chiropractor would tell me that the problem stemmed from the C-4 vertebrae.)

I was finally able to go to sleep but the next day I discovered that the ligaments around my tailbone hurt so much that it was too painful for me to sit for more than a couple of minutes. When I stood up I shrieked from the pain. My muscles were still not getting the message to turn off. I bought a sitz pillow, which my daughter called a butt donut, and I started sitting on that.

One day at my physical therapy I was sitting on an office chair and decided to see what would happen if I spun in a circle. Mary Ann told me that when she worked in the hospital, everyday they would go through the brain injury ward and spin the patients in their wheelchairs to help them learn where they were in relationship to their surroundings—to re-set the brain. Well, I can honestly say that if you have a head injury with balance and vision problems this is probably not the wisest thing to do if you're alone and have someplace to go within the next, say, day or two....

Within a few months, my therapists wanted me to start marching around the house while singing or counting. I could not do this. I could either walk or sing or count or breathe. I could not do two of the things together. As with any of the exercises that I was instructed to do, I simply could not breathe and do the exercise at the same time. Although this doesn't seem like a very efficient way to do something for an extended period of time, it is the only way I could initiate and do the exercises.

It was at about this time that the insurance company decided that they didn't like the fact that the rehab doctor they were sending me to see was actually sending me for therapies and tests that I needed so they decided to have me go for an IME on their own doctor. Until this appointment was completed, the insurance company said that they were going to cut off all of my treatment...again. (See "Indicative and Contributory Signs of Bad Faith", pages 439, 440, 441, 442, numbers 14, 17, 26, 27, 30, 34, and 41).

Of course, by the time they informed me of this, the week before the IME appointment, I had already scheduled my appointments around my Medicaid hearing that was on a Friday in Boulder. They scheduled the IME for a Monday with an IME doctor also in Boulder. All of my appointments had been on Tuesday and Wednesday for over a year. I wondered if I was supposed to cancel all of my therapies or drive to Boulder three times in eight days....

There is no logic, I have found, in the way the managed care manages my time, mileage, motel expense and money they are paying out for IME's. Each IME costs the insurance company at least $800-$2,000 per session (very lucrative—no wonder doctors become insurance whores). My attorney figured that the insurance company will eventually have paid out close to $8,000 to keep me from getting $5,000 worth of therapy.

The funny thing about this was that the IME doctor they sent me to shared an office with my attorney's wife who is a neurologist but has a different last name than my attorney. The insurance company certainly would not know this. My attorney, of course, sent a letter to the doctor stating that he was representing me and would he be so kind as to inform him of any reports he might be missing (since the insurance company seemed to love to send out just the reports that said, basically, that I needed a psychiatrist, even though they still had not approved me for psychological or psychiatric therapy and had admitted long ago that I had a head injury). I was also told that this IME doctor had a rather gruff bedside manner and often got angry with the patient.

When I received the IME notice, my attorney was out of the office on vacation so I spoke with the attorney who had been taking care of most of my insurance problems. He told me that I could go ahead and reschedule the appointment. First I called the receptionist at the IME doctor's office. She said I couldn't reschedule the appointment because the managed care had made the appointment. I called the scheduler at the managed care whose name and number were given to me in case I needed to reschedule my appointment. I waited several days without a return call. Three days before the appointment I called the managed care again and learned that they wouldn't talk to me or reschedule the appointment because they weren't allowed to speak to me even though they had given me a number to call in case I needed to reschedule my appointment. The only thing the person at managed care would tell me was that I would have to have my attorney do the rescheduling.

In the meantime, my rehab doctor wrote a prescription for me to also see a physical therapist, who does ultra-sound on muscles to see if they are working. If a muscle doesn't work she attempts to specifically re-train each muscle. Because I had the IME coming up, the insurance company would only approve four sessions. That would be just enough to find out what muscles weren't working and no time for re-training the muscles. What would the point be, I wondered, in only allowing four sessions?

I met with my Social Security attorney on July 17, 2003 to discuss my Medicaid hearing scheduled for the next morning. She kept telling me that she had never done a Medicaid hearing before and could not understand why we were doing the Medicaid hearing before the Social Security hearing. She even mentioned this to the Medicaid hearing judge before the hearing started.

The Medicaid hearing was done over the telephone and took less than an hour. It was very easy doing it that way rather than having to show up in a hearing room. The Medicaid Judge said it would take a few weeks for her to make a decision.

My daughter and I had to move into a place that, let's put it this way, the rent was only $650 a month in a town where normal rent is about $1,100 a month. This was quite an assault to me—especially to my sense of smell and cleanliness. The stove was so bad that I told the landlord that there was no way we could use it. The landlord took it to the dump. We used oven cleaner on the shower tile to get it clean.

Shortly after we moved, I awoke one morning to a throbbing in my right cheek and pus running out from between my teeth. I called my dentist and he prescribed an anti-biotic and pain meds. Of course I didn't take the pain meds, but I did take the antibiotics. When I went to Boulder the next week, he said that I had an abscess because my teeth had shifted so far forward from the trauma to my jaw that the teeth were now rubbing on the bone. The bone was also shrinking. He also informed me that I would have to have orthodontal work done to correct my bite. He said that my gums on the upper jaw were turning hard and retreating due to the nerve damage.

The dentist re-iterated that I was not to eat anything crunchy or hard such as popcorn, nuts, or other hard or chewy foods because my teeth and jaw just could not take it. He said that it would cause bleeding and leave a build-up of scar tissue in my jaw. He told me that I would probably lose my teeth in that area.

A few weeks later the insurance company wrote a letter to my cognitive therapist and attorney stating that the cognitive therapist had exceeded the 20 authorized visits indicated for oral apraxia as recommended by the IME neuropsychologist—neuropsychologists are testers and are actually not trained in apraxia rehabilitation. The claims adjustor said that if I disputed this decision that I could seek my own IME, but until I got my own IME done, the insurance company would pay no more money for my therapies. My attorney wrote back that I did not have the money to seek my own IME exam and they could not simply cut off treatment after completing a series of recommended treatments since I was still symptomatic. The insurance adjustor wrote back that they were standing firm on their decision.

My attorney wrote a letter back to the insurance company and told them that I had undergone tests at the hospital that showed objective symptoms of apraxia. He stated, "the [Colorado] insurance regulations are very clear that further investigation must be undertaken. Specifically, the language in regulation 5-2-8(E)(1)(b), Unfair Method of Competition and

Unfair or Deceptive Acts of Practices in the Business of Insurance states that presumptive violations include:

> Denying a claim, either in whole or in part, or otherwise reducing payment for PIP benefits arising under automobile insurance policies when the denial is based solely on any of the following: Relying upon utilization review prescribing a prospective fixed treatment plan as a final determination of benefits. Any insurer intending to deny PIP benefits upon completion of a course of treatment over the objection of the claimant shall not deny future benefits upon completion of the course of treatment without conducting further investigation, *including but not limited to, a current evaluation to determine the necessity of further treatment."* (See Bibliography, 16-5). (To find insurance laws for your state, simply go into your computer and put in the name of your state plus statutes plus the keywords for what you are trying to find).

He further told them that I do not want to get into a legal battle with the insurance company. By now I had several points on which I could have sued for bad faith. The attorney suggested that if they wanted to send me back to the IME neuropsychologist that that was their prerogative but that I did not have to seek or pay for an IME at my expense based on the insurance regulation and case law mentioned above. The attorney further stated that the IME doctor had concurred with Mary Ann's finding that I needed this treatment based on the objective tests performed at the hospital and that they now had a duty to either pay for additional treatment or send me back to that doctor for a re-evaluation (cineoesophagram).

The insurance company opted for a letter to the IME neuropsychologist asking for his recommendation for further treatment based on my cognitive, rehab and neurology doctor's reports.

The IME neuropsychologist stated that although he "hasn't seen the records from Boulder Community Hospital" he does "rely on Dr. Keatley's report of the patient's test results regarding her oral apraxia." He made note that I did not complain of symptoms or provide a history as that described by Drs. Keatley and Cohen. (Perhaps that is because he was doing almost all of the talking and we never broached the subject. This is another example of "covering your ass").

He continued, "Be that as it may, I concur that the patient should receive the recommended sessions for treatment of that condition." He back-tracked from his previous cognitive rehab recommendation that I should have only six sessions in a six month period (after returning to gainful employment) coinciding with my oral apraxia therapy and stated that he would not recommend that it be deferred but that, rather, I should be taught cognitive exercises which I could practice at home during the period of treatment for my oral apraxia. He also said that I should do the treatments recommended in his previous reports which included the sleep deprived EEG which my holistic neurologist had recommended also.

I had tried to set up an appointment for a sleep-deprived EEG and left numerous messages with two different doctors. I left messages for five months and, strangely, both doctors called me back on the same day. They said they would put me on the list but the waiting line was six months out. I never did hear back from them and ran out of insurance money so I was not able to go to an appointment anyway.

In the meantime, the psychologist who had me see the EMDR psychologist, still had not been paid based on the IME Neuropsychologist's report stating that I did not need to have any psychological treatment. (Evidently "Dr. Satan" and "Dr. Dapper's" reports were subject to where the insurance company wanted to initiate approval for therapy).

The psychologist was asked to submit a letter to the insurance company justifying ongoing care.

In the letter, the psychologist stated that ten months had now passed since the IME doctor's report and that I was still manifesting "numerous psychological as well as post-traumatic stress symptoms such as anxiety and anger related to her loss of self-sufficiency, cognitive functioning, self-worth, and pre-accident health. She is also unable to participate in pre-accident social, recreational and family activities. Her mobility is limited and she cannot work. Her occupational future is uncertain and anxiety about her ability to support herself overwhelms her." He recommends "the resumption of psychological counseling in or to help identify and release triggers, which revolve around the memories associated with her accident. She would also benefit from intervention that would focus on coping strategies that deal with her shaken sense of self, the physical, emotional and cognitive losses she has suffered and better anger management." He recommended another six to ten sessions with reassessment at selected intervals.

The insurance company said, "No."

The annual net profits of three of the largest insurance corporations: State Farm-$2.4 billion, Allstate-$2.2 billion, Farmer's-$320 million. The net worth of these three insurance corporations shows a value greater than some countries: State Farm-$74 billion, Allstate-$34.2 billion, Farmer's-$12.1 billion.

Total: $120.3 billion. That is just the value of the three largest companies. (See 16-6). The following is the most recent ranking of auto insurance companies as of March, 2011 by a Consumer Report. These rankings are subject to change. (See Bibliography, 16-7).

| Hall of Shame<br>Non-payment of Claims<br>*Bad-faith Practices* | Hall of Fame<br>Payment of Claims<br>*Good-faith Practices* |
|---|---|
| 1. Hartford (the top 3 vary between 1, 2, and 3 worst) | 1. Amica |
| 2. Allstate | 2. Chubb |
| 3. State Farm | 3. Credit Suisse |
| 4. Berkshire Hathaway | 4. Royal and Sun Alliance |
| 5. CNA (U.S. Insurance) | 5. GMAC-major interest in Geico |
| 6. ACE Re-insurance | 6. Swiss Re America |
| 7. American Family | 7. Electric Mutual |
| 8. Liberty Mutual | 8. Cuna Mutual |
| 9. Unitrin | 9. Quincy |
| 10. Zurich/Farmer's (Farmer's has been consistently one of the 5 worst for most years) | 10. North Carolina Farm Bureau |

(The 50 worst and 50 best insurance companies can be found on the internet at www.fightbadfaithinsurancecompanies.org).

In Colorado, major insurers have lobbied hard for caps on damages and for higher thresholds for filing a lawsuit, arguing that excessive litigation drives up the costs of insurance. Studies indicate that soaring premiums have far more to do with the rising cost of auto repairs than with personal-injury lawsuits. In fact, the number of civil cases filed in Colorado has dropped dramatically in the past decade, even as the population has surged.... At trial, no one is allowed to mention whether a defendant even has auto insurance, which leaves the jury with the impression that the victim is going after some ordinary joe rather than a multi-billion dollar corporation.... "Here's the effect of the propaganda," says Denver personal-injury attorney Steve Kaufman, "People believe that everybody who sues is looking to win the lottery and that all these frivolous lawsuits are driving their premiums up. It's ridiculous. Compared to when I first started practicing twenty years ago, you settle cases for half of what you use to. You work on a contingency basis so, why would ever take a case that was frivolous? The costs alone would wipe you out." Sixty percent of the civil trials in Colorado last year resulted in defense verdicts. (See Bibliography, 16-8). What kind of profits do auto insurance companies get? A recent study performed by the Christensen Law firm revealed that the most profitable auto insurance company in the United States in 2010 was State Farm Insurance, pulling $1.8 million dollars. There were several others that weren't far behind. Farmers Insurance came in at $1.686 billion and Liberty Mutual at $1.678 billion. Auto insurance profits total in the hundreds of millions to low billions every year. According to the American Association for Justice profits for the auto insurance industry as a whole total close to $3 trillion dollars annually. (See Bibliography, 16-9).

# Chapter Seventeen
## How to Do the Tango in 5/4 Time

I continued going to my physical therapies and by then my right leg was hurting so much that lifting and bending my leg to tie my shoe would cause me to break out into a sweat.

My new physical therapist, Kristie, did ultrasound on my transverse abdominal muscle and found that it worked somewhat but when I was commanded to engage the muscle, it took a long time before anything happened (apraxia).

I quickly learned in this therapy that a lot of my movement problems were caused from just not understanding how to do the movement. For example, I was using my back muscles to try to do some of the exercises instead of my abdominal muscles.

During the second session, she found that the small muscles in my back didn't work at all and that the large back muscles were doing the work. These small muscles had atrophied, which is exactly what my first acupuncturist had told me and that not one of the medical doctors believed. She also stated that she was amazed that I could walk.

Kristie taught me how to stand up straight, which had been a total mystery to me before then. All week between sessions I practiced being "long" and was surprised at how much better my balance was. I could now walk almost three blocks before my muscles fatigued and I started falling over. I still had to avoid getting near a curb, walking along hedges, especially with the sun shining through the branches, and walking on uneven, uphill or downhill surfaces.

During the next sessions, she found that the small muscles in my legs also didn't work and were atrophied. When she put my legs up in a harness apparatus and instructed me to spread my legs, lift one leg, or whatever, nothing happened. I told her that I knew that my legs didn't work. She wrote in her report for that day that she had never seen me "more apraxic or ataxic".

In my other physical therapy with Marianna, we were attempting to dance to classical music as that was the only music that didn't make my brain schiz out. She had to hang onto my hands unless my feet never left the floor and my hands were crossed, over my head or at shoulder level. The placement of my hands depended totally on whether my foot was moving forward, backward or sideways. If there was movement requiring my foot to be lifted, I just could not move.

In our silliness, we tried to mimic Martha Graham, Twyla Tharp and Josephine Baker. I couldn't get my hips to shake like Josephine and decided to give it up because I didn't have a grass skirt or a pineapple atop my head. We then decided to try the tango. I just could not get the timing—we were counting in 4/4 time with three steps forward, one step sideways, and the other foot brought even. I couldn't even get it when humming Hernando's Hideaway!

Marianna came to the session the next day quite excited about a program she had heard the night before on NPR. She told me that Dave Brubeck had talked about how he was now writing music to 5/4 time instead of 4/4 or 2/4 time because of the midbrain cross-over. (Eastern music is in 5/4 time as is some music by French composers). He said that people did not want to record his music because they thought that Americans would not be able to understand it or dance to it.

I immediately said that I could do the tango to 5/4 time and, sure enough, I could get the steps to the tango in 5/4 time. We started experimenting with other dance movements, including walking and, sure enough, if I did these things to 5/4 time I could move better. In other words, if I walked while counting, 1, 2, 3, 4, 5, 1, instead of 1, 2, 3, 4, 1, I did much better. Thank you, Dave Brubeck!

One day I said to myself, "Screw it. I'm going to heal myself." I realized I had to start "accepting" the therapies I was being given and that it was only I who could integrate those therapies into my being. For some reason, the thought of getting better had become frightening for me. There is a saying that a problem might be like being in a pile of shit. It may stink, but it's warm, soft and familiar.

One day in biofeedback therapy, Jackie hooked the electrodes to my face. We found that the right side of my face was extremely weak and had virtually no strength, or muscle tone, after twenty minutes of facial exercise to correct my droop. The next week we did the same thing on my neck and found that the right side of my neck also lost its oomph after about forty minutes of exercises.

My vision therapy was moving along fairly well considering where I was when I started. For the first few weeks when I went to the office, I bounced from one wall to another in my attempt to maneuver the hallway. I had to stop where carpet colors changed to figure out if I needed to step up or down, and the "downward" non-existent steps made me feel like I was falling.

We did a timed exercise where I had to find the sequential letters of the alphabet in a grouping of nonsensical words. It took me four times longer to find the letters than is average. When I tried to track anything with my eyes, such as the lines around the door, my eyes bounced everywhere but at what I was trying to look at. My vision was so wacky that my therapists were careful what they wore on the days I was there. One day, however, one of my therapists wore a black dress with a raised white pattern. She ad-libbed and took off the dress and put it back on inside out so I wouldn't throw up on her. How creative...and smart.

I had another meeting with my rehab doctor. On that particular day, my right hip joint was so swollen from dragging the left leg around that she said we needed to do injections in it. She warned me that the injection was extremely painful after about four hours. Since she was the first person I had seen during my two-day therapy marathon in Boulder I told her that I would like to wait until the following week and schedule it for the end of the therapies. She agreed to that. An appointment was made for the following week to see the physician's assistant for an injection.

Mumblings were also being made about doing surgery on my back and putting rods in to keep it in alignment.

Mary Ann had often talked about apoptosis. She believed that my brain cells were continuing to be "injured" even though the mechanics of the injury had stopped. Because this was happening new symptoms would crop up unexpectedly.

> Apopsis of neurons and glia contribute to the overall pathology of TBI in both humans and animals. In both head-injured humans and following experimental brain injury, apoptotic cells have been observed alongside degenerating cells exhibiting classic necrotic morphology. Neurons undergoing apoptosis have been identified within contusions in the acute post-traumatic period, and in regions remote from the site of impact in the days and weeks after trauma…. While excitatory amino acids, increases in intracellular calcium, and free radicals can all cause cells to undergo apoptosis, in vitro studies have determined that neural cells can undergo apoptosis via many other pathways. (See Bibliography, 17-1). Cerebral apoptosis is a prominent form of cell death in the PCZ of human traumatic cerebral contusions, and high rates of in vitro apoptosis are associated with a poorer prognosis after TBI. (See Bibliography, 17-2).

That afternoon I had an appointment with the acupuncturist. He put needles into the hip joint, and I immediately got a nasty taste in my mouth.

The next day I could actually walk without grimacing with each step.

The next Monday my chiropractor adjusted my back a different way. My lower back "let go" and cracked like someone snapping a faggot of sticks in two. The next morning my leg pain was gone except for stiffness on the outside and inside of my thigh.

The next day I went to Boulder for my physiatrist IME. The doctor had a stack at least eight inches deep of reports from the insurance company. He told me that he had spent over an hour and half reading the reports the day before and only was able to get through about two inches of them. He said he decided to wait to ask me what was going on with my injuries and therapies to save him time and because patients usually had a better grasp of their injuries and treatment than what a report could tell him.

The gods work in mysterious ways…. At 4:00 in the morning before my IME, I awoke after having a nightmare that my daughter who lives in the D. C. area had been killed in a revolutionary uprising in Chiapas, Mexico, where she was currently visiting for her work. The dream was so real that I couldn't stop crying for about an hour and was left shaken and dumb. When I went into the IME doctor's office

I had more trouble than usual putting a sentence together let alone getting a word out coherently.

I was pleasantly surprised that the doctor never blew up at me for being unable to do half of the things he instructed me to do due to my apraxia, and from being "dumb". I often got stuck in the exercise I was doing even though it was completed. When he turned around I would still be standing there, perhaps with my eyes closed with my arms out. He would just patiently tell me that I could stop that now. He realized I had apraxia and ataxia, speech and cognitive problems. It got to a point where he finally told me he wasn't going to have me do anymore because he saw that I had head, back and neurological injuries and didn't want me to hurt myself. (Evidently he didn't graduate from Haaavard or Mayo Clinic).

The doctor was also somewhat mystified that they asked him to evaluate and recommend treatment for my speech and cognitive problems. He told me that he knew nothing about oral dysphagia or apraxia of speech and he was also not trained in cognitive issues. He was trained in physical rehabilitation. He said he would have to recommend that the insurance company refer me to other doctors who knew about these issues.

I told him that my speech/cognitive therapist's doctoral thesis was about apraxia and that she is probably the specialist for apraxia in

Colorado. He shook his head but was non-committal as to what he thought of the whole issue.

I went for my appointment for the injection in my hip. I told the PA that I no longer had severe pain in my hip since the acupuncture and chiropractic adjustment. She ordered an MRI (at about $5,000 a pop) instead of the injection and wrote a prescription for a gait analysis. I told her that I had not had any blood work done since the accident, and wondered if I was getting some arthritis in my lower back, hips and neck from the trauma. She ordered blood work to be done including testing for both osteo-arthritis and rheumatoid arthritis.

> The insurance corporations claim that our auto premiums continue to climb higher and higher because of lawsuits. The fact is that lawsuits are rarely filed from auto accidents in Colorado—fewer than 1% file lawsuits—out of 289,904 drivers in accidents. Less than 15% of all auto accidents involve anyone getting hurt. This means only 2,548 of the injured filed lawsuits. The fact is that lawsuits are actually decreasing by more than 25% over the last ten years even though our premiums have not decreased. (See Bibliography, 17-3).

The following is from one of many speeches given by George W. Bush where he hammered away at the citizen's right to file a lawsuit by completely denigrating the validity of an injured person's condition. W. changed the face of lawsuits in our country for a good ten years. He mentioned the words frivolous lawsuit, junk lawsuit or lawsuit more than forty times in this speech. If you mention something a few times, the listener will start to believe it is true. If you mention it forty-plus times it becomes a fact or the listener realizes they are being given a snow-job. Which did you believe?

> First, we can control rising health care costs by cutting down on **frivolous lawsuits...** Yet, no one was ever healed by a junk or **frivolous lawsuit**... For Baptist and other hospitals across the Nation, **frivolous lawsuits** have dramatically increased the cost of medical liability premiums... In order to protect the doctor-patient relationship, Congress should pass medical liability reform that removes the threat of **frivolous lawsuits** and the needless costs they impose on our health care system... And that's the fact that we've got too many darn **lawsuits**, too many **frivolous lawsuits** and **junk lawsuits** that are affecting people... One of the reasons people are finding their premiums are up and it's hard to find a doc

these days is because **frivolous** and **junk lawsuits** are threatening medicine across the country... People just filing the **lawsuits** right and left, and it's running up the costs... Yet these **lawsuits** are making it hard for docs to practice their business in the State of Arkansas and other States as well... One of the major cost-drivers in the delivery of health care are these junk and **frivolous lawsuits**... The risk of **frivolous** litigation drives doctors—and me out on this—they drive doctors to prescribe drugs and procedures that may not be necessary just to avoid **lawsuits**. That's called the defensive practice of medicine. According to a survey of the Arkansas Medical Society, 90 percent of Arkansas doctors say the fear of **lawsuits** have caused them to do unnecessary procedures... See, **lawsuits** not only drive up premiums, which drives up the cost to the patient or the employer of the patient, but **lawsuits** cause docs to practice medicine in an expensive way to protect themselves in the courthouse... Medical liability reform is a national issue because medical liability **lawsuits** raise the Federal budget... **Lawsuits** don't heal patients... We've got a culture of **lawsuit** here in America, a culture of **lawsuits**, a litigation culture, which is driving a wedge between the doctor and patients, and that's not right...

These **frivolous** and **junk lawsuits** are not only driving up the costs, but a lot of docs are thinking about quitting the practice of medicine... **Lawsuits** drive up the affordability... **Lawsuits** are driving the docs out of the practice, which means there's less availability... They don't want to spend their time defending themselves in the courthouse because of the **frivolous** and **junk lawsuits** that are too prevalent today in America... But her premiums continued to rise, and Dr. McBee has stopped delivering babies, as a direct result of too many **junk lawsuits**, and that's not right... These **junk lawsuits** not only are running up the cost of medicine; they're making the quality of life of some of our citizens—diminishing the quality of life... There's just too many **junk** and **frivolous lawsuits**... These **junk lawsuits** have raised the cost of delivering babies such that they no longer do so in his hospital... See, too many **lawsuits** affect the lives of a lot of good people, and we need to do something about it... **Frivolous and junk lawsuits** make it hard for those who get injured to have their day in court, for starters... They just don't want to be run out business because of these **junk lawsuits**, just filing suit after suit after suit... See, what happens is some of these **junk**

> **lawsuits**, they'll just file against everybody... These Senators have got to understand no one has ever been healed by a **frivolous lawsuit**. (Jan. 26, 2004) (See Bibliography, 17-4).

One of the most personal injury unfriendly states in the US—Arizona—is actually talking about lifting the Bush-era $350,000 cap on personal injury lawsuits. I wonder if it is because the state is realizing that the injured are now being supported by Social Services and it is taxing the budget....

(Insurance companies cry "insurance fraud" about people who cheat them—very few. I call what they did to me "reverse insurance fraud" and the insurance companies do it all the time to injured people. I have talked to only two people with a closed head injury who have not been flat-out lied to or excluded from treatment by their insurance company. Of course, that is that they knew of).

> Moreover, a certain number of analysis including the well-known study by the US Institute of Medicine (IOM) in 1999...stress the increase in the number of medical errors in hospitals and in physician's practices. The IOM report in particular estimated that 44,000 to 98,000 hospital deaths per year in the US

could be attributed to medical errors. (See Bibliography, 17-5). Insurance companies contributed $2-million—65% to the Democrats and 34% to the Republicans. Lawyers and law firms contributed $112 million, 69% to the Democrats, 30% to the Republicans. (See Bibliography, 17-6). Now, President Bush is working to advance insurance company interests in yet another way: By campaigning for cruel limits on patient compensation from hospitals and HMOs whose medical negligence causes injuries and death. The $250,000 cap on non-economic damages advocated by Bush and Senate Majority Leader Bill Frist (R-Tenn.) would have the greatest impact on the most severely injured Americans – quadriplegic workers and brain-damaged children who suffer most and suffer for a lifetime. As the following list shows, some insurance executives make more than this in a single week, without any pain, injury or suffering. Despite being one of the most detested industries and worst corporate citizens in the country, insurance companies have bought access to the White House and to Congress, and insurers are just beginning to see their contributions pay-off. (See Bibliography, 17-7).

## Chapter Eighteen
### Social Security, Medicaid, Medicare and HUD

My Social Security attorney called me and said that Medicaid had approved my claim but that Social Security denied Medicaid's approval because the Social Security claim had to be approved first. That is exactly what my social security attorney had tried to tell the Medicaid judge during the hearing.

My attorney spoke to the Judge who told her that the reason the Social Security claim had not been approved sooner is because I had put down my disability date as the date of the accident, but worked for a few more months. They did not take into consideration that I could only work a few hours a day a couple days a week. The only issue during this time was a date issue. The Judge said that if I would agree to the new date as my disability date he would go ahead and approve the claim without doing a hearing.

Well, gee, why didn't they tell my attorney that back in March of 2003 instead of waiting six months to tell her? I had received only $277 a month for four months and $135 a month for the remainder of the time in welfare and $144 in monthly food stamps income since November of 2002 when my lost wages benefits ran out. My twenty-three year old daughter was trying to make a life of her own and had gotten stuck taking care of me. She had become quite anxious about the whole situation and said that she felt trapped. I could understand how she felt because I felt trapped also. I could no longer get essential services money to pay her because those funds also ran out back in November of 2002.

    I would now have to wait for the Social Security judge to fill out the necessary paperwork and send the paperwork to me. This would take four to six weeks. My monthly income on Social Security would be $632 but would go up to $645 at the beginning of the year with the cost of living increase. I would have to take the paperwork to my local Social Security office and wait until the Social Security office filed the necessary paperwork for me to start getting benefits.

    A strange snafu in the law required that I would have to be disabled for five full calendar months after June 6, 2000 making my actual eligibility date December 6, 2002. I would also have to prove that I had no assets over $2,000, less my old car. The total amount of disability I would receive from December 6, 2002, until October 6, 2003 would be about $6,947. Twenty-five percent of the $6,947 would be deducted and sent to my attorney (by law there is a maximum that an attorney can charge you on Social Security Disability cases. The amount may not exceed the lesser of $5,300 or 25% of the combined past due benefits, 2002). Social Security charges a service charge of 6.3 percent of the fee amount they pay. (Can you believe that?) This amount is to be taken from the amount payable to the attorney.

Social Security reviews each case once every three years and a person may be considered disabled or considered able to work, in which case a person would have to reapply and start the whole process over again.

I learned that if I had been approved for Medicaid benefits instead of Social Security Disability, the most I could receive monthly would have been $500. If I was approved for both, I would receive the amount which was higher--$500 or, in my case, $632. I would not be eligible for Medicare benefits until two years, five months after my approval date.

The money I had left for the time period of June 6, 2002, and December 6, 2003, was approximately $5,200 after paying the attorney. I think that put me in the below poverty level. Also, Social Security figures your benefit amount on the monies paid in for the forty-quarter period before the disability date.

If a person is self-employed and doesn't send money into Social Security or their employer does not send in any money to Social Security during that forty-quarter period, there will be no benefits available. Or, like in my case, I took some time off to travel. Add this to the fact that I was only working a few hours a week for several months before June 6 and couldn't work at all for almost two quarters so that is why I was only eligible for $632 a month in benefits.

I also found out that when my ex-husband and I owned a business together that all of the Social Security money went into his account so for years I was given no credit for having paid in toward Social Security benefits. This would not have made a difference in my disability case since we had been divorced since 1987, but it would have made a difference when we retired. If we had only been divorced a short period of time, there would have been no money in the account for me. It is required that we be married a minimum of twelve years to collect off of the ex-husband's Social Security. However, if my ex-husband was dead, and since I was not re-married, I could file for a Disabled Widow's Benefit and could receive funds from whichever account would pay out the most monthly wage. In order to file for the Benefit, I would need my marriage license, divorce decree and have to know where and when he died.

I was instructed by a very helpful lady at Social Security to check every three months with Social Security to see if my ex-husband was dead. In this case, I would be eligible to collect on his account if he had paid anything into Social Security in the last forty quarters. (I found out later that from 1992 forward he had not paid any money into Social Security. Most likely he had been working under the table because he owed me about $40,000 in back alimony and child support).

The saddest part of social security benefits is that the benefit is so low that most people cannot possibly survive on that amount. I have talked to numerous people, especially women, whose benefit is quite pitiful since many women fifty years ago did not work outside the home. The wages back then were so much less than today and women's salaries were and still are smaller than men's salaries. If a woman divorced her husband and had no money paid into her account, she would receive nothing and end up on welfare. Social Security has an inflation adjustment each year (except 2011), but the adjustment still doesn't provide adequate coverage because the base is still so small. I talked to one woman who received only $428 a month in social security. Because she owned a thirty-year old condo, she was not eligible for welfare which would have paid her a whopping $500 per month.

About Congresswoman Gabrielle Gifford's treatment: Legislative Assistant Lauren Alfred stated, "Congresswoman Giffords was injured while she was on the job and her rehabilitation is covered by workers' compensation under the Federal Employees' Compensation Act." The Department of Labor website explains that FECA is administered by DOL's Office of Workers' Compensation Programs. The "Injury Compensation for Federal Employees" publication (CA-810) describes the entitlement this way: The FECA at 5 U.S.C. 8103 authorizes medical services for treatment of any condition which is causally related to factors of Federal employment. No limit is imposed on the amount of medical expenses or the length of time for which they are paid as long as the charges represent the reasonable and customary fees for the services involved and the need for the treatment can be shown. Federal employees are entitled to all services, appliances, and supplies prescribed or recommended by qualified physicians that, in the opinion of OWCP, are likely to cure, give relief, reduce the degree or the period of disability or aid in lessening the amount of monthly compensation. Medical care includes examination, treatment and related services such as medications, hospitalization, as well as transportation needed to secure these services. Preventative care may not be authorized, however. The type of acute rehabilitation she receives - involving speech, occupational and physical rehab - costs about $8,000 a day, according to the Brain Injury Association of America. Post-acute rehabilitation can range in cost from $600 to $2,500 daily. The expenses leave the treatment options well out of reach for most patients whose insurers won't pay for the services. (See Bibliography, 18-1). Gabrielle Giffords was covered under Federal Workmen's Comp because she was speaking with constituents.

Please take note. In the above, it states: *No limit* *will be imposed on the amount of medical payment or the length of time for which they are paid...*

Now, can someone please explain all of this to me? First of all, I wish the best for Gabby. I am simply going to use Gabby's situation as an example.

If Gabrielle Giffords had my insurance instead of the Federal government employees' insurance which taxpayers' money pays for, her money would have been gone within the first few days (my maximum benefit of $100,000) because of the extensiveness of her injury. Or she could have gotten twelve and a half days of therapy at $8,000 per day. When her insurance policy limits ran out, she could go on Medicare but would have to wait **two years and five months** after the date she applied for disability for the Medicare to kick in. First, if she was a regular citizen, she would have to prove that she has a brain injury which could take over a year and several appeals. Even after she proved she was disabled, she would not be able to collect Social Security Disability cash benefits until a full five months after her disability **request** date. For example, she was shot on January 8, 2011. Most likely no one would have filed for Social Security Disability until long after her injury as her life and death struggle was foremost in her family's mind. So, if no one filed until, say, August 2011 and she was approved immediately, she would have to wait a full five months before her benefits would actually start. In other words, she would get zero money for that five month period and zero money for the period between January 8 and August. If she went on Medicare, she could receive occupational or speech-language pathology therapy, but only intermittently and would have to pay a twenty percent co-pay. She would receive no cognitive or vision therapy. She could, however, get a whopping thirteen chiropractic adjustments but all thirteen would have to be in a single pod taking no more than five weeks. She would get only 12 sessions a year of physical therapy or up to $1,800, one or the other, plus would have to pay a twenty-percent copay under Medicare. Now, does that seem right? Although a strong proponent for equality in health care, Congresswoman Giffords would have been screwed if she had been me.

I have found that sometimes a caregiver has given all that they know how to give. I decided to change chiropractors after hearing a chiropractor tell someone that she used to teach chiropractic. The first session I went to with the new chiropractor, she was able to pop L-4 back out to where it was supposed to be and shove C-1 and C-2 back over to the left somewhat. Of course, she adjusted all of the other vertebrae, also.

Within a few days I noticed that I could walk better without falling over as much and that my eyes did not pop around like Bingo machine balls. Unfortunately, these areas had been misaligned for so long that within the week, they were pretty much back to where they were to begin with. She adjusted them again and I felt that I had reached nirvana. The trick now was to develop new habits to keep these vertebrae from going out again. I was, however, still so dizzy when I rolled over that I felt like I had for the past year and a half since the accident. I guess my brain would just have to re-establish plumb.

My new chiropractor also discovered that my shoulder blade was out of alignment as was my shoulder and collarbone. My collarbone was up, out and rotated and actually did not move at all. After she adjusted these areas, I found that I could now lift my right arm while it was bent just to chin height without grimacing and shrieking.

I applied for housing assistance and was told that there was a three-month wait, which is a lot better than in most counties where the wait is several years.

When I got home from my next trip to Boulder, I had a message on my answering machine from the physician's assistant. She reported that my blood work looked great, that I tested negative for osteo-arthritis, but had tested positive for rheumatoid arthritis but they weren't sure if it was rheumatoid or lupus. Well….

I was quite sad for a few days after this latest news. I looked in all of my herb books to find out what I needed to take. I found that the most logical information was by Peter Gillam (The Gillam Health Series, Bulletin No. 1). In his article he wrote that water-soluble magnesium will help the body absorb calcium rather than store it in the joints and muscles, which is what causes the arthritic condition to begin with. I also learned that the magnesium helped me sleep deeper and my seizures came less often. I did more research and found that lobelia helps minimize seizures and that sage can cause seizures.

The chiropractor adjusted my jaw and my teeth now seemed more lined up even though my teeth in the back had become so crooked that my bite was still off. I could now chew off a hangnail, which I hadn't been able to do since the accident. Ah, the simple pleasures of life! I could open my mouth further (I was now up to 45 mm from 33) and continued to have my mouth splint re-fitted every month. Unfortunately, just like my neck and spine, my jaw wouldn't hold an adjustment because of the muscle spasms, the big muscles overworking, the small muscles not working and because of the muscle weakness on the right side of my face.

The insurance company told me that I could only go to one of the physical therapists. They did not realize, or probably didn't care, that each of the therapists were working on completely different functions. I had to quit going to Marianna since the doctor's script stated that I was to have sessions with Kristie who wasn't nearly as much fun and didn't seem to understand that traditional exercises made my muscles turn on but not turn off.

I finally received my Social Security paperwork stating that I was now completely and totally disabled.

The Judge's findings stated that I had the "medically determinable severe impairments of a traumatic brain injury/closed head injury, and an organic mental disorder. Organic mental disorders, listing 12.02, require psychological or behavioral abnormalities associated with a dysfunction of the brain caused by a specific organic factor and medically documented persistence of at least one of the following: disorientation to time and place; memory impairment; perceptual or thinking disturbances; changes in personality; disturbance in mood; emotional lability and impairment in impulse control; or loss of measured intellectual ability of at least 15 IQ points from premorbid levels or overall impairment index clearly within the severely impaired range on neuropsychological testing. Listing 12.02B requires that the abnormalities result in at least two of the following: marked restriction in daily living activities; marked difficulties in maintaining social functioning; frequent deficiencies of concentration, persistence of pace; or repeated episodes of deterioration or decompensation in work or work-like settings."

He made his determination based on whether or not I could retain "the residual functional capacity to perform the requirements of her past relevant work or can adjust to other work.

Social Security Ruling 96-6p states that findings of fact made by a State agency medical and psychological consultants and other program physicians and psychologists regarding the nature and severity of an individual's impairment(s) must be treated as expert opinion evidence over non-examining sources to be considered and weighed along with the medical evidence from other sources. It is noted that the residual functional capacity determined by the undersigned is different from that provided by State agency non-examining medical consultants. (The same State agent who claimed I did not have a head injury because I had not lost consciousness.) The residual functional capacity determined by the undersigned has considered the record as a whole, including new medical evidence, and is thus based upon evidence, which was not available to State agency medical consultants. Moreover, the undersigned has assigned greater weight to the opinions of physicians who have examined the claimant."

"For the purpose of this decision, she is considered to be closely approaching advanced age."

"Because the claimant's significant non-exertional limitations only further limit the number of jobs which the claimant could perform, the undersigned concluded the claimant is unable to perform any job existing in significant number in the national economy. A finding of "disabled" may therefore be reached within the framework of medical-vocational rule 201.14."

I found this finding interesting since Mary Ann had told me the week before that I should be able to work in four or five years. My eyes about popped out of my head when she said that. "I'll be fifty-nine in four years!" That's the age when most companies are trying to dump people, not hire them.

Regardless, now I would at least have an income.

I went for my massage. My therapist was quite upset. He had finally been able to get a hold of my claims adjustor to find out why he hadn't been reimbursed for six weeks. She sweetly told him that it was because I had run out of rehab money and then said, "I was going to send you a letter." I found that odd since two weeks prior to that I had over $3,000 (out of the $50,000) left for my rehab based on a letter that she had sent to my attorney.

The week before this I realized that it was quite possible that my insurance company had been misappropriating payments. Chiropractic, dental, medical, optometric, podiatric, hospital, nursing, x-ray, surgical, ambulance, and prosthetic services, and non-medical remedial care and treatment in accordance with a recognized religious method of healing, performed within five years after the date of the accident were to be deducted from the medical portion of funds. I was pretty sure that they had been taking funds out of rehabilitation for chiropractic and possibly dental. I called one of my attorneys and they went to work to find out if this was true.

The day after I met with the massage therapist, I went to Boulder for my therapies. My physical therapist, Kristie, pulled me into the conference room and showed me the letter she had received from the insurance company stating that my rehab benefits were exhausted. She said that she just wanted to warn me that I would be getting billed for the seven sessions at $180 per hour that the insurance company hadn't paid. My mouth fell open. I had no clue that they were charging $180 per hour for my therapy. I told her that I had an appointment with my attorney that afternoon and would get back to her about whether or not I could continue my treatment.

My cognitive, biofeedback and cranial sacral therapists worked on me, and I signed liens with them. The liens were sent to my attorney, who was to sign the liens agreeing to reimburse them out of my settlement money before I received my money, and then a copy was mailed back to the providers.

That afternoon I met with my main attorney. I told him that I wondered if the claims adjustor had been charging almost all of the therapies to rehab instead of medical. This would not be a big deal if rehab and medical rolled into each other. However, if you run out of medical benefits, you can borrow from rehab benefits. If you run out of rehab benefits, you cannot borrow from medical benefits.

Our guess was that they ran me out of rehab benefits so that they wouldn't have to pay out any more money other than going to "medical" appointments, or a medical doctor. They also used this excuse to not reimburse me for my mileage expense and my motel expense including the trips that I went to the dentist and the rehab doctor, whose money came out of medical, but saw the therapists who were considered rehab.

In the first letter that my attorney sent to the claims adjustor on the day before my visit, he stated, "Under the PIP statute, chiropractic care is considered medical treatment. Section 10-4-706(b)(I) provides that no fault medical benefits include up to a limit of fifty thousand dollars per person for payment of all "reasonable and necessary expenses for medical, chiropractic, optometric, podiatric, hospital, nursing, x-ray, dental, surgical, ambulance and prosthetic services… The treatment of neurologic injuries also known as closed-head injuries and their sequelae, vestibular, auditory or visual disorders, psychological disorders, and cognitive disorders that are reasonable, necessary and arising out of the use or operation of a motor vehicle, shall be considered covered medical or dental procedures. 10-4-706(b)(I)." (Colorado Statute). (Each state will have different statutes).

    I told my attorney that I had heard that a claimant could "buy out" the balance remaining on their policy if it was known that the claimant would eventually use all of the money in the policy. He said that that was true, but it would take away my right to sue them for "bad faith". By taking the balance of the money, I would also sign with the insurance company that they had no more liability for the accident. On the up side, I would be able to choose my own doctors and therapists, would never have to go for another insurance IME, and it would take a lot less work for my attorneys. Unfortunately, in many cases, this would also mean that this added asset would exceed the $2,000 limit that Medicaid allows a person to have. Regardless, as stated in the first letter about this subject to the insurance company, my attorney wrote that I "still have almost $16,000 remaining in medical benefits and that should be sufficient to cover a substantial portion, if not all of, the treatment recommendations made by the" IME doctor.

    Miracle of miracles! I was approved for housing in less than two months. My daughter was considered my live-in caretaker so her income was not considered. We would now only have to pay $119 a month rent instead of $650.

In my vision therapy we realized that I could not see out of the bottom quadrants of my eyes. (Eyes are divided into quadrants). This is not to say that the world was black from halfway down as it is with some people, but when I looked straight ahead, there was an angle of my vision that was not being processed by the brain. For example, I might see a kid with his leg sticking straight out at a restaurant or the bag of potatoes leaning against the wall that hadn't been there that morning and fall over them because my brain wasn't registering to change my walking pattern.

When I would fall over these objects, such as the potatoes, it would whip my head hard enough that the dizziness and speech problems would crop up again and last for several days.

Also in my vision therapy, I still had suppression, especially when working with red/green glasses—one lens is green, one lens is red. The object that I was looking at that should have looked red or green would blink out or turn yellowish-white, then turn back on. A hat on a snowman picture would look like it was sitting up off of the snowman's head until I got within a few feet of the snowman. When I tried to look at a fixed object and walk, I discovered that the object swayed with my walk rather than looking stationary. Each week I was given different exercises to try to get the part of the brain to trigger that held the vision memory.

I started cutting back on my therapies because of the lack of money issue. I knew that I would soon not be getting mileage or motel reimbursements and without those, I would not be able to afford gas to drive to Boulder even though my therapists had told me that I could sign a lien with them and continue my treatments.

For two months I did not have the money to go to Boulder for my therapies since Social Security pays the first check at the end of the month following their award letter. Based on my date of birth my name did not fall into the payout category until the fourth Wednesday of the month. My $134 in welfare and $144 in food stamps had been stopped in November because of the Social Security approval so had no money or ability to buy food for about three weeks. I received my first check on December 24. I then received a notice from welfare that said I had to reimburse them for the $134 in welfare and the $144 in food stamps that I had received in November because the SSDI check I had received at the end of December was for the month of November.

# Chapter Nineteen
## Class-Action Lawsuits, Housing Snafus and NAET

Another difficulty with current models of TBI rehabilitation pertains to the issue of access to rehabilitation services. Specifically, there is a wide discrepancy in the availability of TBI rehabilitation programs across geographic regions and a lack of knowledgeable professionals able to facilitate community-based rehabilitation. Frequently, there are problems accessing rehabilitation services in a timely manner, and major financial barriers make access to TBI rehabilitation services difficult for many individuals. (See Bibliography, 19-1).

During the period of time that I was not going to Boulder for my therapy, I noticed that my speech became more difficult. I had trouble holding thoughts together and trouble communicating. I knew that I had to find the answer to getting my body strong enough to heal itself.

I learned about a doctor in the Vail area who does a program called NAET (Nambudripad's Allergy Elimination Technique) to de-sensitize a person from allergies. I found that when I took supplements, such as Vitamin C and B's, I often felt worse than if I didn't take them at all. Because of my neurological problems, when I sneezed or coughed my muscles would spasm. I knew I had to get my allergies under control to keep the muscles calm.

I had also started to realize that I no longer had a "filter" system. Every sound, movement, thought came at my brain full force and caused brain exhaustion and a depressed immune system. At the same time, I was not able to filter what people were good for me to be around and what people were not good for me to be around.

The first day I saw Bruce for my NAET, he checked me for food allergies with a computer program that contains over 4,000 possible allergies. We got as far as the basic foods and found that I was allergic to calcium, vitamin C, sugar, grains, nuts, and enzymes. The sixth allergy was to the hormone estrogen.

Now that was no big surprise although I didn't know a person could be allergic to estrogen. They can also be allergic to progesterone, testosterone, and other hormones. (These hormones are also found in meat). Then, of all things to be allergic to(?)...spices and water. Good Lord! I could basically eat, well, nothing. It also answered a lot of questions about my hormone problems since the head injury since I was basically allergic to myself.

After doing the de-sensitization, I was not allowed to eat or even touch the foods in that category for 25 hours. I went for weekly treatments for six weeks and after each session I felt a little bit better. The most noticeable thing to me besides being able to eat foods without becoming ill was that my muscles started relaxing more. After we did the physical aspect of the allergy, Bruce tested for mental and emotional aspects. I had an emotional reaction to every one of the food groups so was desensitized for the emotion component.

One day I saw an ad on television about a law firm that was filing a class action lawsuit against insurance companies who had not offered enhancements. Enhancements include such things as additional coverage on your policy.

My therapist gave me a copy of a page from an article about the enhancement. For example, my insurance company did not offer extended benefits. Many upgraded policies would have included another $100,000 in rehabilitation and medical for up to ten years; work income loss replacement for life of 85% of lost gross income per week or the policy's ex-benefit aggregate limit, whichever is reached first; loss of essential services expense benefits of up to $25 per day for a period of 364 days from the date of the accident or the policy's all-benefit aggregate limit, whichever is reached first; and a death benefit in the amount of $1,000 payable to the estate of the deceased for death resulting from the operation or use of a qualifying motor vehicle or the policy's all-benefit aggregate limit, whichever is reached first. The all-benefit aggregate limit is $200,000, and operates to cut off further benefits once PIP payments in whatever benefit combination reach the total sum of $200,000. (HP Opt-Up Options, Named Insured and Resident Relatives.)

  I called the class action law firm and spoke with an attorney for several hours who used to work for insurance companies and knew how devious they are. I had previously spoken to my personal injury attorney about filing a lawsuit against my insurance company for bad faith, but he said he would only take the case on an hourly basis because the insurance companies keep plaintiffs in court for years as they have a bottomless bank account, ergo the lack of individual lawsuits for bad faith.

  After speaking with the attorney at the class action law firm, I had my personal injury attorney read my contract so that I wouldn't make an error. It was fortunate that I did. They had sent me a standard contract that also covered the personal injury aspect of my accident. After asking the class action firm to revise the contract, I joined the lawsuit.

The reason you don't hear very much about Bad Faith Insurance is that upon losing the decision and case and as part of the terms and conditions of settling the case, the Insurance Company agrees not to appeal the decision only if the plaintiff agrees to a gag order and that the court's decision be vacated and the information surrounding the case be kept confidential. All of this contributes to the Industry's "rule of secrecy", sometimes also referred to as "the wall of silence". In so doing, experts estimate that 50-80% of all cases and case laws that were decided in favor of plaintiff policyholders are erased from court records (e.g. vacated hence the legal term "vacatur"). So in essence the insurance industry at the same time in fact is also buying the legal system as these are the very same cases which mold common laws which would be used by lawyers and judges to decide future court case decisions that is if these common law case decisions had not been erased from all court records. (See Bibliography, 19-2). (Also read The Rainmaker by John Grisham, Bantam Doubleday Dell Publishing Group, Inc, 1995).

An attorney from the same law firm called me a few months later and said that they noticed on my record that I had purchased a different vehicle in December the year before. They asked if I had sold my original vehicle or kept it. I said that I had sold it several weeks after I purchased the newer vehicle. He asked me to check my policy to make sure that the insurance company had not cut my liability in half. He said that there was a lawsuit in California that involved a man who purchased a second car. When he added the second car to his policy, the insurance company cut the liability from $250,000 to $125,000 on the first car without the owner's approval or knowledge. The man had an accident in the original vehicle which now only had $125,000 liability insurance.

I told the attorney who I was talking to that what the insurance company had done was drop my liability on the first car when I asked them to drop the collision. When I got my new policy I called them and told them that they had made a mistake and to reinstate the liability or I wouldn't be able to allow someone to test-drive the car (several people had been driving the car without liability insurance which is quite illegal and stupid). I checked my corrected policy and, sure enough, they had dropped my liability from $250,000 to $125,000.

The chiropractor took new x-rays of my lower, mid-back and neck which included the skull. L-4 was now at "stage 1" out of five stages for spondylolisthesis while standing up. The x-rays also showed that an area of my skull from the center of the top of my forehead just past the center of the top of my head was now calcified so there had to be some pretty severe trauma to have caused that.

The chiropractor got x-rays from the hospital in Chinle and questioned how they could possibly have stated that I was okay because she said the x-rays were so poor that they were practically unreadable. She showed me how out alignment C-1 and C-2 were. It is no wonder I could not walk without falling over. I was able to see why my therapists had said they were amazed that I could walk. My brain stem had to have taken a severe beating. I asked her what she thought when she did the physical exam the first time she saw me and she said, "Whoa, where do I start?"

When my insurance expired, I signed a lien with my chiropractor so that I could continue doing chiropractic with her. We also started doing resistance exercises for the arms and legs. My apraxia still was in full force, but I was learning ways of getting the limbs to move by saying words like "chicken" or crossing my arms over my head, or by crossing just one arm over, or combinations of numerous pretzel-like movements.

My chiropractor went to Boulder with me for my therapies one week so that she could learn more about head injury and apraxia. She said that she wanted to see how my brain reacted while I was doing my exercises. While I was doing biofeedback, she had me do some of the exercises. We discovered that if we started with the limb on the right side, the brain waves went nuts and would not settle down for several minutes. If we started with the limb on the left side, however, the brain waves stayed calmer and relaxed faster. The limbs also did not spasm as badly.

I went to Boulder in May for my therapies. Jackie had been hooking up the biofeedback electrodes from the middle of my forehead and straight back to the crown of my head and then a few inches past the crown. The brain waves for this area were almost non-existent. This is the area for apraxic tendencies or where messages cross over from right to left and left to right—the corpus collosum. For the most part, that part of my brain was sleeping. The theta waves were shooting off the graph and the beta waves would give out a little hiccup when I tried to speak or move a body part.

> TBI represents an evolving dynamic process that involves multiple interrelated physiological components that exert primary and secondary effects at the level of the

individual nerve cell (neuron), level of connected networks of such neurons (neural networks), and the level of human thought (cognition). Many damaging changes to the connections among neurons (axons) and to the neurons themselves have been described. These include chemical changes to the basic molecules of metabolism (especially calcium), to mechanisms of the human cellular response to injury, and to the quantities of certain molecules that can be dangerous in excess (oxygen free radicals, nitric oxide). A protein substance that is present in Alzheimer's disease (beta amyloid) also can be deposited in neurons. Communication molecules in the brain (neurotransmitters) have either excitatory or inhibitory effects. The most prevalent of these excitatory molecules are the amino acids glutamate and aspartate, which can occur in massive amounts following TBI, leading to overexcitation and ultimately the death of neurons. At the cognitive level, alterations in neural networks and neurotransmitter systems (especially ones involving the transmitters acetyl choline, dopamines, and serotonin) can affect cognition and behavior. (See Bibliography, 19-3).

I started to become more aware of symptoms leading up to seizures. For several days before the seizure, my muscles would become quite rigid. I felt like I was drooling out of my lower left lip and would often reach up and wipe my mouth but nothing was there. I also noticed an itchy burning sensation on my left lower lip.

One day I lay down on the chiropractic table and the chiropractor started to adjust my neck. I told her to wait, and then said, "I know what this is. I'll be back in a minute." Sure enough, I went into a seizure that mostly involved my left arm and leg. When the seizure was done, I could not move for about a minute. By this time, I had learned to relax through the seizure. They did not last as long and were much less traumatic. After the seizure, I felt tremendous relief. The rigidity in my muscles was gone. I had not had a seizure for quite some time and had not been taking the magnesium that I was supposed to take.

Strangely, I started noticing that my chiropractor was looking at me in a way that I can only describe as calf eyes. Then one day, she turned around, looked at me and said, "I love you." I didn't know what to think. I had gone to lunch with her one day to discuss brain injury and we discussed her woes. My cognitive therapist told me that she had seen cases thrown out of court because someone went to lunch with their massage therapist and she also informed me that my attorney would dump my case if he found out.

The dire nature of my lawsuit came to me finally and I earnestly set out to get her to tell me that she was no longer going to be my chiropractor.

Several months later I had started hearing from people that she had been talking about me. I stopped speaking to her except in short answers when she asked me a question during the adjustments. I stopped doing physical therapy with her and got in and out of her office as quickly as I could.

Even after this, it still took another four months before she finally informed me that she was no longer going to be my chiropractor. I left the office and did a brain injured, semi-Rocky type exultation. I almost wish I had been at the top of a long set of steps. So much for patient-doctor boundaries!

This woman would come back to haunt me.

Another thing I started to notice was how electrical storms affected me. For some bizarre reason I thought I could go to the town's summer celebration. Fortunately, it was only a block from where I lived so I could walk there and return home if I became too fatigued. I went with my daughter and met some friends there. I was having a great deal of trouble maneuvering over the uneven, grass-covered ground. There were many display booths that were over-stimulating to me visually.

A thunderstorm crept up. The storm was so close that there was no delay between the lightning and thunder. I stood under one of the tents and when the storm was over, moving people looked like flares shooting back and forth in front of me. My depth perception was completely gone, and I could not walk because in my mind I knew that I was falling.

The next day, I slept for several hours during the day and ten to twelve hours at night for several nights. After that, I spent more than a week unable to sleep for more than three to four hours at night. When I went for my next NAET treatment, Bruce checked me for electricity, and I was full of it! He ran through the tests, and I tested positive for reactions to lightening, high voltage wires, remote controls, x-rays, and several other electromagnetic fields.

During my next NAET session, Bruce checked my brain chemicals. My calcium, dopamine and serotonin levels were quite high. He did the treatment for those, and I have not had a seizure since. The next time I went, he tested me and found that I was allergic to L-tryptophan and melatonin, which aid in sleep. He de-sensitized me for that and my sleep sequences improved. (Keep in mind that if you go on the internet to look up some of these treatments I have mentioned there will also be articles by a medical doctor who calls these alternative treatments Quack Medicine. Don't be alarmed by this. Allopathic medicine is trying very hard to get alternative treatments completely expunged).

    I received a letter from the housing authority in April stating that my benefits would be stopped on May first because of HUD rules. These ridiculous rules state that a live-in aid, which is what my daughter was considered, could not work outside of the home more than twenty hours per week or earn more than $28,000 per year. My daughter worked thirty-six hours and her income was just over the $28,000 limit.

    I had my therapists and doctors write letters to the HUD worker stating that I did need to have a live-in aid. We were trying our hardest to figure out how a person could pay a live-in aide who was required to be in the home 148 hours a week times $20 per hour on my $645 per month income (plus I was eligible for $23 per month in food stamps). My daughter could not back her hours up to 20 hours per week because she had student loans, car payments, insurance, and other bills to pay and barely made ends meet while we were on HUD because she was also paying a lot of my bills so that I could do the few therapies I was doing.

After jumping through all of the hoops required of HUD we were still denied because my daughter was ineligible to be considered as a live-in caretaker. My HUD caseworker told me that when the new HUD rules under George W. took effect 135,000 people lost their vouchers.

The US Conference of Mayors estimates that more than 3.5 million people, or 1.25 percent of the US population are living in city streets or homeless shelters, a number equal to the populations of Albania, Uruguay or Lithuania. In addition, the number of Americans living below the poverty line jumped by 1.3 million to 35.9 million or 12.5 percent of the population last year, according to the US Census Bureau. (See Bibliography, 19-4). Each year, approximately one percent of the US population, some 2-3 million individuals, experience a night of homelessness that puts them in contact with a homeless assistance provider, and at least 800,000 people are homeless in the US on any given night. (See Bibliography, 19-5). More than half of the people who are homeless in Toronto are suffering from a traumatic brain injury, according to a new study that suggests early diagnosis and treatment may help stem the number of homeless people in major cities…What's more significant, 70 per cent of the people had the injury before they ended up on the street…"That really raises the intriguing possibility that perhaps the brain injury in and of itself is a risk factor for becoming homeless," said Hwang…Brain injuries, especially those involving the frontal lobe behind the forehead, often go undetected for years. The injuries can lead to cognitive problems and unpredictable or impulsive behavior—traits often found among street people. "One moment they might be acting normally and in another moment they might be screaming in an uncontrollable rage." Hwang said. "So you can imagine that these kinds of behaviors might put someone at risk for losing their housing, and certainly once a person becomes homeless, might increase the risk that they stay homeless for a long time."(Bibliography, 19-6). (TBI statistics for the U.S. are woefully unavailable for homelessness and actually difficult to find. Most articles quote the Toronto or Australia study).

# Chapter Twenty
## The Mind Versus the Brain—
## Are You Willing To Drink the Water?

Well, my pink cloud or bubble finally burst about twenty-eight months after the accident. I found that I was starting to mope and get moody. A profound grief and sadness started to overwhelm me. The last kick was losing our housing. I was now feeling like I was a total burden to my daughter. She kept telling me that she would be able to handle things financially, but that really was not the point. I had always been so independent and this was the final kick in the gut. I actually started thinking about dying and reminded myself about two Psalms—23 and 91—that I read years ago when I was going through a difficult time in my life.

I realized that a head injury is like walking through the valley of the shadow of death. I had been murdered but my body was still moving around with snippets of the past for a memory and hardly anything of a personality that I had known. I knew that somewhere in this newly found feeling was a gift that I had to look for.

I remembered how many people I had spoken to with head injuries who were still angry years later for having their life snuffed from them and told me quite indignantly that they had had a wonderful life before their accidents and surely did not consider this new existence as a gift. I had tried to convince them that they could now become who they wanted to be, not who their parents and brothers and sisters and classmates and teachers and the rest of society had taught them to be. The problem I now had was what in the world or who in the world I wanted to be. My direction meter was out of plumb, I was fifty-four years old and knew that I could not do the things I used to do and felt that I was too old to start something less demanding at this point in my life. Besides, I realized that the "stuff" I used to do was just "stuff" and actually pretty pointless.

I remembered a wonderful black psychology teacher I had whose mother went to college when she was 72. I had already earned five college degrees and certifications in my other life and figured out after years of working in the counseling arena that I no longer needed to do that.

The existence I was now in felt like I imagined limbo must feel—I was caught in the middle of life and death but still stuck on the earth plane while wondering why I hadn't sprouted my wings yet so that I could fly.

I wondered if I would ever find my lifetime relationship and wondered who in their right mind would want to be with someone who was without her brain. I grieved over the fact that I might not ever be able to pick up or carry or be left alone with my grandchildren, if they ever came along. This was the one thing that broke my heart the most—the one thing that made me weep....

I pulled out my book I'll Carry the Fork! by Kara Swanson (See Bibliography, 20-1), who also has a head injury, and started to read it again. I remembered that the first time I read it I laughed at her line about finding her bras in the silverware drawer.

I got up and walked into the kitchen to put my neck warmer in the microwave. I was chuckling to myself and shaking my head and thought, "At least I'm not that bad." After a few baffling minutes, I realized that I had put the neck warmer in the freezer and that is why I could not find the buttons to set the timer on the microwave for two minutes. This time when I read the book, I realized that the "bras in the silverware drawer" was the only thing I remembered about the book and that I really was that bad. At the end of the book, an attorney wrote a few paragraphs and mentioned Matthew 25:35-36. What the attorney said was, "...I had a brain injury, and you tried to help."

I was getting blubbery about seeing little children play and was in a funk for several days after playing with our friends' two little adopted children. When my daughter and I talked about how funny they were, my eyes would tear up. I couldn't sit through a movie without crying. I hated this new "part" and wished I could send it back and order the correct "part". I had been warned that this would probably happen when the emotional part of my brain started to wake up. They forgot to mention that I probably wouldn't like it.

On one particularly bad day—I was having a lot of trouble buttoning my pants—I remembered the words, "...and acceptance is the answer to *all* my problems today. When I am disturbed, it is because I find some person, place, thing, or situation—some fact of my life—unacceptable to me, and I can find no serenity until I accept that person, place, thing, or situation as being exactly the way it is supposed to be at this moment. Nothing, absolutely nothing happens in God's world by mistake. Until I could accept my [head injury], I could not stay sober; unless I accept life completely on life's terms, I cannot be happy. I need to concentrate not so much on what needs to be changed in the world as on what needs to be changed in me and in my attitudes." (See Bibliography, 20-2).

I do not like cold water in my face....

I was also feeling extremely vulnerable now. My heart, which had been closed down for more than two years, was just starting to open. One day while I was driving to my chiropractic appointment, I saw Pam driving her car down the street. The awful feelings came up—betrayal, fear, grief, self-esteem and self-worth issues. I cried like I haven't cried in years. I felt like my heart was breaking into a million pieces over what I had lost.

The following Thursday I went to the NAET doctor and did an emotional release on the accident. I felt like a thousand weights had been lifted from me. The next week, I ran right into Pam in the grocery store. When I left the store, I started shaking, sweating and got a nasty taste in my mouth. Within an hour the feeling was gone, and I felt tremendous relief, like something deep within me was shaking its self lose. I knew that both of those instances were healing moments, even though they were disturbingly uncomfortable.

I had been working at developing new friendships and rekindling old ones. I found that I was so much more aware of the "games" people play. I more keenly felt and saw manipulations and had no tolerance whatsoever for people who said one thing and did not follow through or unceremoniously decided to do something more exciting or familiar to them. At first, these sudden plan changes didn't seem to affect me but when the same person did this over and over I became quite upset and would bluntly ask them if they were communicating with themselves.

One of the things I learned through years of working as an EMT and a drug and alcohol counselor was to listen closely to what people said. Throughout my recovery, I noticed that people didn't really hear what I said to them and I would ask them to repeat back what I said to them. It was like the old game where you told someone a sentence, they whispered it to the next person and by the time the sentence got back to the beginning, it did not resemble what was said by the first person. I found that the sentence didn't even get to the second person before it was messed up.

I spent many days and nights worrying that people wouldn't want to be around me or talk to me. I knew I was different and weird and felt constantly alienated from society. Having a brain injury is a lot like being a minority. I always felt like I stuck out like a sore thumb, especially since I fell over a lot and had bouts of loss of eye control.

Well, I would just have to snap out of it.

I found out that I could have reapplied for Medicaid after my Social Security approval. On June 1, I reapplied for Medicaid and got accepted. I had fallen through the cracks and should have been on Medicaid for several months. Someone else told me that I would be eligible for Medicare two years after my disability date. When June 6, 2004, rolled around, I was excited that I would be able to begin my therapies again with therapists who would accept Medicare so that I could stop running up obscene medical bills.

I called Social Security and got walloped again. I had forgotten that it is two years and five months after the disability date so I would not be eligible until December 6, 2004, for Medicare. Now, tell me how intelligent it is to proclaim someone disabled and then leave the person without any medical insurance for twenty-nine months!

I found out caregivers as a rule would not take Medicaid because of the extensive paperwork and the approximate $7 Medicaid paid on an office visit. The $7 did not cover the cost of the wages of the bookkeeper who filled out the paperwork. Basically, I would be getting a call button to use in case I fell, a cane if I wanted one (probably a helmet, too), and $7 an hour for my daughter up to 36 hours a month for her assistance. Once I got on Medicare, it would pay my monthly Medicare insurance fee of $85, but I would have to continue to use a call button or have someone clean or have a live-in aide.

The second month after losing our housing we did not have enough money to pay our rent. My car insurance was due. I went to Catholic Charities, and they paid $400 toward my rent for that month. The lady there was extremely helpful and also gave me a $20 voucher for gas. She said that the following two months the Salvation Army would cover some of our rent. I also learned from a neighbor that her son got assistance from a fund at the hospital but when I inquired at the hospital I was told that only happened if a person had been hospitalized. I also learned that if I had been correctly diagnosed at the Chinle hospital as having a brain injury that I would have automatically been immediately eligible for Medicaid and other benefits.

The Salvation Army could not help with the rent the next two months as I had been told.

I was frustrated now by my life and could only think of how I used to climb rock cliffs without equipment and balance on one foot on the very top of a folding ladder where it said, "This is not a step!" I was deeply frightened that I would never be able to do just simple things again, like walking up the side of a hill without having my diaphragm spasm. I went into a crying jag out of frustration and self-pity and had to constantly check my butt to see if I had a ring around it from sitting on the pity pot.

The next day I was higher than a kite and giddy with happiness. A few days after that, my intellectual brain kicked in and I couldn't read enough about how vaccines possibly cause autism, MS, Crohn's Disease and other nasty problems.

I read about Chelation Therapy and wondered if it would help people with brain injuries because some of the same basic problems occur in the brain in head injuries as in mercury poisoning from vaccines and in Alzheimer's and many of those patients are greatly helped with Chelation Therapy. I wondered if the calcium that absorbs heavy metals and turns them into a "gumball" (See Bibliography, 20-3) in Alzheimer's did the same thing in head injured people either with the metals or with the other chemicals released in the brain during a trauma to the head. I wondered if the calcium "gumball" that caused brain damage could be dissolved using the de-ionization machine or with Chelation Therapy. Within three days I was back to being just dull.

I spoke with my attorney a few days later and found out that Pam's company had been served papers and she was being served "as we speak". I was excited, yet scared to death that the next time I saw her she would try to run over me.

A thought had been creeping through my mind since the accident about the brain versus the mind. I started to understand that the brain is just another organ. In our society we have been taught to think with our brain instead of with our mind or intuition. Over the years, I realized that my experience of the world around me, emotion and knowledge came from my brain and wisdom came from my heart. I wondered which was more important—knowledge or wisdom. Knowledge gave me the ability to think—or intellect (the masculine), but wisdom gave me the understanding of the thought—intelligence (the feminine). As Eastern philosophy teaches, we all contain the whole of creation within us. The test for me would be whether I could develop the ability to "think" by using my "whole" instead of my brain. I had spent years exercising my brain muscle. Now it was time to exercise my mind muscle.

Joseph Chilton Pearce states, "intellect, on the one hand, looks through its tunnel vision and asks only *Is it possible?*, and creates disaster. Intelligence, on the other hand, that mysterious "forward movement from above" asks *Is it appropriate?* and will, if developed, use intellect to complete the movement from the "concrete to the abstract" as evolution intends." (See Bibliography, 20-4).

I had noticed since the accident that I was becoming more and more psychic or "in tune" with people. A friend of mine had told me that autopsies done on psychics revealed that their pineal gland, where it is believed psychic ability comes from, was either tipped or enlarged. It made sense to me that people with head injuries would become more psychic because of the pressure placed on the gland.

Nevertheless, I started to wonder if the phenomenon continued after the swelling of the brain went down, or had I simply started to think with my mind instead of my brain. My intent from the day I first learned that I had a brain injury was to make myself "well". Was that "well"-ness to return to who I used to be or was the intent to make myself whole by becoming one with my mind instead of with just the part of my body known as the brain? Perhaps my brain injury was a way to initiate my higher intelligence (mind).

Then I wondered if the unconscious mind is injured along with the brain. Is the unconscious mind in the brain or is the unconscious mind a part of the spirit/the whole? If we had been taught as children to use the "mind" or the unconscious as well as the conscious, or intellectual, part of the brain, would we be better balanced and able to continue functioning in a "normal" way after a brain injury?

Are the two million people who sustain a head injury each year being given the opportunity to learn to develop their "mind"? If so, I tried to imagine what it would be like if the two million people brain injured each year started to question, "Is it appropriate?"

I found that the most humiliating thing that could happen to me as someone who was stumbling and falling and had my eyeballs rolling about was for someone to look at me with disdain or pity. Such projections stymied my quest for "well"-ness and put me back into the intellect part of my brain rather than allowing me to experience the intelligence part of my mind.

And, what was the "gift" that I told people I believed I had been given and why did many of my therapists call my head injury a gift? Most assuredly it was not the $645 a month I was receiving in disability. The disability, on the other hand, was a gift as I was being given recovery-time to seek the intelligence I had always wanted but that I had allowed society to keep snatching away from me. Was this brain injury to be considered an earthly, physical thing or something experiential or was it mundane? Was I living in the truth of the mind, was this just plausible, or was I living in the illusion of the earthly realm?

What is the truth of the mind? Where does it come from? Today I pictured the silver thread connecting me to "home" and found that, not only was it still connected, but I was again reminded that "home" was a place of total serenity and pure love. I wondered then, as I nestled within the all-enfolding arms of total serenity and pure love how I could incorporate my physical, intellectual self with the intelligence of the heart and the life goal of finding the "mind". I questioned if that was the ultimate goal of achievement—to learn to live within the mind and just have complete and full realization that my body was and is just an illusion.

I know that somewhere in the midst of all of this experience, I will find perfect peace. When walking through a scorching desert, the mind contrives an image of a waterhole or a palm tree. Is that the image or is the true image what we think we are looking at every day? Within the mind of a head injury exists a whole new realm or reality. I lived with an earthly image for so long that I was not sure where I was. Once the barrier of the brain was removed and the shock of being torn from my reality settled in, I began to realize that I was being pulled closer to that which we all seek—Oneness with self.

As a head-injured person, it seemed that everything I had ever known was taken away from me. Were these things something that I actually needed or was I recognizing that those things really had no value to begin with? Somewhere in the midst of this, I remembered that misery is optional. As I mentioned before, my glass was never half empty or half full. It has always been full, the question again was, "Am I willing to drink the water?"

"Sow a thought, you reap an action,
sow an action, you reap a habit,
sow a habit, you reap a character,
sow a character and you reap a destiny.

Samuel Smiles
Nineteenth century author
And philosopher

# Chapter Twenty-One
## If Your Guts Say Don't Do It...Don't Do It

My rehab doctor wanted me to see a neurologist to find out what tests could be done to find what was causing the apraxia and balance problems. She asked me if I knew any neurologists. I told her about the holistic neurologist that the insurance company wouldn't let me see again. I told her about a neurologist who I had heard was supposedly a good neurologist but that I had been told by many of my caregivers was a nightmare on wheels if you insulted his ego. This particular neurologist was also a psychiatrist, which most of them are.

I will call this doctor "Harry". If you knew his last name, you would understand the connotation.

I met with my therapists and told them that my rehab doc wanted me to see a neurologist. I, once again, mentioned Dr. Harry to them and they all expressed dismay at my seeing him. They said he had wrecked many an excellent case because the patient had done or said something to diminish or assault his enormous ego.

I met with my attorney shortly after the meeting with the rehab doc and told him that my doc wanted me to see a neurologist but that I had heard nothing but bad about Dr. Harry so didn't want to go see him. I asked him who he would suggest I see. He said that Dr. Harry was an excellent doctor, had four or five board certifications in neurology and psychiatry and that he had used him on several head injury cases. I told my attorney what my therapists had said about Dr. Harry, but he said he wanted me to see him anyway.

I made the appointment for several months down the road with Dr. Harry, received the intake form from him and filled it out, putting my attorney's name in the spot of referral. This would come back and bite me in the butt within a few months.

On the day of my meeting with Dr. Harry, I arrived twenty minutes early for my 10:00 appointment after a one hundred and sixty mile drive. I asked the receptionist if she wanted my Medicare or Medicaid card. She told me to ask the doctor. I filled out some paperwork and sat and waited and waited. Finally, at about 10:22 the doctor came through the waiting room, introduced himself and said it would be just a few more minutes. I asked him if he wanted my Medicaid or Medicare card. He said, "Neither. I spoke with your attorney and he asked me to exam you and to bill him." I almost fell over. I said, "You did?" He assured me that he had.

I sat and waited some more.

Finally at 10:46 I asked the receptionist how much longer it would be. She told me that it shouldn't be much longer. She said the appointment would take two hours. I explained to her that I had back-to-back appointments in Boulder and had to be at the first one in order to accomplish anything in the second one. I asked her if I should reschedule. She assured me that I would be in to see the doctor any minute. Five minutes later I was ready to hurl a chair through a window. I was now an hour behind my allotted appointment time. I asked the receptionist again how much longer it would be. She finally said she would go ask him.

A few seconds after the receptionist left the area another woman came through and asked me if she could help me. I told her that I had been waiting over an hour for my appointment and was going to be late to my other appointments if I didn't get in to see the doctor immediately. She turned and as she walked away said she would go check. Oh, Christ, I thought. I tried to stop her, but she was already around the corner.

The receptionist returned and said that Dr. Harry was going over my records and would be out in a few minutes. Talk about not being prepared! Several minutes went by. Dr. Harry finally appeared at 10:54. I followed him into his stark little exam room. He told me to sit on a chair next to him at his computer desk. He asked me what he could do for me. I started out by telling him that I had four appointments that afternoon in Boulder starting at 1:00 then I told him that my rehab doctor wanted me to see a neurologist to find out what tests she needed to order for my apraxia and speech problems. (Neurologists do not specialize in cognitive rehabilitation).

He started asking me the usual questions about the accident, how it had affected me, who I was seeing for medical care, what drugs I was taking and the usual gamut of questions that I had answered a hundred times before. During this questioning, he never once looked at me. He had his computer in front of him and typed continuously.

When I started talking about my speech problems, I told him that if I talked with my tongue in the middle of my mouth I sound like I've had a stroke. I told him also that my tongue deviates to the right when I stick it out. I demonstrated my slow and slurred speech and showed him my tongue. I had the thing hung out for several seconds before he tore himself away from his keyboard.

I was taking a lot of short cuts in my answers and would later realize that that was a grave error. I told him about the accident but left out the part about wanting to pass out and how foggy I felt.

I asked him about having a Brain Function Image test done. He snorted and said that that test was useless. Good Lord, I thought, did he go to Haaarvard also or was "useless" a medical term that I hadn't learned when I was taking medical terminology in college. He also was not impressed with the idea of a PT scan or CT scan and was more impressed with the MRI. I told him that I understood that the MRI rarely showed head injury. He gave a little shrug and pursed his lips a little tighter and kept typing.

> Myth #3:
> Unfortunately, both CT and MRI scans can only detect macroscopic injuries that can only be seen by the naked eye. What that means is that the two most common diagnostic tools used by doctors to detect brain injury are not sensitive enough to actually detect the microscopic effects of mild traumatic brain injury! In the textbook *Neuropsychology of Traumatic Brain Injury*, the author states, "Many patients with a history of "minor" brain injury will not have abnormalities on their MRI, yet can manifest clear evidence of functional impairment on neuropsychological measures." The authors of this textbook point to the old medical saying: "Absence of proof is not proof of absence." (From the textbook *Medical*

*Rehabilitation of Traumatic Brain Injury* by Lawrence J. Horn, MD and Nathan D. Zasler, MD.) In other words, just because you can't see any evidence of brain injury on a CT scan or MRI scan, does not mean that it isn't there. In my view, the only way to conclusively rule out the possibility of a mild traumatic brain injury is through a comprehensive neuropsychological examination in order to determine whether or not the person is exhibiting any cognitive deficits which may have been caused by a traumatic brain injury. (See Bibliography, 21-1).

Myth #4:
However, CT and MRI scans can only detect macroscopic injury. In other words, injuries that can be seen by the naked eye. Unfortunately, mild traumatic brain injury occurs at a microscopic level in the cells of the brain. (See Bibliography, 21-2).

I told Dr. Harry that my holistic neurologist wanted me to have a sleep deprived EEG for seizures and uro-dynamic studies done to find out if I had apraxia that was causing the urinary problems or if it was the L4 area of my spine causing the problems. He asked me if they had been done. I told him that I had run out of insurance money before I was able to have them. I then mentioned to him what had been found during the biofeedback. He informed me that biofeedback is not medically accepted as a viable test.

During the history part of the questioning, he asked me if there had been any abuse in my childhood. I asked him what kind of abuse. He named physical, sexual. I told him that there had been some sexual abuse when I was young that involved the family friends' boy who was a year older than I was. I was four at the time. I told him that I also had a history of alcohol and drug abuse and had been clean and sober for twenty years. I explained to him that I had done years of therapy to resolve these past issues and told him that I felt completely whole before the accident because I had done integration work. He said he had never heard of it.

When he got done with his questions, he got up and started looking through my x-rays and MRI's. He had me stand up and, with my feet together, hold my hands out in front of me and touch my nose with my right forefinger first, then my left forefinger. As I mentioned before, I cannot do this exercise. When my right hand gets halfway to my nose, I lose track of where it is and think I am only centimeters away from my nose. My left hand does not move toward my nose at all and goes counter-clockwise in an arc. I lean my nose toward my hand and never get within two feet of my nose.

He then had me walk with one foot in front of the other starting with my feet together. All I can say is that I hope I never get pulled over and have to do the drunk-driving test. I would go to jail. This exercise is so difficult for me that I shake and sweat and it takes minutes to walk three steps. All of my large muscles turn on and fight each other—co-constriction.

He stuck a bottle of something under my nose. I could barely smell it out of the right nostril and could not identify the smell.

Dr. Harry finally finished the physical aspects of the exam and told me to have a seat.

I looked at my watch and found that I had fifteen minutes to drive to Boulder, which was twenty miles away. Dr. Harry, without looking at me, of course, said, "You'll be glad to know that you don't have a brain injury. You have psychological stress caused by the accident."

I looked at him slack-jawed and said, "You've got to be kidding. Are you saying that I'm nuts?"

He seemed to get a big kick out of this and laughed then told me that I had PTSD (post-trauma stress disorder) from my childhood sexual abuse, that I was not nuts. I asked him how that could be when I had no symptoms of PTSD and had done years of integration therapy and resolved the sexual abuse issues. He said it was because I remembered what happened during the accident. I told him that disassociating was unfamiliar to me because of the previous therapy I had done so stayed in my body. He shrugged his shoulders and with that stupid grin on his face said that that was his diagnosis. "Oh, ____(my attorney's name) is going to love this," I told him. I thought for a few seconds and then said, "Wow, what's this going to do to my case?"

He then told me that that was his diagnosis also because I remembered "every iota" of the accident.

Dr. Harry smirked and said, "Oh, I've seen cases won on psychological grounds. And, by the way, these therapists have been treating people for brain injuries who really have psychological problems." Before I could respond, he started laughing and walked out of the room shaking his head.

I was furious. I wondered if perhaps this guy was part of the New World Order

Talk about having the last word.

I left his office and went to my first therapy and arrived almost a half hour late. I told my therapist what Harry had said. She just shook her head and said that he hadn't seen me when I couldn't walk without falling over and couldn't talk without stumbling and mixing up words.

The next therapist I went to just shook her head and said that she told me not to go to him. She then said that she believed that "psychological stress" must be the catchphrase for that month.

My dentist said that you don't get jaw problems like I have without a head injury.

I insulted Dr. Harry's ego by pushing my way into his office and now my butt was about to get bitten. (The psychologist who I worked with in the 1980's had a sign hanging inside of his door with a finger pointing up a flight of stairs. The sign said, "Psychiatrist—one flight up.")

I called my old therapist who I hadn't seen in years a few days later and told him what had transpired. He told me that a whore by any other name is still a prostitute. He thought that Dr. Harry was an IME doctor. I told my old therapist that Dr. Harry was not an IME doctor. He was actually surprised and told me that under no circumstances did I have PTSD from childhood as those issues had been completely resolved.

I was also told by someone that when I went to Dr. Harry or any doctor to just tell them that I was foggy after the accident and didn't remember that much about it. Unfortunately, I could not do that. It seems that the accident knocked any lying I could have done right out of my system.

Anecdotal evidence from within the homelessness/SAAP sector as well as empirical research in the criminality field points to the fact that the disabilities arising from Acquired Brain Injury are often either overlooked and/or included under the category 'psychiatric or mental illness' or 'intellectual disability'. Both clinical and non-clinical workers often assume that the presence of a 'traditional' functional disorder is evidence of a mental or psychiatric illness. The Federal Government's SAAP national data collection has not included people with Acquired Brain Injury although it has included other disability fields such as psychiatric, intellectual and physical disabilities. (Australian study). (See Bibliography, 21-3).

## Chapter Twenty-Two
### The Lawsuit Begins—
### First Set of Discovery Requests

Even though the lawsuit was filed with the court on the day before the statute of limitations ran out, my attorney did not serve the papers immediately. I found out that a plaintiff can leave a lawsuit sitting on a judge's desk for quite some time before the judge will ask the attorney what he plans to do with the suit. My attorney opted for letting the suit lie pending further side effects of the injuries that I had sustained. In July the court asked my attorney to do something with the case.

The defendant's insurance company was served toward the end of July and in August, 2004 the defendant was served with her papers. I'm sure there was a fireworks display in the area around her. Ironically I had called to question my attorney about the sequence of events I was to expect and was told, "She is being served as we speak." My mouth went dry, my head started spinning and I realized that the moment I had been waiting for with anticipation had finally arrived. I just had a different reaction than I thought I would have. I thought I would leap for joy, if I could have, but instead I went into fear mode.

The defendant's attorneys asked for a change of venue to the county where we both lived and was granted the change since, as I've stated before, lawsuits are to be filed in the county where the defendant resides. My attorney had filed the suit in a county where very wealthy people live saying that wealthier communities usually give more generous settlements.

For me, all was quiet for five months.

During the quiet time the defendant's attorney sent an offer of $500 to my attorney to settle the case. My attorney slid the offer across the table to me when I met with him in February of 2005 and said that he didn't think that I would accept the offer but that he had to show it to me. I would have laughed if it hadn't been so pitiful. Of course, I rejected the offer.

My attorney explained to me that if an offer was made and I declined the offer and we went to court and the jury found the defendant to not be liable and ordered no damages, then the defendant's attorney could sue me to recoup their attorney's fees. If no offer was made then the defendant's attorney could not sue for attorney fees even if I lost. The defense attorneys could say that they offered a settlement and I refused so litigation and debt increased. Therefore, they could say I was liable for the increased debt. On the other hand, if I asked for more money than the defendant offered and a jury awarded more money, I could request attorney's fees from the defendant.

Personally I believe that this should be changed and a scale set up where a minimum offer can be made according to the injuries sustained such as in an insurance policy where if you lose a leg, an arm, your eyesight or became incapacitated in some other way there is a minimum amount that is paid without question. Full disability would have a much higher minimum amount that could be offered.

The next step in the game for me was receipt of what is known as the **First Set of Discovery Requests to Plaintiff**. The Discovery consisted of three parts: **the Pattern Interrogatory, the Non-Pattern Interrogatory and Requests for Production**. The Pattern Interrogatory also will arrive from the District Court with a very intimidating front page. The document may be in any format with boxes around the document, stars around the document or just plain as in this example:

District Court, County, State
Address
City, State

Plaintiff(s)          Court Use Only
Address
v                                        Case #:
Defendant(s)                             Ctrm:

Address
City, State        Div.#:

The Law Offices of….
Address
City, State
Phone #
Atty. Reg.#

## DEFENDANT SUZIE HOMEMAKER'S FIRST SET OF DISCOVERY REQUESTS TO PLAINTIFF

The Defendant, Suzie Homemaker, by her attorneys, The Law Offices of J. Smith, submits the following written Interrogatories and Requests for Production to Plaintiff, to be answered within thirty (30) days of the date of service of these Discovery Requests, by the Plaintiff, under oath, pursuant to Rules 33 and 34 of the Colorado Rules of Civil Procedure.

Of course, your state's Civil Procedure Rules will look differently. The **Pattern Interrogatory Instructions** looked like this:

(a) An answer or other appropriate response must be given to each interrogatory checked by the asking party.

(b) Within 30 days after you are served with these interrogatories, you must serve your responses on the asking party and serve copies of your responses on all other parties to the action who have appeared. See C.R.C.P. 33 for details.

(c) Each answer must be complete and straightforward as the information readily available to you permits. If an interrogatory cannot be answered completely, answer it to the extent possible.

(d) If you do not have enough personal knowledge to fully answer an interrogatory, say so, but make a reasonable and good faith effort to get the information by asking other persons or organizations, unless the information is equally available to the asking party.

(e) Whenever an interrogatory may be answered by referring to a document, the document may be attached as an exhibit to the response and referred to in the response. If the document has more than one page, refer to the page and section where the answer to the interrogatory can be found.

(f) Whenever an address and telephone number for the same person are requested in more than one interrogatory, you are required to furnish them in answering only the first interrogatory asking for that information.

(g) Your answers to these interrogatories must be verified, dated, and signed. You may wish to use the following form at the end of your answers: "I declare under penalty of perjury under the laws of the state of Your State that the foregoing answers are true and correct."

Along with the questions was a set of definitions.

"Words in **BOLDFACE CAPITALS** in these interrogatories are defined as follows:

**INCIDENT** includes the circumstances and events surrounding the alleged accident, injury, or other occurrence or breach of contract giving rise to this action of proceeding.

**YOU OR ANYONE ACTING ON YOUR BEHALF** includes you, your agents, your employees, your insurance companies, their agents, their employees, your attorneys, your accountants, your investigators, and anyone else acting on your behalf.

**PERSON** includes a natural person, firm, association, organization, partnership, business, trust, corporation, or public entity.

**DOCUMENT** means a writing, as defined in CRE 1001 and includes the original or a copy of handwriting, typewriting, printing, photostating, photographing, and every other means of recording upon any tangible thing and form of communicating or representation, including letters, words, pictures, sounds, or symbols, or combination of them.

**HEALTH CARE PROVIDER** includes any **PERSON** or entity referred to as a "Health Care Professional" or "Health Care Institution" in C.R.S. section 13-64-202(3) and (4).

Each of these definitions may vary according to whatever state you reside in. Because I was a resident of Colorado, this is the way the wording was and the definitions that were given. Instead of C.R.S., your definitions and questions may have, perhaps, N.Y.R.S. for New York."

The **Pattern Interrogatory** looked like the following:

### PATTERN INTERROGATORY DEFINITIONS
2.1  State:
    (a) your present residence **ADDRESS**;
    (b) your residence **ADDRESS** for the last ten (10) years;
    (c) the dates you lived at each **ADDRESS**.
2.2  State:

(a) the name, **ADDRESS**, and telephone number of your present employer or places of self-employment;

(b) the name, **ADDRESS** dates of employment, job title, and nature of work for each employer or self employment you have had from five (5) years before the **INCIDENT** until today.

2.3 State:

(a) the name and **ADDRESS** of each school or other academic or vocational institute you have attended beginning with high school;

(b) the dates you attended;

(c) the highest grade you have completed;

(d) the degrees received.

4.1 At the time of the **INCIDENT**, was there in effect any policy of insurance through which you were or might be insured in any manner (for example, primary, pro rata or excess liability coverage or medical expense coverage) for the damages, claims or actions that have arisen out of the **INCIDENT**? If so, for each policy state:

(a) the kind of coverage;

(b) the name and **ADDRESS** of the insurance company;

(c) the name, **ADDRESS**, and telephone number of each named insured; the policy number; the limits of coverage for each type of coverage contained in the policy; whether any reservation of rights or controversy of coverage dispute exists between you and the insurance company;

(d) the name, **ADDRESS**, and telephone number of the custodian of the policy.

6.2   If you sustained any physical, mental, or emotional injuries as a result of the **INCIDENT**, identify each injury you attribute to the **INCIDENT** and the area of your body affected.

6.3   Do you still have any complaints that you attribute to the **INCIDENT**? If so, for each complaint state:

(a) a description;
(b) whether the complaint is subsiding, remaining the same, or becoming worse;
(c) the frequency and duration.

6.4   Did you receive any consultation or examination (except from the expert witnesses covered by C.R.C.P. 35) or treatment from a **HEALTH CARE PROVIDER** for any injury you sustained in the **INCIDENT**? If so, for each **HEALTH CARE PROVIDER** state:

(a) the name, **ADDRESS**, and telephone number;
(b) the type of consultation, examination, or treatment provided;
(c) the dates you received consultation, examination, or treatment;
(d) the charges to date.

6.6 Have you taken any medication, prescribed or not, as a result of the injuries that you sustained in the **INCIDENT**? If so, for each medication state:
    (a) the name;
    (b) the **PERSON** who prescribed or furnished;
    (c) the date prescribed or furnished;
    (d) the dates you began and stopped taking it;
    (e) the cost to date.

6.7 Has any **HEALTH CARE PROVIDER** advised that you may require future or additional treatment for any injuries that you sustained in the **INCIDENT**? If so, for each injury state:
    (a) the name and **ADDRESS** of each **HEALTH CARE PROVIDER**;
    (b) the physical or emotional complaints you provided to the **HEALTH CARE PROVIDER**;
    (c) the nature, duration, and estimated cost of the treatment.

6.8 If you attribute any loss of income or earning capacity to the **INCIDENT**, state:
    (a) your work duties,
    (b) your job title at the time of the **INCIDENT**;
    (c) the date your employment began.

8.8 Will you lose income in the future as a result of the **INCIDENT**? Is so, for each item of damage state;
- (a) the nature;
- (b) the date it occurred;
- (c) the amount;
- (d) the name, **ADDRESS**, and telephone number of each **PERSON** to whom the obligation was incurred.

10.2 List all physical, mental and emotional problems from which you suffered during the ten (10) years prior to the **INCIDENT**.

10.3 At any time after the **INCIDENT**, were you involved in any other incident in which you sustained injuries of any kind? If so, for each incident state:
- (a) the date and place it occurred;
- (b) the name **ADDRESS**, and telephone number of any other **PERSON** involved;
- (c) the nature of any injuries you sustained;
- (d) the name, **ADDRESS**, and telephone number of each **HEALTH CARE PROVIDER** that you consulted or who examined or treated you;
- (d) the nature of the treatment and its duration.

11.1 Except for this action, in the last ten (10) years have you filed an action or made a written claim or demand for compensation for personal injuries? If so, for each action, claim, or demand state:

(a) the date, time, and place, and location of the **INCIDENT** (closest street **ADDRESS** or intersection);

(b) the name, **ADDRESS**, and telephone number of each **PERSON** against whom the claim was made or action filed;

(c) the court, names of the parties, and case number of any action filed;

(d) the name, **ADDRESS**, and telephone number of any attorney representing you;

(e) whether the claim or action has been resolved or is pending.

State the name, **ADDRESS**, and telephone number of each individual:

(a) who witnessed the **INCIDENT** or the events occurring immediately before or after the **INCIDENT**;

(b) who made any statement at the scene Of the **INCIDENT** by any individual at the scene.

(c) who **YOU OR ANYONE ACTING ON YOUR BEHALF** claims to have knowledge of the **INCIDENT** (except for expert witnesses covered by C.R.C.P. 26(a)(2) and b(4).

12.1 Have **YOU OR ANYONE ACTING ON YOUR BEHALF** interviewed any individual concerning the **INCIDENT**? If so, for each individual state:

(a) the name, **ADDRESS**, and telephone number of the individual interviewed;
(b) the date of the interview;
(c) the name, **ADDRESS**, and telephone number of the **PERSON** who conducted the interview.

12.2 Have **YOU OR ANYONE ACTING ON YOUR BEHALF** obtained a written or recorded statement from any individual concerning the **INCIDENT**? If so, for each statement state:
(a) the name, **ADDRESS**, and telephone number of the individual from whom the statement was obtained;
(b) the name, **ADDRESS**, and telephone number of the individual who obtained the statement;
(c) the date the statement was obtained;
(d) the name, **ADDRESS**, and telephone number of each **PERSON** who has the original statement or a copy.

12.3 Do **YOU OR ANYONE ACTING ON YOUR BEHALF** know of any photographs, films, videotapes depicting any place, object, or individual concerning the **incident**. If so, please state:
(a) the number of photographs or feet of film or videotape;
(b) the places, objects, or persons photographed, filmed or videotaped;

(c) the date the photographs, films or videotapes were taken;
(d) the name **ADDRESS**, and telephone number of the individual taking the photographs, films, or videotapes;
(e) the name **ADDRESS**, and telephone number of each **PERSON** who has the original or a copy.

12.4 Do **YOU OR ANYONE ACTING ON YOUR BEHALF** know of any diagram, reproduction, or model of any place or thing (except for items developed by expert witnesses covered by C.R.C.P. 26(a)(2) and b(4) concerning the **INCIDENT**? If so, for each item state:
(a) the type (i.e., diagram, reproduction, or model);
(b) the subject matter;
(c) the name, **ADDRESS**, and telephone number of each **PERSON** who has it.

12.6 Was a report made by any **PERSON** concerning the incident? If so, state:
(a) the name, title, identification number, and employer of the **PERSON** who made the report;
(b) the date and type of report made;
(c) the name, **ADDRESS**, and telephone number of the **PERSON** for whom the report was made.

12.7 Have **YOU OR ANYONE ACTING ON YOUR**

BEHALF inspected the scene of the **INCIDENT**? If so, for each inspection state:
>   (a) the name, **ADDRESS**, and telephone number of the individual making the inspection (except for expert witnesses covered by C.R.C.P. 26(a)(2) and b(4));
>   (b) the date of the inspection.

When you first get this interrogatory, it will scare you. That is exactly what it is meant to do so that you will settle the case. What you have just read is only the first third of the interrogatory. Some of these questions might be on the interrogatory and some may not, depending on your situation and the **INCIDENT** that occurred.

I found that every time I got to the word **INCIDENT** I would cringe and become angry. The word incident seems to minimize the impact of the accident as well as its validity, which I am sure the defense attorneys are well aware of. I mentioned to my paralegal the fact that there were no typos and that the document seemed well organized and thought-out. She informed me that these questions came off of a computer program. For some reason, that helped to settle my fear. I had thought that the attorneys I was up against were quite structured and must be from some prestigious firm. I learned later that it was a two-attorney firm and they were probably trying to make a name for themselves on my case plus get a free trip to our little town where they could vacation for a week.

**CERTIFICATE OF MAILING**

I HEREBY CERTIFY that on this _____ day of (Month, Year), a true and correct copy of the foregoing DISCOVERY REQUESTS was placed in the U.S. mail, postage pre-paid, addressed to the following: _____.

Make sure that the waivers you sign clearly states that the person receiving the waiver is to not speak to the defense team without the presence of your attorney.

Pattern interrogatories help the defense attorneys establish a pattern of consistency and behaviors over the years up to the incident. For example, my high school transcripts resembled someone who kept their grades up just enough to play basketball, which I did. I could not understand why they wanted the high school transcript other than to intimidate. I graduated from high school in 1967. Obviously, if I had college transcripts, I graduated from high school.

I attended many colleges and schools after I graduated from high school that were scattered out over the years. I went to a University for one semester after high school and lost interest in basketball so I figured, why bother with college. Besides, I wanted to travel.

Five years later I went back to college and did one more year. It was not until 1984 that I knew what I wanted to do with my life, or so I thought. I went to University and received my certification in drug and alcohol counseling. During that period of time I started taking other classes and graduated in 1989 with bachelor's degrees in Psychology and Sociology, a Certification in Criminology and Corrections as well as a Certification in Drug and Alcohol Counseling, which I received in 1985. The next year I graduated from a law school with a Certification in Dispute Resolution.

Did I use any of these degrees? I worked in methadone clinics for a couple years then decided to do restoration work on buildings because I had moved to an area where there was no methadone clinic, and I wanted to do something that was not so political.

The second part of the interrogatory is called the **non-pattern interrogatory**. The wording in the instructions and definitions of the non-pattern interrogatory are questions that are deemed continuing. "If any information sought by said Interrogatories is not learned until after the Interrogatories are answered, or if the answers for any reason should later become incorrect, there shall be a continuing duty on the part answering said Interrogatories to supplement or change answers previously submitted pursuant to Rule 26(e) of the Colorado Rules of Civil Procedure and applicable Colorado case law."

(Once again, this rule may be different in your state.)

"The definition of ""you" or "your" or any synonym thereof is intended to and shall embrace and include, in addition to the named Plaintiff, counsel for said Plaintiff and all agents, servants, employees, representatives, private investigators, and others who are in possession of or may have obtained information for or on behalf of the named party.

On the question about my injuries I wrote five pages. I took most of the answers off of my doctors' reports or off of psychological/cognitive/head injury questionnaires. My attorney, of course, had his paralegal break this down to a very short answer, telling me that I needed to avoid sounding like my own expert witness. Basically the five pages became traumatic brain injury, headaches, back pain, neck pain, vision problems, right shoulder pain, jaw pain and Posttraumatic Stress Disorder.

When asked to "identify" a person or entity in these Interrogatories, identification should include the full name of the person or entity, along with the last known address and telephone number."

This is an example of the second part of my Discovery:

**NON-PATTERN INTERROGATORIES**

1. Set forth in detail your version of the accident, including from where your trip began, where you were going, the speed you were traveling at impact, the direction or directions in which your body moved at and following impact, and any objects that you struck within your vehicle.

2. With regard to those persons you believe to be witnesses in this case, please set forth for each person you identify the substance of the facts and opinions to which those persons may testify concerning your injuries, change in lifestyle, financial and job related problems, social life and physical and/or emotional problems following the accident.

3. Please identify all damages for which you are making a claim in this lawsuit and as to each item of damages, identify the amount claimed and how such amount was calculated.

4. Please set forth a complete list of all hospitals where you have received treatment for any reason during the ten (10) years **preceding** the accident.

5. Identify all doctors, dentists, osteopaths,

chiropractors, psychiatrists, psychologists, or any other health care providers whom you have consulted for any reason during the ten (10) years **preceding** the accident.

6. At any time **prior** to the incident, were you involved in any other incident in which you sustained injuries of any kind? If so, for each incident state:

(a) the date it occurred;

(b) the name, address, and telephone number of any other person involved;

(c) the nature of any injuries you sustained;

(d) the name, address, and telephone number of each health care provider that you consulted or who examined or treated you;

(e) the nature of the treatment and its duration.

7. If you have received any type of financial assistance from any insurance or government entity since the incident, please identify the company, agency or entity, include the claim number or benefit number assigned to the assistance, and state the monthly amounts you have received from each company, agency or entity since the accident.

8. Identify by name and relationship all persons who have resided with you during the five (5) years prior to and following the accident.

The third part of the **Discovery** asked me to produce within thirty (30) days of the date of service of this document the following and gave, once again, definitions. Do not get concerned about this. All I did was sign the waivers. I actually didn't have to do anything. I am simply showing this to you so that you don't become intimidated when you receive it. Don't let them get into your head. Just be aware that each of these items will be a part of the defense's defense.

## REQUESTS FOR PRODUCTION

Privilege. If the Plaintiff considers any document of thing requested by the Defendants to be privileged from production, Defendants request that within 33 days of the date of service hereof, the Plaintiff serve on the Defendants a written list of all documents and things withheld from production, identifying each document as follows: date, address or author's name, title and address; addressee's name, title and address; the name and address of each person to whom a copy of the document has been sent or shown; the general character of the document; and the legal basis on which each document is considered to be privileged from discovery.

Duty to Respond. Plaintiff is hereby notified that Plaintiff's duty to respond includes the duty to supply any and all documents and things not in Plaintiff's physical possession but which can be obtained from sources under Plaintiff's control. Please produce the following:

    1. Copies of all medical and psychological treatment notes, test results and treatment records from all hospitals, doctors, dentists, osteopaths, chiropractors, psychiatrists, psychologists, or any other health care providers whom you have consulted or treated with for any reason **since** the accident. (Without waiving its right to obtain the requested records from the Plaintiff, Defendant attaches a blank medical records release form for its use.)

    2. Written and recorded statements of witnesses and expert witnesses, expert witness reports, notes, diaries, memoranda, and all other records prepared by or on behalf of you concerning any and all allegations contained in the Complaint.

    3. All drawings, diagrams, photographs, vehicle damage photographs, accident site photographs, graphs, charts, videotapes, computer-generated data, tape recordings, statement transcribed from recording devices and other tangible things which you, your attorney, or representatives thereof have in their possession, custody, or control with reference to any of the allegations contained in the Complaint.

    4. Copies of any and all diaries,

journals, or personal notes maintained by or at the direction of Plaintiff in which are described events which Plaintiff contends relate to the incident which is the subject of this lawsuit or otherwise gives rise to this litigation.

5. Produce a copy of each and every accident report you or anyone else generated or drafted concerning the accident.

6. Copies of all medical and psychological treatment notes and treatment records from all doctors, dentists, osteopaths, chiropractors, psychiatrists, psychologists or any other health care providers whom you have consulted for any reason during the ten (10) years **preceding** the accident. (Without waiving her right to obtain the requested records from the Plaintiff, Defendant attaches a blank medical records release form for her use.)

7. Copies of all documents, statements and other written and/or recorded material identified in your response to Pattern Interrogatory no. 12.3.

8. Copies of all complaints, demands and letters of demand submitted on your behalf which are related to the lawsuits and claims identified in your response to Pattern Interrogatory no. 11.1.

9. Copies of any and all accident

reports, written statements or other Documents related to the **subsequent** accidents identified by you in response to Pattern Interrogatory no. 10.3.

10. Copies of any and all accident reports, written statements, or other Documents related to the prior accidents identified by you in response to Non-Pattern Interrogatory no. 6.

11. Copies of all applications, statements, questionnaires and other Documents submitted by you when applying for unemployment compensation, Medicaid, disability and/or social security benefits following the accident.

12. Copies of the entire contents of your personal injury protection (PIP) file. (Without waiving her right to obtain the requested records from Plaintiff, Defendant attaches a blank insurance records release form for her use.)

13. Copies of your income tax returns from 1997-2003, including any W-2 and 1099 forms. (Without waiving her right to obtain the requested records from Plaintiff, Defendant attaches blank IRS 4506 for her use.) (Also, the dates on yours will be different.)

14. Copies of the entire contents of your employment files and records kept by your employers during the five years prior to the accident to the present. (Without waiving her request that Plaintiff produce the records, Defendants attach a blank employment records

release form for Plaintiff to execute and return for Defendant's use.)

      15. Copies of the entire contents of your file from Social Security Administration concerning benefits you are currently receiving from that agency. (Without waiving her right to obtain the requested records from Plaintiff, Defendant attaches a blank Social Security records release form for her use.)

      16. Copies of your current resume or curriculum vitae, and any resume or Curriculum vitae from 1997 to the present.

      17. Copies of all business advertisements, resumes, and biographies for any self-employment you have had from 1997 to the present.

      18. Copies of all customer contact lists for any self-employment you have from 1997 to the present.

      19. Copies of your high school, college, or other educational transcripts. (Without waiving her right to obtain the requested records from Plaintiff, Defendant attaches a blank school records release for her use.)

Respectfully submitted this \_\_\_\_ day of January, 2005

      THE LAW OFFICES OF J. SMITH
      By:_____
      J. Smith

## Chapter Twenty-Three
### How to be Prepare—
### What I Needed to Know

By now your head is probably spinning. In my case, the Discovery was sent on January 10 to my attorney. By the time I received the Discovery, it was January 21, leaving me only nineteen days to complete the Discovery. I had to ask for an extension. This will definitely slow up your case if you don't already have your information ready and it will anger the Judge.

From the very beginning of your injury, set up a three-ring binder, or some other type of file system that will include the following so that when the Interrogatory Discovery arrives, you will know how much you paid out-of-pocket. This should include a section for Medicaid and Medicare. You will have to pay some back to Medicaid and Medicare out of your settlement before you receive any settlement money. I was told that I would have to put my settlement money into a trust fund and could only receive up to $2,000 per month or would become ineligible for social services the month I took out more than $2,000. I saved the following:

1. motel receipts, gas receipts, and food receipts that I paid for out of pocket;

2. AFDC—food stamps, public welfare;
3. private welfare such as Catholic Charities, other church charities, food banks, the Salvation Army for items such as rental assistance vouchers, gas vouchers, food vouchers, clothing vouchers, or auto repair vouchers that were paid for by a charity;
4. Social Security Disability;
5. Medicaid and Medicare;
6. HUD (Section 8 or city rental assistance programs)
7. Heat assistance program;
8. Food bank programs;
9. Copies of every report written about me from doctors, therapists, psychologists, and any other health care provider who I saw. If you do not have these, your attorney should send you copies of these reports before you do your deposition. The defense will have this information and they will pull out something that you thought was trivial and question you about it during your deposition.

Many times the health care provider does not want to give your information to you, but it is your right to have it. Try to avoid asking for a lump of reports as you will probably be charged for the copying—one doctor charged me $250 to send me copies of reports that I gave to him! If you get a copy of your report after each visit you will have an idea of what you were told versus what is in the report. As I mentioned before, I found that several of the health care providers I saw told me something other than what they wrote in the report. If this happens, confront the doctor with what you were told versus what is in the report. The best way to avoid this snafu is to take someone to your exams and therapies with you if at all possible.

I also learned that the physician's assistant whom I had seen wrote in a report, "Unfortunately, the patient is quite against traditional medicine." This will not help your case. After reading this in the report, I refused to see the physician's assistant again and would only go to the actual doctor.

To me, society has traditional and alternative medicine backwards. Traditional medicine is what is natural, such as herbs and bodywork. Alternative medicine should be called what is known as allopathic medicine/traditional. That is an alternative to what a Power greater than our selves put on the earth to heal and what that Power gave to individuals to work with through their hands and senses. Traditional allopathic medicine uses chemicals to alter your body's reaction in the form of prescription drugs and it seems to me that these chemicals usually treat the symptom, not the problem.

Remember, the defense team will look at every word and scrap of information that is in a doctor's possession. One of my doctors refused to accept a doctor's report that negated my case because she did not want the defense to find the letter in her records. On the other hand, my attorney wanted me to make sure that all of my medical providers knew of the contents of the report.

Be careful what you write in any letters or notes to your providers. Your attorney is the only one you have complete confidentiality with. Your psychologist/psychiatrist has confidentiality leeway, not absolute confidentiality.

I decided to sign the waiver for the medical records request. Each health care provider that I saw charged $25 to $120 per set of records. By this point in time, I had seen approximately forty health care providers. The health care provider will also charge your attorney for records and he/she, in turn, will charge you a copy fee, plus postage to send the records to the defendant's attorney and that will come out of your settlement.

Your insurance company most likely will charge the defense attorney and your attorney for copies of their records, which will be monumental in size if you have a brain injury or any other serious injuries. In my case, my insurance company had approximately 6,000 pages.

Be prepared with the following:

1. Every place you've ever lived.
2. All educational transcripts.

This can take up to a whole day if you are over thirty years old. My high school does not, in essence, exist anymore. It was part of a consolidation. The college where I took EMT classes and was certified does not have a record of me even though I worked as an EMT at the hospital where the classes were held. The massage school I went to is no longer in business. Most colleges require a $2 to $10 fee for a copy of your transcripts. Some colleges require you to fill out a form off of the computer. Some colleges request a letter in writing with your social security number, address, the dates you attended, and verification (driver's license copy) of who you actually are.

1. Records of all injuries sustained in the accident;
2. Insurance records/declarations;
3. Employment records from employers five years previous of the accident;
4. Records and copies of all prescription drugs and receipts of all herbal and vitamin supplement purchased as

prescribed by health care providers. (Most insurance companies in most states will not reimburse you for food expense or vitamins and herbal supplements but I personally believe that these amounts should be owed to you as part of the settlement if they were prescribed by a health care provider);
5. If self-employed, have self-employment records ready;
6. Income Tax Returns from five years prior to the accident and from the time of the accident to the present time even though you will have to sign a waiver for the attorneys to get the records directly from the IRS;
7. Have prepared the amount of income that will be lost due to the accident with records to back up your claim;
8. Ask health care providers how many months or years of treatment to expect.
9. Know how much health care providers charge per session. If liens have been signed, know how much is owed.

In my case, I was told that it would take four to five more years of cognitive therapy and/or speech therapy before I would reach "maximum". My jaw will probably never be right. I will have to have orthodontal work done by a dentist who specializes in neurological jaw problems. It will probably take years of physical therapy to re-train my brain and muscles. This may never be achieved. My small muscles were still in spasm while my large muscles were still just trying to hold things together at the time of discovery. My optometrist told me that their goal was to teach me remedial measures because my vision will most likely never be corrected. The time and cost are unknown.

10. If there have been other accidents or there have been other damages that are attributed to the accident, have the cost and monetary loss available as well as physical, emotional, and psychological costs;
11. Keep a record of your complaints. Is there improvement in areas? Are some areas getting worse? Journal, journal, journal. If you keep a diary, be careful about mentioning if you feel like you want to take revenge on the person who caused your injury or that you wish harm to them. The defense will grab this and say that you are not truly injured and only want revenge. Remember, nothing is sacred in a court case. Your diary and notes will be requested;

12. Records of all medical, psychological and emotional problems ten years prior to the accident;
13. Lawsuits other than the ones filed against a defendant for the ten years prior to the accident and since the accident;
14. If there are witnesses, know who they are and all other pertinent information about them, including what they saw and heard;
15. Interview records and transcripts of witnesses or others in relationship to the accident;
16. Notes and videotapes, audiotapes and photographs including those from anyone acting on your behalf;
17. Reports of the accident made by anyone including those who may have inspected the scene.

If you have not already done so, begin to think about the sequence of events leading up to the accident. If you remember the accident at all, start writing down your memories. If this process is too difficult for you, or if it causes too much emotional and/or mental distress, do this in the presence of your mental health provider. If you have not already done some psychological counseling, do it now. During the deposition, there is no judge to stop the defense from asking questions that might be stopped in a courtroom. From here on, you, as the plaintiff, will be treated as a defendant. Don't allow yourself to get sucked into this pit. You are the plaintiff, and you need to be compensated. Make this your mantra. If you have not already done so, you need to stop being in the victim role. Try to envision a stop sign held up in front of you when this "stinkin' thinkin' creeps in.

    I set up a daily affirmation for myself and read this before I did anything else for the day.

## Activating Event
I have a head trauma and I need to be financed and compensated for my injuries.

## Old Belief System
We had no money. The labor was hard. There was more labor than fun. It was my responsibility to keep the family together. Don't trust authority.

## New Belief System
Shift 12% of my consciousness to 88%.

The spiritual concept is one of old ideas and thought forms born on the farm. The new spiritual concept is one of liberation of those old concepts starting today.

1. Spiritually I liberate the old ideas today.

2. Liberation of the sea-saw thought effect (that I am undeserving).
3. Within ninety days I begin to receive an annuity which is more than my old belief system would have allowed me to believe plus a one-time settlement of $75,000-$90,000.
4. And if more is possible, I accept that.

The consequence of my new belief system is that I receive me and I open to the flow of abundance coming toward myself. I have grown up from that little girl on the farm to a conscious adult who receives benefits from my maturity.

When I wrote this new belief system, I was having a terrible time conceiving of a monetary value that I deserved to be compensated for my injuries. My past beliefs dictated that I was an undeserving person. I ran the gamut of believing that I would get no compensation to the other end of the spectrum believing that I should get the maximum amount available. The words adequate versus exorbitant crept into my thinking.

What most juries are not told is that the defendant most likely will not have to pay a penny out of their pocket. The juries are also not told how much the person is insured for or even that they have insurance. The balance in the equation is that if an award is given above and beyond the amount the defendant is insured for, there is a big chance that the defendant will file for bankruptcy and you will get nothing. Therefore, the word adequate became the motivating factor in what I would choose to settle for.

When you receive your Discovery papers, remember to pull yourself into the Now. If you begin to feel fear, you are living in the future or the past. Do not get pulled into this addictive behavior.

# Chapter Twenty-Four
## Attorney v Psychiatrist—
## And the Loser Is!...me

The week before I met with Richard (pseudonym), my personal injury attorney, I met with a tax attorney because Richard wanted me to revamp some things on my taxes. The tax attorney just kept asking me why Richard wanted me to change some items because it was not in my best interest. The tax attorney also said that he was much more interested in helping me with my settlement monies, as his specialty was investments. We decided to call Richard and find out what his objective was.

Richard told the tax attorney that my case wasn't worth anything (because of the supposed PTSD diagnosis) and there would be no money to invest because the defendant only had $100,000 in liability. I told Richard that she had at least $300,000 in liability. He argued with me and finally agreed to go look. When he returned he said that he stood corrected. She had $300,000 in liability and a $1,000,000 umbrella policy. So, suddenly, the amount of possible money went from $100,000 to $300,000.

The following week I met with Richard and his latest assistant and was informed that they did not know that I had an appointment. This lady was now the seventh person I had been presented with as his assistant in the two years since I had signed on with his firm. The others had been fired or quit. I was beginning to understand why. When I met with Richard a few months before that, the paralegal who was taking notes asked him a question. He jumped all over her and told her to not talk unless she was told to.

I was quite shocked and felt like I felt in grade school when a mean old teacher came storming into the bathroom, glared at the poor little girl who had been in there too long and started wailing on her. I would imagine that the poor child wasn't able to go to the bathroom for another twenty years or so without having an image of hawk eyes and lace-up, big soled high-heeled shoes.

While the paralegal and I were working on my discovery, Richard came marching in and told her that it was taking her way too long to complete her task. (The next week I learned that he fired her.) I was beginning to wonder if this guy who had wined and dined me, so to speak, to get me signed on was a wolf in sheep's clothing and passive-aggressive to boot.

Before this aforementioned foray occurred, I had met privately with Richard for about a half hour. It was during this meeting that he slid the $500 offer from the defendant's attorney across the table to me. He also said that he didn't think that my case was worth much and that it would be terribly expensive to go to trial because most of my medical providers lived on the eastern slope and the trial was going to be held hundreds of miles away. That day he seemed to find every excuse in the book to get me to throw in the towel. (One of my therapists who knew him personally said Richard tends to play the devil's advocate).

    I then told Richard about my experience with Dr. Harry. I told him what was said in Dr. Harry's waiting room and that Dr. Harry said that he had spoken to him and that he had told Dr. Harry that he was paying for the exam. Richard told me that no such thing had happened. He said that he never referred anyone to a doctor because it would look like he was trying to buy testimony. (Richard is the one who told me to go to the rehab doctor I chose). Then he sat back and thought about what I had told him and said that he might have seen Dr. Harry one night at a dinner and said that he wanted him to examine me, but he had certainly never told him that he would pay for it.

    I went over the exam with Richard and said that Dr. Harry spent the first hour typing and not looking at me. Richard seemed miffed about that but was furious when I told him about the conversation Dr. Harry and I had at the end of the meeting. He asked me to relate parts of the conversation twice and quizzed me about my comment pertaining to the fact that Richard would not like the diagnosis.

I told Richard about my inability to perform the heel to toe exercise and the nose touching exercise. He asked me to demonstrate the toe to heel exercise. I did and broke into a sweat, got the shakes and took a long time to accomplish the feat. He then told me to walk across the room, which was only six feet wide. Of course I could walk across a six-foot section without stumbling or falling. I was now up to more than twenty steps before I fell over unless I was leaned forward and walking very fast.

Richard said that because I could walk normally he believed that Dr. Harry's report was correct and that I was suffering from psychological trauma. I told him that I had worked in physical therapy for months learning to walk across a room but had not worked on walking heel to toe or drawing my finger to my nose.

I could not figure out why this whole conversation had set his teeth on edge.

We briefly discussed my discovery and then he dismissed me to his paralegal.

The discovery was due the next day. I had mailed my answers to the discovery to the attorney the week before. They had plenty of time to dissect it and re-write it with answers shorter than mine were. They took exception to some of my answers. For example, in Non-Pattern Interrogatory question number 1, I was instructed to give in detail what happened before the accident. I guess I was a little too detailed. I was told to not perjure myself and to answer as completely as possible so I did!

At any rate, the Discovery was not ready so we had to ask for an extension.

The next week I started thinking about how annoyed I was that the Discovery had not been ready when I got to Richard's office. I know that it is not polite to offend the Court. I tried to call the woman with whom I had worked on the Discovery, but after much hemming and hawing by another paralegal, I learned that they couldn't get the Discovery off of the computer of the woman who I had worked with because she was no longer employed there and they didn't know her password. So now I had to start over with another person.

I called an attorney that my daughter knew and spoke with him about what had been happening. He said to begin with if he was my attorney he would get Dr. Harry's testimony suppressed because the doctor had not seen me until more than three years after the accident so wouldn't have a clue what I looked like at my worst. I asked him about doing a settlement with a smaller lump sum payment and an annuity that I would receive monthly. He said that he had done that before.

I wrote a letter to my attorney and suggested a mediation settlement. I also told him that I was not happy about the way phone calls were not returned and the fact that every time I met with him I had to start with a new paralegal because the old one was gone. I mentioned also that he had not known how much the defendant had for insurance and that I felt like he did not believe in me. I also told him that I had spoken with one of my medical providers and she had told me that the toe to heel and touching the nose exercises entail three parts: vestibular, vision, and proprioperception. I am lacking in all three. I also sent to him names of articles and authors who back up this claim.

Three days later I received an eleven page letter from my attorney telling me that he was withdrawing from my case.

Holy crap!

And he was sitting on my Discovery. He did inform me in his letter, however, that he had requested another extension. Richard requested that I reimburse him $2,514.18 that he had paid for court case monies advanced. He sent copies of the letters he had sent to my providers stating that he was not going to honor the liens that had been signed. Included also was the notice to the Court and the defendant's attorney that he was no longer my attorney. In the real world I thought that people sat down and discussed their differences and tried to come up with a solution. Not so with this guy. It was suggested to me that I file a complaint with the Bar Association.

He said that one of the reasons he was quitting the case was because of the episode with Dr. Harry. He said I should never have told Dr. Harry that he referred me to him, even though he did. That's the only reason he gave for backing out of my case.

And now I was left out in the cold without an attorney.

I called the attorney who my daughter knew. I was to send files to him to look over and he would let me know in a week if he wanted the case.

I called Richard's office and left a message that I needed my files ASAP. I received a letter from Richard stating that my file was so massive that he would just send the attorney information he felt the attorney needed to see and would send the bulk of the file to me. He stated that several of the doctor's files were an inch to several inches thick. Gee, and I thought Dr. Harry said there was nothing wrong with me.

I spoke with my tax attorney and he gave me the name of another trial attorney. I set up an appointment to meet with his staff. No one wanted to take my case because Richard had dumped me. The attorneys I spoke to said that it gave the defense the idea that I did not have a case. Fortunately, the attorney who my daughter referred me to took the case and partnered with an attorney he knew in Denver and they took over my case.

I received a nasty letter from the courts about my deposition and that I was going to be held in contempt. It was now four months past due. The new attorneys worked feverishly to get the deposition done and the contempt charge against me was dropped.

In the meantime, my deposition date was set and would occur in just over two weeks.

# Chapter Twenty-Five
## Durable Power of Attorney—
## A Trust Fund for My Settlement Money

Even though I should have set up a Durable Power of Attorney years ago, I waited until after I got my Discovery, for actually no good reason other than reality hadn't yet set in. I was told that there should be two parts to a **Durable Power of Attorney**, namely, a **General Durable Power of Attorney** and a **Medical Durable Power of Attorney Including Medical Directives**. A **Durable Power of Attorney** was in my best interest for several reasons:

1. If I do not have a Power of Attorney set up and something happens to me that incapacitates me or I die, there will be no one who can transfer my funds to pay for my debts or take care of my financial situation.
2. No one will be authorized to make medical decisions on my behalf.
3. It would be quite expensive to go to court to declare a power of attorney after my death and quite expensive to go to court to appoint someone to take care of my medical, legal and financial situation in a medical emergency. This would be over-burdensome to my children who would probably rather be

with me than tracking down an attorney or sitting in a courtroom.
4. My children would not be strapped with the extra burden of trying to figure out who is responsible for mom.

The **General Durable Power of Attorney** designates my older daughter to be **attorney-in-fact** (subsequently called **agent**). If my older daughter dies, becomes incapacitated or resigns, my younger daughter automatically is the successor agent.

In essence, my daughter can do everything necessary in my name and in my benefit, which I would normally do for myself if I was present and able to do so. This authority is intended to relate to any person, transaction or interest concerning real and personal property, including intangible property interests, which I may now own or acquire in the future. My daughter could also delegate authority to others.

I was advised to have my Social Security Disability checks deposited directly into my bank account to avoid any mix-up with the bank. This would include all other checks that I might receive. She can open and close accounts in my name and her name will be added to my accounts.

If I owned a business my daughter would be able to operate the business just as I would operate it if I were able to. This would include hiring and firing employees, management responsibilities, and the financial end of the business as well as deal with the IRS.

Basically, she becomes me without actually being me. When I first read what my daughter could do, I was a little unnerved. However, the last paragraph put to rest any unease I felt. In signing, she agrees that she will not use the powers written in the agreement except for my benefit. As my agent, she has the responsibility to account to the beneficiaries of my will or of any trust created by me. An hourly rate can be paid to her but only at a rate that someone performing the same job would be paid in the geographic region where my agent resides. If any personal benefit were to be improperly received as a result of exercising the power of attorney, those funds would have to be returned.

At any time I can revoke the agreement.

The **Medical Power of Attorney** outlines what I would want to happen to me in case of an emergency but only if I am incapacitated. As a believer in alternative health care, my daughter can override recommendations given by health care personnel including my attending physician. She has access to all of my medical records that are protected under HIPAA (Health Insurance Portability and Accountability Act). As an example:

By agreeing to the terms of the **Medical Durable Power of Attorney**, my agent can:

1. Employ health care personnel as she deems necessary for my physical, mental and emotional well-being;
2. Give medical consent for treatment. She has absolute discretion to give, withhold, or withdraw consent to any medical procedures, tests or treatments, including surgery. She may arrange and contract for hospitalization, convalescent care, hospice or home care as I may require.
3. If she determines that certain medical procedures will no longer benefit me or that the burdens outweigh the benefits, she may, in her sole discretion, but only after making every effort to communicate with me first, revoke consent to such procedures, tests and treatments, as well as hospitalization, convalescent care, hospice or home care.
4. Authorize relief from pain, including unconventional pain-relief therapies which my daughter believes may be helpful, even though such drugs or procedures may have adverse side effects, may cause addiction or may hasten the moment of (but not intentionally cause) my death;

5. Grant releases to any physicians or medical personnel, which has the effect of implementing my wishes regarding health-care treatment or withholding health care treatment.
6. Provisions for residence and transportation. She will set up where I live, what health care facility I go to and can withdraw me from a hospital or care facility and allow me to die in my home.
7. Anatomical gifts may be given at the time of my death. My eyes have already been willed to the Lion's Club Eye Bank.

**CPR Directive**:

1. CPR is not to be given unless it is likely to be successful and likely to result in my recovering normal function and independence and enable me to be discharged home from the hospital. In general, CPR must be initiated rapidly and followed by prompt defibrillation and when the cardiac arrest is a consequence of a cardiac problem and not of a progressive debilitating or poorly treatable condition such as severe trauma, stroke, senile dementia, cancer, or AIDS.

2. Specific instructions and limitations come into effect if I am gravely ill and with available treatment I am unlikely to recover in a reasonably independent function, if I am in a terminal condition that responds poorly to treatment, or I am in an irreversible coma or am unlikely to recover reasonably independent function for any reason and I am unable to make decisions about my health care treatment, after consultation with my physicians and family members, I be allowed to die by discontinuing any and all medical treatment including artificial hydration and nourishment, antibiotics and life-support systems. Pain medications and other comforts may be administered as long as they do not prolong my life. I wish to be as conscious as possible at the time of my death.
3. Specific health history contains the physicians I am currently seeing and the name, address and phone number of the physicians.
4. Long-term care insurance, if I had any, would contain the insurance provider, policy number, and contact information.
5. I prefer residential care and hospice care over a hospital. I have requested that a referral be made to hospice soon enough that their

supportive services would be a benefit to me and my family;

**Relationship to Living Will**. This document acts as my living will.

1. I authorized my daughter to submit this document as a declaration of my wishes in the event I enter a permanent vegetative state or a terminal condition as defined in the document. If I become unconscious or incompetent in a state where this declaration is not honored, my daughter can transport me to a jurisdiction where it will be honored.
2. **Third Party Reliance**. As long as a person, facility, institution or entity relies in good faith on the authority of my daughter, they will not incur any liability to me, my estate, my heirs, successors or assigns. If I revoke any part of the document without the person, facility, institution or entity's knowledge they will be held harmless.
3. Immunity for my agent. As long as my agent commits no willful misconduct or gross negligence, my estate, heirs, successors and assigns can hold no liability or claims against her.
4. Resort to court. If anyone disputes the document, my daughter can get a declaratory

judgment to validate the document, be appointed the guardian by the court if the court finds that appointment of a guardian is necessary, and seek actual and punitive damages against any party who in bad faith fails to comply with instructions I set forth in the document.

Sobering, but necessary. (Examples of Living Wills can be found on the internet.)

The same attorney explained to me how to set up a trust fund for any settlement money I may receive. If I choose not to set up a trust fund, I will have to pay Medicaid and Medicare the balance due them for any medical, psychological, chiropractic or other healthcare bills. Most likely, the balance left from the settlement monies would put me over the $2,000 ceiling amount allowed by Medicare and Medicaid in order to be eligible for the programs. Since I am quite uninsurable unless I miraculously and "spontaneously" heal and can go back to work where there is a health care plan available, I will not have any insurance. Since I signed a lien with Medicare, the bills from Medicare and Medicaid would be taken out of any settlement I received before I received any of the money.

It was best in my case to try to get doctors and therapists to take Medicaid or Medicare because they pay a fraction of what I would have to pay out of pocket. Therefore, the lien amount that I would have to pay back Medicare/Medicaid would be much less than what I would have been charged as an individual person.

Accidents have a multitude of blind alleys attached to them. Even though a settlement may be forthcoming, it is not without strings attached if you are disabled from the accident.

The attorney drew a picture for me of what he would suggest I do. First of all, I can buy a home with a value limit and a car and still be eligible for Medicaid and Medicare. When buying the house, I was told to take title of the house as [my name]—life estate. My children would be named as owners of the house also, or "remainder intent as tenants in common". If I get mad at one of them, their share or remainder intent is revocable by deed. If one of them dies before I die, their share will go to their "issues" (children). Upon my death, my share in the house automatically goes to my children. This protects their inheritance from being completely swallowed up by debtors.

My attorney signed the document as the notary. Two witnesses came to the office and signed that they had witnessed my signature. The document also needed to be signed and notarized by my daughter. If the document is not notarized at the time of signature, anyone can contest its validity. This is not a huge deal, but could delay treatment in the case of an emergency while the agent tracks down a notary.

The day after I received the letter from my attorney Richard informing me that he was dumping me, I drove ninety miles to meet with a neurosurgeon. He had absolutely no qualms over the fact that I have a brain injury. My rehab doctor had sent a letter of referral to him stating the apraxia, vestibular dysfunction, cognitive problems, and physical problems I had been having.

I asked him several questions about my inability to perform certain exercises, my falls, and spasming diaphragm. He simply said that he could not answer those questions until an MRI was performed. I questioned him about the conclusiveness of an MRI. He told me that an MRI will show brain injury but not always, but that certainly does not mean that I don't have a brain injury. My rehab doctor had told me that the results of an MRI are often different than the one taken shortly after an injury because scar tissue/adhesions can appear months or years later and they will sometimes show up on an MRI.

The doctor ordered an MRI of my brain, brain stem (cervical), and lumbar (lower back) area. Going by the x-rays and the MRI that had been taken the previous year he said that he wouldn't do surgery yet.

## Chapter Twenty-Six
### The Deposition—
### Now You Actually Are In Hell

The date of my deposition was scheduled. My attorney from Denver sent a huge box of medical reports to me to read and videotape to watch as well as a list of items to watch for in the deposition. I was told to read every word that had been written in every report. I spent a couple hours with my local attorney and explained to him what happened in the accident. He also had me watch another videotape about depositions.

Thankfully, my attorney refused to allow the defense to record or videotape my deposition as neither of us wanted to add anymore stress to my system. A very kind court reporter took the notes of my deposition.

I arrived at my local attorney's office about a half hour before the deposition time. I was a nervous wreck. By this time I had lost almost thirty pounds.

Pam showed up with her two attorneys. Now the irony involved here was that one of the attorneys just happened to be someone who I had spent time with two weeks prior to the deposition at my daughter's church. He had just gone to work for the defendant's business (DB) attorney's firm a few weeks before we spoke with him. I spoke with him about a situation that had happened to my daughter and, lo and behold, the second set of questions out the mouth of the insurance company's (IC) attorney was about my daughter. I looked at the DB attorney who I thought was a friend and a friend of my daughter's. He looked everywhere in the room but at me. During the day there was not one time that he could look at me.

Several mistakes had been made on my interrogatory discovery when it was prepared, especially dates of where I lived or worked. The attorney asked me if I had lived at a certain place from a date to a date and I had to answer no because it was not correct on the discovery. He asked me if I had had time to read the discovery and I told him that I had received it a few days before my deposition and there were changes that needed to be made.

I had not signed the discovery physically because by the time my new attorneys received my files and went over everything then prepared the discovery, the defense had filed a Motion to Compel with the court. The attorneys got the discovery to the defense at noon on the day that the Motion to Compel was ordered so I did not get a chance to change any of the answers. The defense attorney requested that I send a signed copy of the discovery to him, which I never did.

In the morning the questions of the deposition seemed pretty benign and time consuming. It did not take long, however, for me to realize that no question is benign. For example, they asked me if I had the telephone number of my friend John who used to be a roommate. Foolishly, I pulled out a list of telephone numbers that I always carried in my pocket. I had been warned about this.

This list had names and numbers of doctors, therapists, friends and attorneys. The DB attorney asked for a copy of the whole list then quizzed me about each of the names on the list. Most of these names had absolutely nothing to do with the case but that does not mean that the defense cannot call these people and ask them questions pertaining to that person's relationship to me. This was a blunder on my part. I should not have pulled the list from my pocket. Any physical item that I used as a reminder for an answer could be taken from me by the defense.

These seemingly benign questions also seemed to me to be a tactic to lull me into a sleep zone and to get me tired enough that by afternoon they could rip into me. I was correct in this assumption. By afternoon, the questions became deeply personal.

The defendant had already lost control of the car during the accident when I said, "Don't hit the brakes" because I didn't want her to lock up the tires. She actually didn't put her foot on the brake pedal at all and later on told me that she had ABS brakes so could have hit the brakes. I told her that I didn't know she had ABS brakes but since she knew she did, why didn't she go ahead and hit the brakes.

The question asked by the attorney, however, was a tad bit different. He asked if I screamed, "Don't hit the brakes." I told him no. He asked, "You didn't scream don't hit the brakes?" I told him no again. Finally he got it that he had been told an exaggeration and asked if I said don't hit the brakes and I told him yes. Of course, sitting next to him was the defendant making snorting sounds and harrumphing. At one point I pictured her teeth growing, her gums pulling back and growing ears like a donkey.

The IC attorney then asked me if I had ever gone in and cleaned the defendant's house when she wasn't there. I answered no but was confused about the question. To me cleaning someone's house meant dusting, vacuuming, mopping floors, cleaning toilets and tubs. Sometimes when I picked the defendant's son up at school, he asked me to go into the house with him. Sometimes I did and helped him do his chores. I should have answered that the question was too vague.

Another set of questions pertained to my motives in the friendship. For example, did you want to move into the defendant's house? I asked him to rephrase the question. He took several stabs at rewording the question and I finally was able to answer that I had mentioned to the defendant that I would consider moving into her basement apartment if she ever completed it. The IC attorney asked me why I didn't move into the apartment and I answered, "Because she's mean." I got one lick in. He then asked if I told the defendant that I wanted a big house someday. I told him no because part of the sentence was left off. What I had told the defendant was that someday I wanted a house big enough where newly divorced women with children could live until they got on their feet.

 I had figured out that I had to mull over every word that was said by the attorney. I know that I had made him mad on several occasions because he couldn't get me to answer his questions the way he wanted me to answer them. At one point he asked me a question with two questions in it. I told him that it was two questions and to ask me the questions one at a time.

 The sick part of the deposition was that I, somehow, had become responsible for causing the accident. Originally they had told my attorney that the wind caused the accident, now it had become me who caused the accident.

 In a personal injury case, it must be proven that the party you are suing was 51% responsible for the accident.

Of course, if the accident had been with a person I did not know, the questioning would have been completely different. Many of the accusations against me—that I was suing her for alternative reasons—would not apply.

The afternoon just got worse for me and by the time the seven-hour limit was rolling around, the second attorney started asking me shotgun questions. I was exhausted by then and was in so much pain from sitting for so many hours that I wanted to get out of there. The rapid-fire questions threw off my equilibrium. I started answering the questions too quickly. I was not allowed to finish answering a question before he went onto another one.

The irony of the deposition is that I was told to never answer a question using more than twenty-five words and to never give them information…period. So, to the question, did you give money to the defendant to pay for motel, food and gas, I had to answer yes even though it was for the second night only and to cover the gas we had used driving around the Chinle area. The first night and the trip home were covered by her business.

Now, the glory of a deposition is that you can go back and change your answers once you get the transcript. I knew that there were a lot of answers that I would have answered differently and some answers that I gave that he could twist up in court.

It is not a good idea to need to change answers on a deposition, however, so I needed to have just slowed down and answered as shortly, vaguely and honestly as possible.

A few days before the deposition I thought about the following and made a list of what I needed to know. I am not an attorney and the following is written as it is to help with clarity, not as legal advice:

1. The scene of the accident. I pictured the terrain, the slope of the ditch, the surface and color of the highway, whether there was a house nearby, and if there were fences, telephone or electrical poles, or road signs.
2. The direction we were traveling. Although I knew that we were traveling north, I got out a map of the area where we were prior to the accident to see if the road we were traveling on was true north, had meandered to the northeast, northwest or what the road did. On the map, it showed the direction we were traveling on was going north with no apparent curves in the road.
3. Weather. The weather in my accident was one of the most important issues.

Lately, many cases have been lost because of the icy road defense (an act of God) even though the driver of the vehicle at fault was going too fast. In this case, the opposing attorneys told my attorney before my attorney would even take the case that the defense believed that the accident was caused by wind shear. After the opposing attorneys got the reports from my insurance company, they decided that the cause of the accident was an icy road as well as the wind. They were looking for anything other than speed and the fact that the driver was not paying attention. The night before the accident, a snowstorm had blown through depositing only a skiff of snow but had a vicious wind pushing the snow, thus causing the white-rock surface of the road to become icy. As we left Chinle driving north, the wind was violent but as the wind started to die down, the defendant drove faster in correlation to the wind's cessation. The clouds were just starting to clear a bit as they do at the end of a storm front.

4. Road conditions. Think about what the road conditions were. In my case, it was icy and the defendant knew it but about a week later stated that she thought she could drive faster on ice because she had a 4-wheel drive vehicle.
5. Time of day. This information will most likely be on the police report. Be careful in answering this question. The defendant and I

might have a different idea of what time it was. Unless I looked at my watch or at a clock at the moment of the accident, I had to make sure that I used the word "approximately" or just said that I did not know the exact time and would not want to guess. I thought the accident happened around 9:30 a.m. but the police report showed that it occurred about fifty minutes earlier.

6. Damage to vehicle. There is a good chance you will not have a clue what the damage to the vehicle was, but in my case we went to the wrecking yard and actually saw the vehicle. As I will explain shortly, the pictures of a vehicle versus the reality will be different. Pictures cannot have the impact of the actual visual witnessing of the damage to the vehicle. You might notice something odd like the ignition key could not be pulled from the switch or the insurance company might know that and you don't. If you tell the questioner only what you remember and he then asks if that is all and you answer yes you will have boxed yourself into an answer. I had to remember to answer that that is all I remembered or that is all I was aware of.

7. Speed. If you are a passenger, there is a good chance that you will not know how fast you were going. In my case, I knew pretty well

how fast we were going because I actually looked at the speedometer at about the time my butt muscles were clenching. Unless the speedometer is a digital speedometer and gives an absolute number, remember that you cannot possibly say with certainly how fast the car was going because you will have looked at the speedometer from the side. The opposing attorney asked me if I was sure that I wasn't looking at the tachometer when I said that we were going between 55 and 65. Saying sixty miles per hour would have been too much of an absolute. The attorney, I believe, asked the tachometer question to set me up for later on when he would ask me if I know the difference between a tachometer and a speedometer. Since I am a woman, I anticipated that he would assume that I was just a dumb female and wouldn't know the difference. Little did he know that my ex-husband and I owned an auto repair business and I could tear the engine out of the attorney's car and rebuild it if need be.

8. How far from the other vehicle. Go to the scene of the accident and look around. Take a tape measure with you so that you can use the word "approximately" if you feel that you must. I had to answer that I didn't know and that I wouldn't want to guess. Do not get

caught in saying that you guess you were going a certain speed or give a number that you are not sure of. This number can be calculated to say that you were traveling 60 mph when you were only going 35 mph. The attorney asked me how far away the ambulance was from where we were pulling out of the driveway and how far ahead of us the car was traveling that we were coming up behind. I told him that I could not guess that number of feet. (Another question was about my falling over. I told him that when I walked I had to have my head tilted or I became nauseous. He wanted to know at what degree I had to have my head turned. I tipped my head in my chair and he said, "So, what, about 20 degrees?" I answered that I wouldn't know that because I didn't have a mirror to see how far my head was tipped).

9. Obstruction of view. Notice whether or not there were signs or anything else that may have obstructed your view. Remember if there were any cars or trucks coming or going that may have obstructed your view. Was any road construction going on at the time of the accident? This is a question that might box you in if you are not careful. You may not be aware of the fact that at the time of your accident there was a sign standing that is no

longer there that may have obstructed your view. Call the highway department and make inquiries. If the accident occurred near a business, go to the business and make inquiries. I had to remember to avoid saying that there were no obstructions and so would have needed to say that I did not recall any.

10. Property damage. Know whether or not there was a fence ripped out or a road sign hit. I do not know if we plowed over a mile marker sign, or not. I do not know if we landed upside down on top of a telephone box or a rancher's dog. I was not asked this question, but you might be.

11. What did you observe before the accident? I went over and over what was said and what I saw prior to the accident. Each time that I did, something new came up. The IC attorney asked me if there were any other vehicles on the road. I answered yes. He asked where the vehicles were and how fast they were going. I stated that there was an ambulance driving east toward the canyon that was going exceedingly slowly and that I saw a car going south by the Burger King that was driving exceedingly slowly. I anticipated that he might eventually ask me that question during the trial. As I stated in the first chapter, there

was a highway patrolman parked on the shoulder of the road. He was not driving on the road. I was not able to give testimony that the patrolman was even in the equation. I also anticipate that he will say that I did not mention that patrolman during the deposition. My answer then would be that he did not ask me if I saw any cars pulled off onto the shoulder of the road.

12. Job and wage loss. You need to write out the date you started your job, the hours you worked, the place you worked and whether you lost wages and know how much was lost due to the accident. Include benefits and tips.
13. Prior accidents. Write out any prior accidents you may have been involved in during the ten-year period before the accident that you are being deposed for and memorize this information.
14. What could you do before the accident that you cannot do now? In my case, the first and foremost answer was: walk without falling over, but there was so much more involved. I lost any sexual interest that I had, could no longer go on hikes or read books and remember the characters twenty pages later. I had trouble going to movies without coming out totally annoyed. I could no longer go to social gatherings without becoming so

exhausted that I slept for hours afterwards. This particular one is difficult to take. I seemed so normal to the people I was socializing with a few years after the accident, but they did not see what happened to me when I went home.

The following is a guideline I used for preparing for my deposition:

1. The first and most important rule is to tell the truth. Believe me, this is not easy. You must listen carefully to each question and examine each word in the question. For example, you might be asked a question with a double negative—"Did you not...".
2. Understand the question. If you do not understand the question, ask the questioner to make the question clear and do not answer the question until it is clear to you about what is being asked. I have a serious problem with answering people before they finish a question because I assume to know what the question is going to be. If I had answered most of the questions before they were finished I would have blundered because many times the question didn't go where I thought it would. Make sure the questioner used the right reference. An

example was about the amount of time that the defendant's daughter and I were gone to pick up a book. If I had agreed to the two-hour time that the attorney gave and later the daughter said that she had checked the time before we left and when we got back to her house and it was one hour and fifty-seven minutes, the defense could say that I had lied and therefore none of my testimony was the truth. Do not answer a question that used the words, "she," "there," "this," and "an hour later," as given to me by my attorney as an example. You cannot assume that you know what in the world they are talking about. "She" could be anyone, etc.

3. Think about the question before answering. One of the questions that the IC attorney asked me was if I went to someone named Lee Purvis. I sat there with my brow furrowed and could not figure out who he was talking about. Finally he asked me if I went to an attorney named Lee Smith. I answered yes. Later on I realized that I do not know anyone named Lee Smith, including all of the attorneys I interviewed with. His first name was not Lee. This, believe it or not, could have blown my case. It was a lie on my part and would have to be changed on the deposition. Another example was a copy of

an insurance paper that I supposedly filled out. True, it appeared to be my handwriting but I did not remember filling it out. If I had answered yes that I remembered the paper, it would become solid evidence. Instead I answered that I didn't recall the paper. He could have gotten me, however, when he asked if that was my handwriting. I told him that it appeared to be instead of saying yes. Use the words, "I am not sure" if you are not sure.

4. Do not accept opposing counsel's statements just because he/she says it's true. An example that my attorney gave to me was: <u>Question:</u> You discussed the problem with Mr. "Smith" when YOU reviewed this letter with him, didn't you? While you may have discussed "the problem" with Mr. Smith, if you do not recall having reviewed the letter with him, say so. This is also a two-part question. The question should have been: Did you discuss "the problem" with Mr. Smith? (and know what the problem is that the attorney is referring to). And did you review the letter with Mr. Smith? If the question asked in the second part had been, did you review the letter with him, you do not know who "him" is.

5. Do not try to become a lawyer. If you do not understand a question, don't try to figure it out. Ask the questioner to repeat the question so that you can understand it. What I found in my deposition is that the lawyer many times did not have a grasp of the situation or of what actually happened. An example was that the IC attorney asked me many questions about the test scores on a Woodcock-Johnson Battery Test that, to a layman's eye, appeared to be quite high. I could not tell him that the scores were actually quite low because education and age are taken into consideration when ranking the grade percentile. In other words, a percentage score of 87% may rank me in the nineteen-percentile grade wise. The questioner could not get me to admit that the scores were high but I finally conceded that they appeared to be high but that he would have to ask my therapist since I was not qualified to answer his question. I understood that what the attorney was trying to get me to do was admit that I do not have a head injury.
6. Focus on the question being asked. What I found is that I was asked numerous questions that seemed irrelevant to the case, especially in the morning. They are most likely testing

you for honesty and to get you to be flippant and blasé. As my attorney told me, "There are no irrelevant questions." One flippant answer I could not resist was a question about where someone now lives. I answered "heaven". Well, I heard my attorney give a little snort, but it seemed that I annoyed the opposing attorney because he rudely said, "What?" I then answered, "She's deceased."

7. The first rule is you are not required to know everything. Answer, "I don't know" if you don't know. If the truth is that the answer is no then answer, "No." Just be accurate and tell the truth. You are not in this deposition to try to get the other side to like you or to become friends with them. Remember, these people's lives are about money, not humanity, and they will do everything in their $500 an hour lives to save their company money or they will become a $150 an hour attorney and not be showing up at a deposition wearing an Armani suit and driving a Lexus. In both of the videotapes that I watched, schmoozing examples were given of opposing sides swapping compliments to each other about their cars. Believe it or not, the IC attorney's Lexus became a schmooze subject as did my attorney's office, which is located in his barn on his ranch. The IC

attorney was really stroking my attorney's ego about what a great place it was, even though the smell of horseshit was the number one evidence in the room. My attorney's bow tie became a topic. The defendant even got in on the conversation and talked about her good friend who lived just up the road from my attorney (so when you do my deposition be nice to me or your neighbor will be mad at you). I was thinking about a vomit bag from all of the atta-boy quips going on before they realized, I think, that I wasn't going to get pulled into their crap. I just sat and stared at the wall. Anything you might say can be used against you during the deposition, so even if you know "the neighbor", do not jump into the conversation. The neighbor might now have a bias against you because of the friendship with the defendant. The most important thing about this area is that there are going to be jurors who are taking time from their lives and, most likely, losing a bucket-load of wages to sit and listen to your story. So be honest about what happened, respect these jurors and remember how much you hate getting a jury notice or this will come back and bite you in the end.

8. Review all of your documents and statements before your deposition. I read every word that was written about me or that I wrote to the insurance company or to my caregivers, I thought. When a question seemed to come from out of the blue, it surprised me and I discovered that I had a tendency to panic. I also wanted to give an answer that would hide my ignorance. Don't do this. These answers were another thing that I would have to change when I got my deposition back. One of the seemingly innocent questions was about a roommate that I had. I had told my psychological therapist that my roommate had been behaving inappropriately. If I had not re-read the reports and remembered this incident, I might have answered that I didn't remember this incident and the defense could have assumed then that the roommate in question was one of my prime witnesses. Instead, I was able to answer that it was a female roommate that I had for only a short time who was sneaking men into her room in the middle of the night and smoking in a non-smoking condo. I couldn't remember her name and told them that I could not remember her name.

9. If a document is presented to you, analyze it carefully before answering questions about it. For example, as I mentioned before, a document was stuck under my nose that I had evidently signed for an insurance report. At the bottom of the document a question was asked, "Was the accident anyone else's fault?" I checked no and underneath had written "Icy". Now, obviously the defense is going to try to get me to admit that I was saying the defendant was not at fault and that it was the fault of the icy road. In my shorthand way, what I understood the question to mean was there another car involved. I wrote icy to say that the driver of the car I was in was driving too fast. I was not able to get either of those things out because the IC attorney stuck the document under my nose, asked if I signed it and told me to look at the last question. I told him that I didn't remember the document, but he, of course, said, "Well, isn't that your hand writing?" I had to admit that it appeared to be. For his question about the "Icy" comment I was barely able to say that I would have to guess that the question meant… and he asked me another question. This document was not in the file of paperwork that my attorney sent to me.

10. Do not bring any documents with you to any deposition or court hearing unless you have been subpoenaed to do so. Remember, the defense can get copies of anything you have with you. If your attorney is up on things, if you are asked for a copy of the phone numbers like I mentioned before that I had in my pocket, your attorney should request that everything else be blocked out except the number that opposing counsel asked you about. Leave your purse and wallet outside the room the hearing is being held in.
11. Analyze any documents presented to you carefully before you answer any questions. The document may resemble another document that you are not aware of. As my attorney told me, look at (a): the letterhead, if any; (b) the date; (c) the person to whom it was sent; (d) the recipient's full address, (e) the name of the author of the letter; and (f) persons to whom copies are noted. Don't just glance at the report. Take all the time that you need to review the document and let everyone else wait. Do not let the defendant's attorney rush you into an answer. You have the right in this deposition to take as long as you want.
12. Do not argue with the attorney. From your daily life experience, you know that when

you argue with someone, you are simply trying to be right, not necessarily honest. Assume that the opposing counsel is going to try to bully and upset you to get you to say something that is not honest or to volunteer information that could hurt you. Let the opposing counsel be the one who gets upset. As I stated before, I know that the IC attorney was upset several times because he could not get me to say what he wanted me to say or if he asked a question that had just one word wrong in it, I would answer the question no or ask him to re-phrase the question. I absolutely refused to let him bully me into an answer. I, also, did not want to "people-please" him.

13. Do not volunteer any information. If he asks for your name, just give it. Give nothing else. If you were married, don't give your maiden name unless you are asked. I know that it is human nature for many people to be complying, especially for women, and you can bet that the attorney knows that.

14. Do not pay attention to the tone of voice that the attorney uses, his demeanor, or any suggestion of what the answer should be. Focus on the question, not the attitude. Do not get pulled into the opposing counsel's sarcasm, raised voice, or suggestion of what

an answer should be or their posturing. At the same time, be aware of a nice attorney. The IC attorney was very nice to me in the morning and seemed to want to befriend me. I knew what he was up to. What I did was look straight ahead. I got to my attorney's office early and sat in a chair that sat facing a wall. During the deposition, the only time I looked at the attorney was occasionally when I asked him to please re-phrase a question. If I met the man on the street, I would not recognize him. Of course, I will recognize the attorney who I thought was a good Christian man.... Neither one of these men proved to be my friend. They were attorneys out to save money for their company and their client.

15. Concentrate. It is difficult to sit for hours and keep your train of thought, especially for someone with a brain injury. By Colorado law, a deposition cannot go any longer than seven hours (check your state's statutes). Strangely, the attorney's paralegal is the one who caught this and pulled out the law book that bore the rule. Once again, one of the things that I noticed was happening in the morning was that the questions were boring and seemed to be irrelevant. When I found myself getting bored, I reminded myself that

sooner or later a whammy would come my way.

16. Take your time with your answers. I spent a long time before answering each question, especially in the morning. I wanted to tell the truth, but I wanted to make sure that I was telling the truth only to the question being asked, not what I thought was being asked or what I should have been asked. I was also aware of the seven-hour rule and knew that the longer I took to answer the questions, the fewer questions could be asked. I knew that when the boring questions were humdrum, complex questions would be coming up.

17. Correct your mistakes as soon as you realize them. In the afternoon questioning, the IC attorney asked me a question that reminded me of a question that had been asked that morning. I told him that I wanted to correct a statement that I had made that morning. He jumped on that with both feet and asked if the fact that I remembered that morning's question proved that I didn't have a head injury. I told him that it didn't prove anything, and when he asked how I could substantiate my answer I told him that I could remember conversations but could not do lower cognitive skills. Of course, that statement brought up another set of questions about

the difference between higher and lower cognitive skills. I told him that lower cognitive skills (executive functioning) consisted of things like the ability to boil an egg.
18. You're most likely going to make a mistake so interrupt the questioning to correct a statement if you need to or you are not telling the truth. If you remember a mistake after the deposition, tell your attorney as soon as possible.
19. Preparation is an important part of your deposition. I can almost guarantee you that the question will be asked about whether you met with your attorney to prepare for your deposition. Of course you did, unless your attorney is also brain damaged. The ridiculous thing is that if you answer that you met with your attorney before the deposition, the defense attorney can make the accusation that you were coached on what to say. It is a double-edged sword.
20. Answer only the questions that are asked. Most likely your attorney will not ask you any questions. You will not be able to tell the whole story in your deposition. This will come out at the trial if your case goes to trial. The way I understand the deposition, it is a time to let the opposing counsel know as little as possible. This way, they don't have a clue

what might come out during the trial. That is why short answers are so important. Again, my attorney gave me strict instructions to never answer any question with more than twenty-five words. During one of the breaks, he informed me to stop answering questions with a yes or a no. I answered the questions from then on with statements like, "As I recall." Do not box yourself into an answer. If opposing counsel asks if that is all, do not answer yes. Answer the question, "that's all I remember right now." For example, the IC attorney asked me about my injuries. I named brain injury, headaches, jaw, shoulder, neck, spine, digestion, urinary and intestinal problems, and leg problems. He asked if that was all. If I had answered yes, then later remembered that my left arm also still hurt, he would most likely ask during the trial if I was lying now or if I had lied on the deposition. No matter what, the jury will now think that you might not be honest about everything, and you can bet the attorney will paint you as a liar.

21. Know your own knowledge versus what you have heard. If you heard that you traveled 25 feet after the initial impact of the accident, don't answer yes unless you have actually gone to the scene and measured the distance

from the point of impact until the time the vehicle stopped and make sure you don't answer an absolute 25 feet. For example, during my deposition, I told the IC attorney that there was a car traveling in front of us as I already mentioned. He asked me how far away the car was from us. (The defendant, of course, was sitting next to him shaking her head and snorting because she had been looking out the side window and didn't know there was a car that we were about to run over the top of. Also in that part of the country you can bet someone could tell me exactly whose car it was and then it would become apparent that the defendant was not paying attention to the road. The DC attorney also admitted he had never been to that part of the attorney so would not know the culture). I simply told the attorney that I did not know how far in front of us the car was because I did not have a tape measure and any other answer would be a guess. It is in your best interest to use answers like, "not absolutely," "my best estimate," approximately," and "anything else would be a guess." If you have thought long and hard about something that you anticipated being asked, say that you thought long and hard about it and your best estimate would be….

Example: Photographs and diagrams might be requested of you. As my attorney told me, "Do not acquire new knowledge from photographs and do not interpret diagrams you do not understand." Photographs are notoriously unreliable for judging distances or measurements. For example, the pictures that were sent to us by the opposing counsel were Xerox copies of original pictures. On the copy, the destruction done to the vehicle was not as apparent as the reality of visually seeing the vehicle. The copies were grainy and not taken at an angle to show the true cant of the vehicle. So, if the IC attorney asks you if a photograph is an accurate depiction of the car, you can answer that it is generally accurate but that you cannot tell if it is accurate as to specific details. The vehicle I was in looked different than the pictures. The pictures did not show the mud and tufts of grass jammed up into the edges of chrome and bumper. There was also not a picture showing the front of the vehicle. The inside view of the picture did not show the mud that was inside the vehicle or the broken glass or dog food that was scattered all over. Also, by the time the pictures had been taken, we had removed the luggage, cell phone and the defendant's personal items that had been strewn about the vehicle. For all you know, the vehicle in the picture is another vehicle that they have taken a picture of. If you did not know the serial number or license number of the vehicle, you cannot be absolutely certain that the picture shown to you is the vehicle you were in. Use these photographs only to refresh your memory of the events. (It is also my guess that the person from the insurance company who took the picture removed the tufts of grass and clods of dirt).

To cover myself if I was instructed to draw a diagram of what happened during the accident, I practiced several drawings. Each time I drew a diagram, I remembered something else. Remember, if you do draw a diagram and you are asked if that is an accurate description, make sure you answer that that is what you remember right now. Do not answer yes. And remember, the car's insurance company is the one who will be taking the pictures.

22. If you make an assumption in your answer, make sure that it is understood that it is an assumption. I was asked a question that I could have answered that I assumed and instead answered that it would require me to

make an assumption that I did not have all of the facts about.
23. If you feel that a potential question might need an explanation, make sure you speak with your attorney before the answer. I wrote out a list of questions that I thought might be asked and my attorney also gave me questions that are usually asked. Make sure you go over and over these answers. Make sure you give the answer before the explanation. I did not explain any of my answers during the deposition. I made the defense attorney ask me to explain my answers.
24. Do not interrupt opposing counsel and do not let opposing counsel interrupt your answer. If he does, ask that you be allowed to finish your answer. Opposing counsel will interrupt you, most likely, if they do not like your answer. An example I gave earlier about the insurance form was an interruption. I did not get to insert my answer, but I will do so when I amend my deposition but only if it is of great importance to do so.
25. Ask for a recess if you need one. If you are too tired or don't feel well, you will begin to answer questions dishonestly just to get things over with. I found that happening to me at about 5 p.m. after starting the

deposition at 9 a.m. If you suspect that the opposing attorney is asking you questions that are privileged or you just simply "smell a rat", ask for a recess.

26. Don't get mad. Now, unfortunately that is quite difficult to do if your character is in question. When the question came up, "Did you make a sexual pass?" (I asked the defendant for a hug after we were back in the hotel room). I went ballistic. I knew it would probably come up, but when it did it just absolutely rubbed me the wrong way because I felt that it was an attack on me personally and had absolutely nothing to do with the facts of the accident. Of course, in the eyes of the defendant's counsel the whole avenue of questioning was directed at making me look like a scorned lover. The questions about whether or not I wanted a big house had to do with making me look like a gold digger. Remember, there are no irrelevant questions. If the opposing attorney knows they can make you mad, they will use that information to make you mad during your trial. Staying cool will be one of the most difficult things you will encounter during your deposition.

You are in control of the deposition. You may or may not believe this, especially right after the deposition. But the longer you think about, the more you will realize that if you answered the questions as honestly and accurately as you could without boxing yourself in, you will have had control. For several weeks after the deposition I was in a panic state. I mulled over every aspect of every single question and questioned myself until I was about to collapse from exhaustion and lack of sleep. I finally was able to realize that "I did okay."

It is in the best interest of the opposing counsel to intimidate, harass and scare you to get you to settle. A few days after my deposition the opposing counsel made a second offer of $5,000, up from the original $500 offer. I, of course, declined this.

I was rubbing my hands together and licking my chops anticipating the upcoming deposition of the defendant. I wrote forty-four pages of single-spaced information to my attorney about everything that I knew about the defendant. Unfortunately, the attorney did not get the notes until after her deposition.

I was finally able to get a full night of sleep when I completed the report.

When I changed the way I looked at things, the things I looked at changed. I could be as a mad as I wanted at the driver, but was the driver being evil or helping me to fulfill my divine quest? Would I stoop to the occasion or rise to the challenge? I began to realize that the outer never comes together without the inner.

I wondered everyday what would have happened if I had not gotten into the car that day. Would my life somehow have been better, richer, more fulfilled? I would imagine that I would have gone on with my life just as I had. Would I have continued to live in the past, continued to drag along the old garbage of childhood with me until I chose not to anymore or until I died? Or was my life's destiny to start an orphanage for AIDS children in Africa? (That is actually what my daughters and I were discussing doing and looking into funding for).

There is that old saying that sometimes they have to take a baseball bat up the side of your head before you get the lesson. This time I was hit up the side of the head with an SUV.

# Chapter Twenty-Seven
## Mediation—
## The End of the Legal Nightmare

In September I found a dentist who specialized in trauma to the jaw. There are only two dentists in the state of Colorado who do this kind of work. (Remember that I said "regular" orthodontists said that my teeth were fine from a cosmetic stand-point, not a jaw stand-point). Dr. Lausen was a lifesaver for me. I spent several hours at his office working with Tanya who set me up for a splint. When I hit my head on the post of the car, my right lower jaw was thrust back and upwards and was, basically, stuck in that position. On the x-rays, it showed that the jaw was pushing against the nerve bundle that goes down the neck and putting pressure on the eardrum.

Once again a mold was made of my teeth. This time, a "halo" was placed around my head and I held my teeth in the correct position, forward and down, before I closed my teeth into the putty. With the other orthodontist the splint was made without putting my jaw in proper alignment first.

The following week I returned to Denver to get the new splint. They squirted some gel onto the splint and, once again, via the "halo" and computer I closed my teeth into the gel. When the gel set up I was ready to go. I was instructed to keep my mouth closed as much as possible, which is a near impossibility for someone with a brain injury, and also to use a Tens Unit daily on my jaw and neck to break up the lactic acid that was going to be created by the muscles because of the change in position.

Dr. Lausen's comment as to whether or not I had a brain injury was that if someone hit their head hard enough to cause that much damage to a jaw that more than likely a brain injury has occurred. He would testify to the fact that the accident caused the trauma to my jaw if we went to court.

> TMJ, a subtype of tension-type headache, usually results from stretching and tearing the ligamentous structures of the jaw joint. The mastoid muscles are usually tender, with pain, clicking, or popping in the involved joint and limitation of jaw opening. (Bibliography, 27-1).

My vision therapy had stalled prior to getting the splint and I was being taught just remedial measures for my everyday living. The week after I got the splint, my vision therapist was amazed at the remarkable change in me. Within two weeks of getting the splint, I had a vision exam to see if my prescription needed changed. My astigmatism had improved by 50%. Dr. Cecil wanted to re-test me the next week. My vision was 25% better the second test. We compromised between the two and I got new lenses. The doctor was amazed and wanted to speak with the orthodontist.

I went to an orthopedic doctor about my shoulder. He suspected that I had torn the rotator cuff and wrote a script for me to do physical therapy. I went to the physical therapy department at the hospital and told them that I had apraxia. The head therapist did not know what apraxia was. I did not go there for my therapy. It would be months later before I would follow up on the suggested therapy because I was so overwhelmed at the time about the lawsuit.

The day of the defendant's deposition was a turning point for me. I thought that she would lie and she lied beyond anything I had in my imagination. Even though I did not go to the videotaped deposition, I received a copy of the transcript several weeks later. One of my attorneys, Kevin, who had done the deposition, grinned when he handed the transcript to me. I asked him why he was grinning and he just shrugged and was non-committal.

Well, when I read the deposition I realized why he was so jocular about the whole thing. It read like a Jerry Springer Show transcript. She described her emotions and psychological make-up as mine. This was the most blatant display of transference that I had ever witnessed. She interrupted my attorney numerous times, answered questions before Kevin finished the question, did not know the sequence of dates or even when the accident occurred, and went on numerous diatribes giving information that could come back and bite her in court.

Evidently the defendant's attorney realized that she would blow their case and requested a Mediation to be held.

In the meantime, my attorney called "Dr. Harry" and asked him about his testimony. He refused to change his diagnosis even though reams of reports stated that I had a brain injury. He said that he would testify that I had Post-Traumatic Stress Disorder caused by the accident and that I would never be able to work again because of that. PTSD is more difficult to explain to a jury than brain injury evidently. "Dr. Harry" also diagnosed me with what is known as "conversion disorder". In other words, all of my pain was psychosomatic. He gave my attorney the name of a psychologist who tests people for what is known as "malingering". We only had two months to complete the testing before the mediation was to take place.

In the meantime, the defendant's insurance company requested that I go to one of their psychologists. Of course, the psychologist they sent me to agreed with "Dr. Harry" since "Dr. Harry's" report is the one he received. And, that was the only report he got. He kept me in his office for almost eight hours with only a fifteen-minute lunch break. By the time I left there, I could not function and had to sit in the parking lot for almost an hour before I could drive.

The next day I met with my attorney. I was a train wreck. My head was throbbing, my head was canted to the right because of muscle spasms and I kept tripping over my feet and cane.

That evening I met with the psychologist who was going to test me for malingering. The results were that I was not malingering and that I had an organic brain injury. I also did not have any mental illness, including PTSD.

Now we had a standoff. Quite interestingly, the insurance company's psychologist's report was faxed to my attorney the morning of the mediation which made us late to the Judge's office. This was just a blatant move by the insurance company and the defendant's attorney to catch us off guard. Little did the defendant's team know that at no time were we going to dispute "Dr. Harry's" finding. Permanent disability is permanent disability.

What I find biased and unfair is that the defendant never had to take any tests for honesty or behavioral problems.

We met for the mediation at an office in Denver. Before we started, my attorney was quickly reading through the opposing team's psychologist's findings. We both had to sign a lengthy agreement stating that we could not speak of anything outside of the mediation that occurred during the mediation, which really sucks because there were some very interesting happenings that day as well as turn of events.

Basically, I knew within the first half hour that if we went to court that the jury very well could have awarded me a million dollars or thrown up their hands and awarded nothing. My counsel and I knew that the court would become the platform for a TV situation event. I knew that I would sit quietly in court and be respectful, but that was not true for both sides. Not only would the whole thing become a spectacle in the "she said", "she said" context but the fact is that juries usually only award $50,000 for a brain injury unless you're a quadriplegic in a wheel chair sucking life through a straw.

Also, once you leave a Mediation, the insurance company can do this: If they offer you, for example, $10,000, they can also say that if you don't accept that amount that they will make an offer to the Court of $7,000. If the jury awards $6,999.99, the defendant's insurance company can turn around and sue you for their costs, which often amount to anywhere from $80,000 up.

By now you are probably asking how these insurance people and attorneys can live with themselves. Easily! They seem to have no conscience. Besides, I believe that money is their God and so do their stockholders.

The most ironic thing happened during our lunch break. My attorney and I were headed toward a restaurant and, lo and behold, there was the defendant with her latest boyfriend standing in front of the place. She was on her cell phone and smiled at me and waved at me with her pinkie. I was startled and my attorney thought that was one of the strangest things he had ever seen. We made a very smooth U-turn and went to a restaurant across the street.

We sat looking out the window, watching the defendant, making comments like, "Are you even kidding me?" The defendant got off her phone, and they started walking back toward the mediation office. Her boyfriend put his arm around her shoulder then rubbed her back. I looked at my attorney and said, "Settle the case."

I do not know if it was brain damage that made me say that or what came over me. I know that this woman had had a horrendous childhood and here was someone who obviously cared for her. I knew that if we went into court that all of her lies would come out and this man would dump her. For some reason, I just could not be a part of that happening. I also knew that in time the scales of justice would be balanced—maybe not by the court but by a power greater than ourselves or by a circumstance in her life where she would be in the position that I was in or had been in a past lifetime.

When I left that day, a burden that I had carried for four long years had been lifted.

It took almost a month before I received a copy of the settlement agreement from the defendant's insurance company. You can find a copy of a Full and Final Release from a law library, website or ask your attorney for an example of one. This is a copy of a fairly standard full and final release form:

### FULL AND FINAL RELEASE

_____ [hereinafter "Undersigned"], for and in consideration of the sum of _____Dollars ($\_\_\_\_\_), and other valuable consideration mentioned herein, the receipt and sufficiency of which is hereby acknowledged, does hereby remise, release, forever discharge and covenant to hold harmless (name of defendant and the name of the Insurance Company) and any and all other persons, firms, partners, partnerships, associations, insurers, corporations, officers, directors, shareholders, affiliates, predecessors, successors, assigns, heirs, personal representatives, executors, administrators, attorneys, employees, agent and servants whether herein named or referred to or not, and who, together with the parties hereby released, may be jointly and severally liable to the Undersigned, of and from any and all claims, demands, damages, obligations, liabilities, actions, causes of action, suits, judgments, covenants, contracts, agreements, torts and losses of every nature and kind whatsoever in law or equity, including claims for contribution or indemnification, resulting from or arising out of any and all KNOWN OR UNKNOWN, FORESEEN OR UNFORESEEN injuries, damages, and losses, including, without limitation, physical, emotional, psychological, personal or bodily injuries, death, pecuniary losses, increased risk of harm or death, loss of fringe or other benefits, loss of services, loss of income, loss of earning capacity, loss of profit, loss of enjoyment of life, loss of consortium, pain and suffering, damage to property, costs, expenses, attorney's fees, interest, reimbursements and the consequences thereof, which the Undersigned may have sustained or incurred, or may hereafter sustain or incur, by reason of a motor vehicle accident that occurred on [date], [location], fully alleged in the Complaint filed in Civil Action Case No._____, Courtroom__, _____County District Court, State of _____.

The Undersigned further understands and agrees to expressly undertake and assume the risk that the settlement underlying the execution of this Full and Final Release was made on the basis of mistake or mistakes, mutual or unilateral, including but not limited to: the nature of the underlying damages, losses or injuries; the extent of the underlying damages, losses or injuries; the severity of the underlying damages, losses or injuries; the likely duration of the underlying damages, losses or injuries; the temporary or permanent nature of the underlying damages, losses or injuries; the risk of complications from the underlying damages, losses or injuries, the nature or extent of the complications from the underlying damages, losses or injuries; the risk of discovery of other conditions, damages, losses or injuries; the future course of known or unknown damages, losses or injuries; the future consequences of known and unknown damages, losses or injuries; the impression that the Undersigned is fully informed as to the nature, extent, complications, effects, or consequences of the underlying damages, losses or injuries; the extent of recovery or expected recovery from known and unknown damages, losses or injuries;

mistakes not only as to known injuries, damages, losses, loss of services, loss of income, expenses, costs, attorney's fees, liabilities, claims, and the consequences thereof, but also as to the possibility of mistake regarding injuries, damages, losses, losses of services, loss of income, expenses costs, attorney's fees, liabilities, claims and the consequences thereof, which are presently unknown but which the Undersigned has sustained or will in the future sustain. The Undersigned further expressly states that she is fully informed as to the nature, extent and character of her injuries, damages, and losses and as to the nature, extent, severity, duration, risk of complication, risk of consequences, aggravation, recovery and all other known and unknown, foreseen and unforeseen, consequences of said injuries, damages, or losses. The Undersigned further expressly states that she has been advised of her right to consult additional professionals of her choice including doctors and lawyers, at her expense, regarding any and all known and unknown, foreseen and unforeseen, injuries, damages, losses, loss of services, loss of income, expenses, costs, attorney's fees, liabilities, claims, and the consequences thereof, which may, can, or will result from the above-referenced accident. The Undersigned further expressly understands and agrees that the signing of this Full and Final Release shall be forever binding, and no rescission, modification, or release of the Undersigned from the terms of this Full and Final Release will be made for any mistakes.

The Undersigned further warrants that no promise or inducement has been offered except as herein set forth and that this Full and Final Release was executed without reliance upon any statement or representation except as set forth herein, and that the Undersigned is legally competent to execute this Full and Final Release and accepts full responsibility therefore, and assumes the risk of any mistake of fact upon which this agreement may be entered into. The Undersigned further warrants that she has not relied on statements or representations by the party or parties being released or their representatives or attorneys regarding the Undersigned's rights, claims for damages, the facts of the accident, or the nature and extent of any injuries, damages, and losses. On the contrary, the Undersigned has considered all these matters and understands she has or could have relied on the judgment and the advice of any attorney.

The Undersigned hereby declares and represents that no other person, insurer, corporation, or legal entity has received any assignment, subrogation, lien or other right to the claim or claims made or which could have been asserted in Civil Action Case No. (your complete case number and location), and in the event that the persons or parties released herein are subjected to further claims by any person, insurer, insured, corporation or legal entity, under any actual or purported right of assignment, subrogation, lien or other right, the Undersigned will indemnify, defend, and hold the person or parties released harmless from any such claims or demands. The Undersigned further agrees to indemnify and hold harmless the said party or parties released hereby, against injuries, damages, losses, costs, expenses, attorney's fees, interest and judgments, from any and every action, claim, or demand of every kind and character, including actions, claims or demands, claims for contribution, subrogation, reimbursement, or indemnification, which may be asserted by or through the Undersigned by reason of said incidents, or the effects or consequences thereof.

It is expressly understood and agreed that the acceptance of the above-mentioned consideration is in full accord and satisfaction of a disputed claim and that the consideration is not to be construed in any way as an admission of liability on the part of the persons or parties released, but, on the contrary, the persons and parties released specifically deny any liability on account of said accident or any matters related thereto.

The Undersigned considers the consideration now being paid to be fair and equitable under all circumstances and accepts the consideration as a full and final settlement of all actions, claims, rights, and damages which the Undersigned may now have or may have in the future against the party or parties being released.

It is further understood and agreed that this Full and Final Release contains the entire agreement between the Undersigned and the party or parties being released and it is agreed that the terms of this Full and Final Release are contractual and not a mere recital.

The parties to this Release agree they will not disclose the terms of the settlement except to immediate family, legal and financial advisors, or in response to a lawful subpoena or court order. Each party will be responsible for payment of their own attorney's fees and costs.

THE UNDERSIGNED HAS READ OR HAS HAD THIS FULL AND FINAL RELEASE READ TO HER AND THE UNDERSIGNED UNDERSTANDS ITS TERMS AND THAT THIS IS ALL THE CONSIDERATION THE UNDERSIGNED WILL RECEIVE FROM THE PARTY OR PARTIES RELEASED HEREIN AS A RESULT OF THE ACCIDENT REFERRED TO ABOVE AND IN THE COMPLAINT FILED IN CIVIL ACTION _____IN_____COUNTY DISTRICT COURT. THE UNDERSIGNED FURTHER WARRANTS THAT SHE HAS

SIGNED THIS FULL AND FINAL RELEASE OF HER OWN FREE AND VOLUNTARY ACT.

Phew! By now you are probably exhausted from reading this. I was shocked at what all I would have to give up to collect the modest settlement that I got. Wouldn't it have been nice if the Defendant had to sign a contract with me before I got into her car that was similar in nature to the Full and Final Release?

The worst part for me was signing off on the last paragraphs where I agreed that the defendant had no liability, the money amount was fair, and that I could tell no one the amount agreed upon. Of course, pretty soon, if you have any math skills left, you will be able to get a good idea how much the settlement was without me giving a number….

I had ridiculously believed when I paid my car insurance over the past forty-five years that if I had an accident where someone in my car was injured that my insurance company would make sure that the rider was taken care of. Not so. What I learned was that the insurance company offered me just enough to get rid of me and threw me forever and always into the system where you, the taxpayer, would be responsible for feeding and housing me for the rest of my life. I'll bet you never thought of that, did you, when George W. Bush was calling lawsuits flagrant so that the insurance company stockholders could put more money in their pockets—money that the Republicans and Tea Party refuse to tax? And so, just like the bank bail-outs, the money I should have been awarded went for a stockholder's yacht or some other expensive toy while you, the struggling tax-payer picks up the tab for the negligent driver. Now might be the time to reconsider the vacatur law and also to allow jurors to know that the insurance company foots the bill, not the defendant.

Now, most people do not know that attorneys bring in people off of the streets, so to speak, to sit in on mock trials as "jurors". They videotape the "jurors" during the trial to study their posturing and also videotape during mock "deliberations" to see how the "jurors" react to the attorney's posturing, what is said, their comments about the plaintiff and the defendant and how they "think" about what they have seen and heard. When an attorney tells you that most head injury cases settle for $50,000—what a joke—it is because they have held dozens of mock trials to find out what is worth $10 and what is not, so to speak. Attorneys use these videotapes to see how to behave in front of a jury and also what type of jurors they want to choose.

It is not a coincidence that attorneys choose a jury as they do. They use numerous psychological tests to find out how each individual will vote and they use that information to stack the jury and often hire a consultant like [Dr. Phil] to tell them what jurors to choose. My question here is, why is it legal to buy a jury through a consultant but a crime to bribe a juror out-right?

# Chapter Twenty-Eight
## Paying Off My Debts—
## Still More Good/Bad News

I figured, okay, I have signed the paperwork so I will soon receive at least a few dollars from the settlement. I waited and waited and waited.

After I switched attorneys, some of the liens did not get sent to the new attorney. I had to get in touch with the lien holders and have them send their lien to the attorney for settlement. This is a good idea for you to do before your case comes up rather than waiting for your settlement because the attorney can often get the lien holder to reduce their fee. One therapist dropped her charges by 50%, another by 10%.

The biggest hold-up was Medicare and Medicaid. They did not contact my attorney until three months after the settlement was made. Once Medicare and Medicaid heard that I had settled the case, they reported to my attorney that it would take 40-60 days to get their bills sent to the attorney. I couldn't believe it.

We received an outrageous bill from another doctor—the one coerced into dumping me. The paralegal called the doctor and asked her to lower her price. The doctor refused to budge. We requested an itemized statement and found that the doctor had charged me several hundred dollars for a spinal adjustment. I, of course, got on the computer and punched in liens+medical and up popped pages of rulings about how much a doctor can charge per visit. The following was found at: http://www.appealsboardreporter.com/articles/AB R01-20051210-009.htmaspx.

1. ….may take into consideration a number of factors, including but not limited to: (1) the medical provider's usual fee and the usual fee of other medical providers in the same geographical area, which means the fee usually accepted, not the fee usually charged. (2) the fee the outpatient surgery accepts for the same or similar services, and (3) the fee usually accepted by other providers in the same geographical area. (See Kunz v. Patterson Floor Covering (2002) 4 WCAB Rptr. 10,124 Rp.) *Medical Group Ambulatory Surgery Center, Inc., (Bernita Boney) 8 WCAB tr. 10,130 City of Los Angeles v. Worker's Compensation Appeals Board, Bohm* [Writ Denied]

2. Reasonableness of medical provider charges—Once the lien claimant submits his or her lien as evidence, the burden of proof shifts to the defendant to provide evidence that the charges are not reasonable. (See *Kunz v. Patterson Floor Coverings* (2002) 3

WCAB Rptr. 10,024 {en banc}. [In this case, the defendant failed to produce any evidence on which the WCJ could determine whether the surgical charges were reasonable.] *Labor Ready Inc. v. Workers' Compensation Appeals Board (L. C.*

3. Determining Reasonableness of Charges for Medical Treatment-In determining the reasonableness of any medical treatment charge that is not subject to the Official Medical Fee Schedule, the Board must take into consideration a number of factors, including but not limited to the medical provider's usual fee, the usual fee of other medical providers in the geographical area in which the services were rendered, and any unusual circumstances in the case. (See Gould v. Worker's Comp. Appeals Bd. (1992) 4 Cal.App.4th 1059.) The "usual fee" is the fee usually accepted, not the fee usually charged, because that is an aspect of the economics of a medical provider's practice in the current market. *San Mateo County Transit District v. Workers' Compensation Appeals Board (Clyde Wallace)* 6 WCAB Rptr. 10,059.

It is also my understanding that no doctor could take more than one-half of the net recovery. The amount that the chiropractor requested was several thousand dollars more than one-half of the net recovery. Medicare/Medicaid, however are not under the same guideline. They could take all of the recovery.

My attorney had to pay the liens before I was compensated or they could lose their license. (If you are a caregiver and do not receive your payment, you need to file a complaint with the State Bar Association). I knew the ruling but still could not convince all of my caregivers to let me sign a lien with them because most of them said that liens don't work and they trusted me. This was not wise on their part or on my part. From the aspect of the doctor, if there is only $5,000 left, for example, am I going to give the money to the doctor or keep it to regain some of my sanity after what I've been through? Also, if I received the money, I would have to claim it as taxable income unless I put the money in a trust fund, which would take several more months. I will go into this later.

Now, the attorney really had no choice but to pay the bill unless I objected personally to the amount being charged. Of course, that is what I did. I contacted the State Board of Chiropractic Examiners and the State Insurance Commissioner and requested paperwork to file a complaint for excessive billing and excessive treatment as well as unprofessionalism. I then wrote a letter to the chiropractor and told her what I would do if she did not follow the rulings and accept the correct fee.

The chiropractor went to one of the defendant's attorneys who called my attorney and said she wanted to settle but that I would have to sign a waiver. I let the thing sit for about two months just to let her sweat. Besides, we still had not heard from Medicare/Medicaid. Of course, the catch phrase on the waiver said that neither of us could tell anyone the settlement agreement.

Another veil of secrecy plummets down just like a stage curtain dropping with a whoosh.

Unfortunately, there could be no curtain call. The second best part was that if she ever says anything to anyone about me then I can still sue her for libel.

This seems like a good time to mention that invariably a doctor, therapist or some type of worker will make a sexual comment or comments or make a pass at a person with a brain injury. Report this immediately. Remember that people with head injuries don't think quickly and usually don't know what to do with a person who has made these inappropriate suggestions or comments to them. I have heard this from others with brain injuries and have been told this by many of my therapists. This did happen to me. Also, be aware that the head injured person can also be very sexually explicit and inappropriate.

I did not hear from my attorney's office until the end of April. It had now been six months since we settled the case. I just figured that the attorneys had not heard anything from Medicare/Medicaid. Finally, one day the paralegal who had been dealing with the financial aspect of my case called and told me that she had had a heart attack and apologized for not following up on my case. She told me that she had called Medicare/Medicaid and left them messages to contact her. What next, I wondered.

After four months of wearing the oral splint to pull my jaw back down and forward, I went to the Second Phase of my treatment. Once again, a mold was made of my teeth and I was given a retainer to wear along with the splint. I felt sorry for anyone standing within five feet of me because I could not talk without spraying the poor soul with spit who was talking to me. I had now lost thirty-two pounds from not being able to chew and eating only soup as well as because of the stress of the whole situation. Within a month, I lost another five pounds. The rib bones were sticking out of my chest and I was beginning to look anorexic.

Several months before the mediation I had written to Dr. Devi Nambudripad who discovered the NAET treatments and asked what other treatments could be done for brain injury. She sent a list to me and I went to my NAET doctor and asked him to go through the list and test me. Sure enough, brain+neurotransmitters lit up the graph. Bruce did the treatment for that aspect and within a short time my apraxia and ataxia was much less and I was able to start my physical therapy again without such severe apraxic and ataxic symptoms.

Most of the muscles in my arms and back were completely wasted from my not being able to exercise. We started from scratch with the exercises and within a few weeks I started to bulk up. My posture improved and some of the pain in my back subsided. With the help of the oral splint and the NAET, I stopped falling all over the place. I still avoided pivoting to the left because the left foot was still having problems receiving the message to move.

As I mentioned before, my attorneys told me that I would have to set up a trust fund or pay taxes on the settlement money that I would receive. By now it didn't appear that I would get any money after paying the outstanding bills but, in the meantime, I went to an attorney who specialized in financial situations. He asked me if I wanted him to find out about trust funds and I stupidly told him yes. About a month later I got a bill from him for two hours of labor for finding out about trust funds. I questioned the veracity of this so went to the court house. From the time I entered the court house door to the moment I had the paperwork in my hands took seven minutes...the attorney charge me $380. I did not pay the bill.

I was told by my Assistance caseworker that if I didn't put the settlement money into a trust fund that I would lose my benefits for that month and have to start all over and reapply for the benefits. The money would be considered income and an asset. HUD was different. I would not have to reapply to HUD but for one month I would have to claim that money as income and it would make a difference of about $30 in what I would have to pay out of my pocket for my rent. And, I would have to pay income taxes on the money if it was not placed in trust.

The State did not require that the form they sent to me be the particular form used in creating my trust fund, but it was an option. I was told that I could use the form as it was, modify it to meet my requirements or draft my own disability trust form. The only requirement was that the disability trust form must meet the criteria listed in the state's rulings.

Almost eight months after the settlement form was signed I received my money. I immediately placed the money in a trust fund. My portion of the HUD payment went up almost $100 a month. I had enough money to cover a few of my therapies for about a year and then the money was gone.

Every month for another four years, I sent $125 to the orthodontist. I spent money out of my pocket for gas and for my portion of the medical bills. Unfortunately, Medicare and Medicaid do not pay for any alternative medicines or for any therapies such as vision, cognitive and speech. Those therapies would also have to be paid for out of my own pocket.

## Chapter Twenty-Nine
### New Techniques—
### Back Surgery and Nursing Home

My old roommate told me about a chiropractor his friend had seen who did Dr. John Brimhall's technique. I made an appointment and went to see her.

Dr. Robbie was amazing!

After doing a physical exam, she asked me to do some exercises. The first exercise she asked me to do was to march in place. I couldn't do it. She watched my eyes while I attempted the exercise. Of course, they were dancing all over the room. She put a pair of red-tinted glasses on my face. She had me take two pills that were specifically "brain food". She then pointed a laser on the part of my brain that commands cross-crawling exercises. After numerous sluggish attempts to raise my feet and hands synchronistically, suddenly with each step it got easier and easier. Within four minutes, I was actually marching in place! I had not been able to do that for six years!

She then asked me to do more exercises. I was unable to do almost 100% of the exercises until she put the laser on the part of the brain where that particular exercise stems from. I was absolutely joyous and wondered how long the treatment would hold. Each of our sessions lasted for at least an hour.

I finally found a surgeon who could put my shoulder minimally back together. After the surgery, she said, "What in the world did you do to your shoulder? It looked like ground beef in there!"

The anesthetic knocked me for a loop for about six months. I scared my family and friends witless. I behaved like I did right after the car accident and said and did some really ridiculous and inappropriate things. I knew that what I was doing and saying was impulsive but could not seem to stop it. I went to the NAET doctor and had him test me for anesthetics and, sure enough, I came up positive for anesthesia in my system. He treated me for sodium pentothal and within hours the symptoms were gone.

I moved from the state I had been living in to another state. I wanted to be close to where Dr. John Brimhall had an office so that I could be treated by him for the neurological problems. Unfortunately, that would not happen but I was able to see people he had trained. They were nowhere near as good and thorough as Robbie but as long as I got "re-set" every few months, I could manage many of the movement problems I had.

I was still having numerous nerve pains in my back and neck. I found a chiropractor who specializes in a technique called NUCCA which stand for National Upper Cervical Chiropractic Association. The doctor took very specific x-rays of my neck then used a protractor and did measurements. He had me lay on my side and then with the heel of his hand worked the vertebrae into place. I got up from the table and my headache was gone. I felt like my hips were underneath me for the first time in seven years. I was amazed.

I continued to improve. Eight years after the accident, I moved again. I found a new doctor who immediately recognized that I had a brain injury and referred me to a neurologist. The new neurologist answered when I asked if I have a brain injury, "Obviously!" He ordered new MRIs and referred me to a neuropsychologist who wanted me to write an editorial supporting Republicans because the election was coming up. I just sat there and kept my mouth shut. She had me do some neuropsychological tests.

The MRI showed that I had had two small strokes. At the time of the strokes, I knew that I had experienced them. My speech became slurred and my daughter asked me if I had a stroke or something. I told her that I thought I had. I had been hitting my head more often than usual during that period of time and within hours of a very severe hit on the refrigerator door, the first stroke hit.

The neuropsychological tests that I took came back showing that I still had severe impairment in several areas but improvement in others.

Nine years after the accident I moved again. I knew I could no longer put off the back surgery that I needed. I went to two different surgeons. One said the MRI wasn't definitive and he could not tell what was wrong other than left side L4 stenosis. At one point in his examination he said, "Wow, you're really ataxic!" He had me get oblique x-rays taken and the spondylolisthesis of L-4, L-5 was ridiculously apparent. When I leaned over, L-4 slid right out of its area.

The second surgeon I went to read the MRI for twenty minutes and told me more than I could have imagined. I, of course, chose the one who could read the MRI.

The back surgery went great. I was, however, put into a room post-surgery across from a very busy, noisy nurse's station with a ninety-four year old woman who kept pulling her oxygen mask off. Every time she did the buzzers and beepers went off. I was completely over-stimulated and overwhelmed. Finally at 5:30 the next morning I told the nurse that I was going to f....ing start throwing things if they didn't get me out of the room. She knew I was serious and I scored a private room.

My speech problems came back. I found that I was so apraxic from the anesthetics that I could not walk properly. The on-off switch had been thrown and I was jerking along just like I was after the accident. I knew that it would go away and that I would have to be patient. I had a zinging nerve pain in my right thumb and index finger from where they had put probes to test my neurological functioning during the surgery.

Two days after the surgery I asked the surgeon what he had done. He said he removed the disc between L-4 and L-5 then put a spacer in between the vertebrate and rods and screws to hold my back in place. He told me that he could take L-4 and wiggle it around. Evidently the ligaments had been so severely sprained in the accident that they could no longer hold the vertebrae in place. He said, "No wonder you had so much nerve pain. That thing was moving all over the place and rubbing the nerves in that area!" So much for the psychosomatic pain that Dr. Harry had diagnosed me with!

How everything can go haywire at the same time is beyond my comprehension. Since I had no one to help me post-surgery, they decided to ship me off to a Care/Rehabilitation facility.

Three days after the surgery the van from the facility was scheduled to arrive at 11:00 a.m. I was given my last hospital pain meds at 9:00 a.m. with another dose due at 2:00 p.m. An early lunch arrived late and the van from the facility arrived an hour and a half late.

Two women appeared at my door with no introduction or fare thee well. I was moved to their wheel chair and unceremoniously pushed toward the elevator. During the ride through the corridor, the woman pushing me complained about how nauseous she was. She bounced me up over the elevator door crack while I was thinking about how much that bump hurt and was sure that I was a lot more miserable with my pain than she was with her nausea. All narcotics made me sick to my stomach and it had taken two days after my IV was pulled to find a drug that didn't make me throw up.

We bounced and bumped over every threshold and crack in the sidewalk to the van. The pusher lowered the wheelchair ramp, never set the brake on the chair and I rolled around and wobbled precariously as the ramp raised me to back of the van. Now, one would think that a trained person would tilt the wheels of a wheelchair to go over cracks and bumps, but not this woman. The floor in the back of the van had crevices where the wheels from past chairs had smashed down the insulation and vinyl and resembled the wheel ruts made by the settlers crossing the plains. The woman took aim and gave the chair a mighty shove. Of course, it couldn't make it over the first hurdle so she pushed harder the next time and the next. Finally, I was heaved up over the lump and wobbled into the crevice and jolted to a stop. I couldn't say anything…I was in too much pain and stunned.

When we exited the driveway, she gunned the engine to beat a car coming up the street. We nose-dipped, then tail-dipped down through the gutter and she had to jerk the wheel to keep from going up over the median strip. When we got to the first light, she slammed on the brakes. When it turned green, she jack-rabbited the van out of the starting gate. She wove in and out of traffic through town and when we got to the interstate, she decided it was time to snack. When she reached for her food, the van wandered toward the line. She corrected her course by jerking the wheel. When we exited the interstate, we went through a tiny town that's main street had been torn completely out and we bumped and jolted over the ruts and pot-holes.

I was relieved to know that we were only about five minutes from our destination. I just knew it couldn't get worse. How wrong I was!

When we got to the town we were headed for, she took the back way. There is an unfortunate dip in an intersection on that route. The light turned yellow and she gunned the engine. We hit the dip going about thirty miles per hour and I flew up out of the wheelchair. The seatbelt caught me and slammed me back down into the chair. I bent forward in excruciating pain. The little older lady in the passenger's seat looked back and asked me if I was all right. I just glanced up at her and shook my head no. The driver barely glanced in the rear view mirror.

We arrived at the facility a few minutes later. I was jerked and wobbled back through the creviced trail and forced mightily through the crack and out onto the ramp. Just then, the older lady's phone rang. She answered it and walked up the sidewalk talking to the caller. The driver pulled me out into the 106-degree sun and left me sitting there. I demanded that she move me out of the sun. She said she was waiting for the other woman to open the door.

The older lady got off of the phone and opened the door. I was banged over the threshold and wheeled to a room where I and the wheelchair would be weighed. The new older woman in the room asked me if I was okay. I told her that we had gone over that dip in the street by Circle K going about thirty miles per hour and that I had been thrown about 3 inches in the air then slammed back down. She leaned over and said, "You need to file a complaint. A lot of people have complained about this woman. My husband used to be the driver and she lied about him and got him fired from his job so she could have it."

What was I stepping into?

The new woman pushed me to my room. I was introduced to my new roommate who had a cast on her arm and her leg.

I immediately asked for my pain meds. I was now over an hour past due and was in excruciating pain from the seventy mile ride to the facility. And, I was only three days out from a major surgery. I was told, "The nurse is getting it." That did not happen.

They told me I could get in my bed. I said that I couldn't until they raised the head of the bed. The bed didn't work. They pushed and yanked on the head while holding the button on the cracked-cord remote. One of the aides said, "It's probably the plug." The other one said, "It's probably the bed." They argued back and forth and decided to find another bed. They had to wobble push the bed out of the room because without the remote they couldn't lower the wheels. They left and came back up the hallway pushing another bed. Amazingly, that bed wouldn't work either. Finally, the cord was plugged into another receptacle and the bed worked. Wonders….

By that time I could not smile for the life of me. The bathroom smelled so foul that I did not want to go into it without waders and a strong disinfectant.

Another aide started unpacking my suitcase and writing on my clothes in permanent marker. I asked her what she was doing and she told me that they had to write my name in my clothes. "Not in half inch letters!" I told her.

There were no TV's or phones in the rooms. I told the woman that I needed a TV. She said there weren't any more—the ones they had were already being used. I pitched a mini fit and she found a TV. Ha, the joke was on me. There was no remote and the TV was only about 15" and they stuck it clear across the room.

I asked for a cane and the back brace that I had been prescribed. They said I wouldn't be able to get either one until physical therapy got there on Monday.

It was now after 4 p.m. and I still had not been given any pain meds.

A very nice intake nurse came in and I asked her where my meds were. She sheepishly told me that the pharmacy had not filled the order yet. I told her that I knew for a fact that the paperwork had been faxed to the facility the day before and that the meds should have been there when I arrived. This nurse actually got up and drove to the pharmacy to pick up the prescription. Finally, eight hours after my last pain meds, I got a pill—twice as long a time frame in between doses.

They brought some food for me. It was as cold as if it had just been taken out of the refrigerator. My roommate was pushed back into the room from the dining room and left in her wheelchair. She couldn't get back in bed by herself. She turned on the light and no one came to help her. Finally, about two hours later someone showed up to assist her. Oh, boy, this was not looking good….

Sometime in the middle of the night, two aides came storming into the room, switched on the fluorescent lights and loudly said they were there to do vitals. I knew my blood pressure would be off the charts as they scared the crap out of me. I swear that the girl who did my blood pressure was related to Medusa. Her hair stuck out frighteningly in every direction.

The next morning my roommate warned me that I needed to make sure that my bed table was cleared off or they would yell at me when they brought the food tray. An aide flew into the room with a tray and slammed it down on my table and left the room. There was no sugar, salt, pepper or any other condiment. The food was ice cold. The cereal was runny with just a few grains of cereal in it. I couldn't believe it. Fifteen minutes later, someone answered my call light. She left for several minutes, came back in the room and slammed a packet of sugar, salt and pepper on my tray. Of course, by now I had already gagged down what retched food I could.

This was not going well. I knew I had to get out of there. I would be safer in my own home and would at least be able to get my pain pills when I needed them and have warmed up food. I was tired to death already at how snotty everyone was and inefficient.

I told the nurse that I wanted to file a complaint. She said I would have to wait until the next day. I said that there was no way I was staying there another 24 hours. She said I'd have to find my own ride home and sign out against doctor's orders. I told her that my doctor would never order me to stay in that place.

Finally, she coughed up the business manager and I told him what all had happened since I got picked up at the hospital. He cooed and demurred and immediately got two girls to clean to the bathroom. He also tried to bully me during the conversation and I just point-blank said, "Do not try to bully me." He immediately changed his tone and said he would personally make sure I had hot food for lunch, find the remote for the TV and would make sure I got my pain meds at the appropriate time. I demanded hot food for my roommate, also, who had not had a hot meal since she arrived there a month prior. He gave me his cell phone so I could call for a Medicaid van to pick me up and deliver me home. The guy told me that he would personally go wait at the front of the building for the van and come and get me immediately when the van arrived.

The poor old lady next to me was stuck in bed and needed to go to the bathroom. She turned her light on at 7:30 and around 10 woke me up and asked me if I could please go find someone to help her. I hobbled out of bed and went out into the hallway to find a nurse. I found an aide and told her that the woman was about to soil herself. The aide said, and I still can't believe this, "It's okay if she goes in her bed. We would just clean it up."

I was stunned. I said, "Are you even kidding me? Do you know how humiliating that is for a person?"

And then lunch was served. The business manager showed up at the door with two trays perched on his hands like a four-star restaurant waiter—one for me and one for my roommate—her first hot meal since she arrived there a month prior. All I can say is that it was the worst sweet and sour on the face of the earth and the lemon whatever it was like a clot lying in the dish.

I had been hearing the phone ringing out at the nurses' station. I had been told that they received all calls at the nurse's station and would bring the phone to me if someone called for me. After about an hour of constant ringing, I wandered out to the nurse's station. It was dead silent. Not one nurse or aide could be seen or found. I looked up and down the hallways. Not a soul was in sight. I stood there and stared at the ringing phone. I knew it was friends trying to reach me.

I waited and waited for the van. Finally, the business manager showed up with the driver—the same one who had delivered me to the hospital four days earlier. Just as we reached the threshold of the room, the nurse handed the phone to me. I answered it and my friend said she had been trying to call me for hours, that she was about to call the police because she was afraid something had happened at the facility. I told my friend that I had heard it ringing and ringing and when I went out in the hall to see why no one was answering it I found that no one was anywhere around. I then told her, "Here's who you need to talk to." I thrust the phone to the business manager. My friend ripped him a new one and he told her that if she didn't stop yelling at him that he was going to hang up on her. He hung up on her. Not a good idea….

In the meantime, I was being rudely lectured by the nurse about how I was checking out against doctor's orders. I told her that no doctor in their right mind would want me to stay in that place. I told her that I was afraid that if I stayed there I would be dead by morning. She didn't like that.

I got into the van and the driver told me that he had been at the facility for more than a half hour looking for someone to help him find me. He said he actually went from room to room and there was not one nurse or aide in the whole facility. He said he finally found the manager sitting in an office reading a book.

We drove the four blocks to my home and he helped me inside. Again, I was so relieved to be home even if I was alone. I called another friend and she said she had been going crazy trying to call me. "What kind of place was that?" she asked me. I told her what happened and she went ballistic.

I went on the internet and typed in www.(state)gov.org and went to the health department site. On that site I pulled up a complaint form and filled it out. I also went to the site that listed care facilities and their star rating. Imagine this: the care facility I was in only got a half a star. Now, I ask, "Why do Medicare and Medicaid allow their patients to go to facilities that get less than two stars on their list of potential rehab centers?" This needs to change.

Within a month's time, I heard from nurses and therapists who came to my home to work with me that the facility I had been sent to was the worst and that many of their patients now had gangrene or had fallen because of neglect. Then, to top it off, even though the business manager and nurse had told me that new management had taken over and the facility was improving, I found out that they had done a sneaky thing. Two brothers owned this facility and another one that is equally heinous. When the health department came down on them and when debtors came after them, they simply filed bankruptcy and one brother stepped to the other facility and the brother at that facility became the manager of this facility so that they could tell people that they were under new management and also become debt free. I wonder how many times they will get away with doing this.

All I can say is: before you go for surgery, check out care/rehab centers so that when you are presented with a list of potential facilities you know which one to avoid. Back when I was an EMT there was one facility in the town where I worked that reeked of urine and gangrene. Every call I went on to that facility was to pick someone up who had gangrene. The other care centers in that town did not smell like this one facility and we rarely got a call to pick someone up with gangrene.

So, beware of care facilities and do your homework.

Interestingly, after my back surgery the pain in my neck got so bad that I had headaches that were knocking me flat. I convinced a pain management doctor to order a Stand-up MRI on my cervical area. Sure enough, the Stand-up MRI showed exactly the same condition as my lower back. On the laying-down MRIs, my vertebrae would fall back into place so did not show the seriousness of the spondylolisthesis. This MRI showed that the nerve on the left side of the C-5, C-6 space was pinched. No wonder I hadn't been able to straighten out my arm for ten years!

The pain doctor started injections in my neck and they would be scheduled every two weeks for three shots. Of course, the medication he injected knocked me for a loop again. I had night sweats so badly that I woke up drenched. I only slept about three hours at night. I couldn't turn off my mind. I thought about buying a chain and a padlock for the refrigerator. I was antsy and irritated by everything and everybody. I finally called the doctor's office and was told that those are side effects from the injection and usually people only get one or two of them if at all. Well, lucky me—again I was reminded that I just cannot take pharmaceutical drugs.

I spoke with my orthopedic surgeon about getting the surgery done on my neck and he said he wouldn't touch me for at least a year after my back surgery because I was still manifesting apraxic symptoms from the anesthesia given to me during the back surgery. He said I was just too head-injured and too high of a risk to do the surgery yet. I was given a prescription to start physical therapy on my back and also gait therapy to re-teach me how to walk somewhat normally. I was again like a Bobo doll when I walked from the anesthetic shorting something out.

    I started physical therapy three months after the surgery. How I drew this lucky card I do not know. The owner of the physical therapy company had a background in working with people with brain injuries and specifically with apraxia. He was quite impressed with how goofed up my brain was when he told me to do certain exercises. I asked him if he thought I had a brain injury. He barked out a "huh" and said it was obvious. When I told him that several doctors said all I had was PTSD he shook his head and blew out a "ha". He just said, "Some of these doctors…."

# Chapter Thirty
## What Does Everything Mean?—
## Finding Grace Through Humility

Many of my caregivers had made comments to me about not being in my body. I kept insisting that I was and then started to question if perhaps they were right. I know that before the accident I had reached a point in my life where I felt that I was in harmony with the universe. I had reached nirvana. I wondered what my next phase would be and remembered that I had the wish to expand my spiritual self. As the old saying goes, "Be careful what you wish for."

My wish was being fulfilled in an odd way. Evidently I understood that for my spiritual being to expand that my physical being would have to be stilled, as well as my conscious being. As my friend once told me, "You have blown yourself right out of your aura."

This did not mean that I had disassociated. Before I understood what this meant, I thought they meant that I was no longer connected to my soul, that my silver thread was snapped. I knew that this was not so because I watched me fly back into my body via this thread.

Now, I had a decision to make. Did I want to pull myself back into my old auric field or did I want to expand my Self to reach the outer fringes of the new auric field. To stay in the old auric field, I would have to backtrack and go back to who I was before the accident. My wish prior to the accident was to expand. Well, what a seemingly odd way to do it.

I really started to think about the boundaries that had been imposed on me throughout my life and the boundaries that I had imposed on me throughout my life. I had been taught that Christianity was the only way to go. As I got older, I began to study Buddhism, Zoroaster, Judaism and other religions. I started to see the similarities in the religions rather than the differences. I began to see the similarities in humans rather than the differences.

Yes, my deposition seemed like something sent from hell, but once I got over the fear and took care of what I needed to take care of I realized that the defendant's deposition was also coming up. What was hell for me would now become her hell. Everything is relative to what I am experiencing at this moment.

One of the problems I had been experiencing was the inability to understand that just because someone called themselves a caregiver, that the name did not always make it so. I have told you about the cruel-tongued doctors I went to, the neurologists who just didn't get it, and the other professionals who made inappropriate comments. I can blame my failure to recognize these malpracticing individuals on my lack of a filter system caused by my head injury or I can understand that the head injury brought up behaviors in me that I needed to address. My ego, of course, does not want me to speak of this, but the truth of the matter is that these individuals were put in my life to help me learn to set boundaries for myself and to get my approval of myself and acknowledgment as a human being from within, not from without.

I am now at ten years since the car accident. I have experienced more in those years than I ever imagined and been able to withstand more than I thought possible. I cannot begin to count the number of times I questioned why I was to experience what happened before, during and after the accident. I was blessed to have been an EMT for several years and to attend a Law School's Center for Dispute Resolution. If I had not had those tools, I question if I would have made it as far as I have and not have been messed with worse by the medical, legal and insurance people.

By being sat down so abruptly in a chair, I was left with countless hours to wander through the darkness to find answers about the real reason why I was on earth. It certainly was not what I had been told by parents, family, friends, teachers, preachers or any other earthly being. I realized that when I died and came back from the "other side" that it changed my life forever. I was no longer afraid of dying, realized there was no such thing as what humans think of as death, hell or heaven. Hell and heaven can be misconstrued as being "over yonder" or some believe it is here on this earth. The "other side" is just a miniature step through the veil. I know that we have guardian angels or beings from the other side who help us through everything. I learned that I am never, ever alone.

And so, since I wrote this book and left it on the computer for four years, I started another book called *It's Time to Go Now* that I will publish in December 2011. I answer the questions that came up for me during my time walking through the darkness.

While clawing my way up out of the deep, dank well I realized that I was mimicking and doing exactly what the earth is doing. I was thrown into the far dark end of the oval where we/the earth goes before we/it is thrust past the fulcrum and back into the world of light and the living. I realized that it is in that darkness where our greatest healing occurs, where we begin to understand self. It is a process of bringing things together to reach understanding. It was a time when I could work on the inner self even if I was not consciously aware of the work that I was doing.

I no longer question my therapists' remark that a brain injury is a gift. I am awakening, not necessarily to whom I was before the accident, but to whom I have become.

I now know that even in the times of true darkness that humility and grace can and does occur. And that is the "gift".

## Indicative or Contributory Signs of Bad Faith

The following are some examples of bad faith insurance indicators and a few of the signs that may be indicative to make you aware that you are or may be dealing with a bad faith insurer. The following have been identified as some of the potential signs of bad faith insurance practices. These signs are not meant to be offered as legal advice nor should be construed as legal advice. FBIC (Fight Bad Faith Insurance Companies) is neither a court of law nor legal counsel, so accordingly nothing indicated herein should be taken or construed as legal advice. In order to establish whether an insurer is in violation of "Bad Faith" laws or "Unfair or Deceptive Insurance Claim Settlement Practices" laws and/or is not acting in good faith must be decided and is determined by a court of law according to the specifics of the case, the court's applicable interpretation of statutes and case laws which may vary by state. When questioning or in doubt consult your state's bad faith insurance practices and other pertinent statutes, case laws and key applicable court interpretations...and most importantly, if you feel your insurer may be guilty of bad faith, unfair claims settlement practices and/or other pertinent illegal insurance practices and you feel you require legal advice, you should seek legal counsel from a licensed attorney admitted to the BAR and in good standing in your state or jurisdiction who is knowledgeable and familiar with the issues raised (FBIC also has a Legal Disclaimer and Copyright section in this article). As referenced, some of the following signs, although subject to a court's specific findings in your case, have been identified as being potentially indicative if not common or contributory signs of bad faith:

1. An insurer may be acting in bad faith if the insurer delays or denies investigation or payment without a reasonable basis for its delay or denial.
2. Failure of Insurer to acknowledge and reply promptly upon notification of a covered claim.
3. Failure of Insurer to pay a covered claim as a result of failing to do a proper, prompt and thorough investigation as to reasonable liability and damages based upon all available information.
4. Failure of insurer to affirm or deny coverage of claims within a reasonable time upon receipt of claim and/or proofs of loss.
5. Failure to offer or attempt to effectuate prompt, fair and reasonable evaluation of damages and equitable settlements of claims

to insured within a reasonable time where liability is reasonably clear.
6. Insurer attempts to settle a claim for less than the amount to which a reasonable person would have believed was entitled or attempts to substantially diminish a claim requiring an insured to initiate litigation.
7. Attempting to settle claims on the basis of an application and/or policy which was altered without notice, knowledge or consent of the Insured.
8. Making payment(s) for claims without accompanying statement indicating the coverage for which payment(s) are being made.
9. Insurer failure to make known any arbitration award appeals policy in an attempt to settle a claim for less than the arbitration amount awarded.
10. Insurer requiring claimant or physician to submit both a preliminary claim report and formal proof of loss forms which contain substantially the same information.
11. Failure of insurer to promptly settle claims, where liability and coverage is reasonably clear under one portion of the insurance policy in order to influence settlements of coverage for another portion(s) of the policy.

12. Failure of insurer to promptly provide reasonable explanation and basis when denying or making a compromise offer of claim settlement.
13. Failure of insurer, when making a cash payout to settle a first party auto insured claim, to pay the same amount which the insurer would pay if repairs were made.
14. Requesting over-burdensome documentation demands not required by the policy.
15. Reference of focusing on recovering on the uninsured portion of the loss.
16. Using illegal and fraudulent investigative methods and procedures.
17. Using harassing, intrusive or demeaning investigative methods and procedures which victimize the insured.
18. Failure of an insurer to settle a claim directly, when and where settlement is required, and instead requiring the insured to pursue a claim against another party first before offering a settlement. Failure of Insurer to make full and satisfactory payment of a first party claim prior to requiring settlement or exhausting the limits of a third-party insurer (i.e. in uninsured motorist cases).
19. Failure of Insurer to unreasonably refuse to waive subrogation thus hindering or preventing a claimant from reaching

settlement with the party at fault (i.e. in uninsured motorist cases).
20. Unjustifed contention and/or "low balling" regarding the value of a loss.
21. Intentionally withhold, misinterpret or misconstrue claims information and/or failure to not inform insured of provisions and covered benefits under the policy pertinent to the claim.
22. Attempts to use indiscriminate measures, reference and/or procedures that diminish or reduce the top line amount or value representing full payment of the claim.
23. Intentional or irresponsible non-disclosure and withholding of information, misinterpretation of file documents and/or policy provisions that would be in favor of the claimant.
24. Unsubstantiated and unwarranted accusations of arson.
25. Wrongful threats not to pay claims.
26. Utilization and/or development of deceptive insurer schemes or use of outside company services set up or conducted to carry out the same false pretense schemes (i.e. "Independent Medical Examiner Paper Reviews") for the purpose to be able to wrongfully deny or reduce payment of claims.

27. Insurer advice to claimant not to hire a lawyer.
28. Treatment of insureds represented by attorneys as insurer adversaries.
29. Treatment of insureds and claimants as adversaries.
30. Significant increase in amount of premium as a result of making a claim where insured was not at fault and in conflict with industry standards.
31. Cancellation of a policy as a result of making a claim or result of an accident where insured was not at fault and in conflict with industry standards.
32. Failure to live up to, conform or comply to industry standards.
33. Using inaccurate or wrongful information of a factual or legal nature to diminish, deny or delay payment of a claim.
34. Not being forthcoming with facts regarding coverage to deny, delay or reduce the amount of the claim.
35. Using extreme undue persecution, wrongful and victimizing tactics and actions, meant to crush, threaten, thwart, intimidate, oppress, in order to scare away and get the claimant not to make or pursue the claim.

36. Failure to convey to insureds settlement offers and demands of adversaries in accident and liability cases.
37. Changing or altering policy coverage without informing or receiving the consent of insured.
38. Representation by an insurer that an investigation "of fact" is taking place, knowing that no investigation is being done, in order to intentionally stop and dismiss an inquiry by a plaintiff, plaintiff's attorney or DOI examiner.
39. Biased investigation of that which is supposed to be neutral and unbiased.
40. Utilization of internal one-sided or outside companies biased schemes, such as in so-called "IME" bias (independent medical examiner bias), which are supposed to be objective and neutral, in order to wrongfully enable, facilitate and support insurer's position to fraudulently deny, reduce or discontinue payments of claims.
41. Repeated and constant reference and intentional miscommunication and misrepresentation by insurer downplaying the size of a claim to insured's attorney.
42. The same claims person of an insurer handling conflicting and both sides of the same or related claims.

43. Deviating from standard procedures called for in an insurer's claims manual.
44. Attempting to prevent the court or an insured's attorney with due exception from securing a copy of an insurer's claims manual.
45. Abusing and/or misusing the judicial court system in order to delay or settle in good faith payment of a claim where liability to the claim is clear and amount of the claim is reasonable in order to delay insurer's having to make payment of a claim.
46. Fraudulently misrepresenting and revealing various conflicting financial information that mischaracterizes the true financial information and status of an insurer.
47. Attempting to shift blame and responsibility of investigation to insured and away from the insurer.
48. Threatening to harm insured and/or take legal action against an insured to recover amounts paid by insurer as in a short-term workmen's compensation or short-term disability claim in order for insurer to discontinue having to make payment on a longer or long-term basis.
49. Insurer refusal to settle a third party claim against an insured within the limits of the insured's policy thereby exposing the insured to additional liability.

50. Intentionally misinterpreting or misconstruing the law to the disadvantage of the insured and benefit of the insurer.
51. Deny treatment for a covered health benefit because of its expensive cost and instead misrepresenting and suggesting a less costly procedure in its place to be just as effective.
52. Unreasonable denial of a covered health benefit because of its high cost.
53. Unreasonable misinterpretation of policy language.
54. Taking undue excessive advantage of unlimited time when knowing there may be no time limitations established on alleged investigations of such matters of matters of fact.
55. Making health insured patients pay their standard copay when the cost of both the drug and the pharmacy's fee for dispensing the managed care prescription is lower than the copay amount.
56. Causing health insureds to pay a copay that is higher than what the cost of the prescription is to the insurer because of common secretive rebate deals between insurers and drug manufacturers which subsequently are not disclosed and therefore do not accurately represent the true cost of the drug.

57. Health insurers not acting in the best interests of the patient and/or acting for their own self-enrichment at the health expense and disadvantage of the patient.
58. Some health insurer secretive deals are alleged to result in the health insurer selection of a more expensive drug to be on their list of acceptable drugs ("Formulary list"), services or procedures deceptively generating greater insurer profits, excessive higher costs to patients and illegally billing federal Medicare or state Medicaid programs.
59. Good Faith Insurers Look For And Find Ways To Accept And Pay Claims Properly and Promptly...Bad Faith Insurers Look For And Find Ways To Delay, Diminish, Disapprove And Deny Payment Of Claims.
60. Good Faith Insurers Look For And Find Ways to Accept And Pay Claims Properly And Promptly...Bad Faith Insurers Look For And Find Ways To Delay, Diminish, Disapprove, And Deny Payment Of Claims.

(FBIC: Fight Bad-faith Insurance Companies. http://badfaithinsurance.com/. 7/1/2004).

# Bibliography

Quote
Keller, Helen. The Story of My Life, Classic Reissue, pp. 155, Nov 2005.

Chapter 1
1. Brain Injury Association of America, 105 North Alfred St., Alexandria, VA 22314, March 2001.
2. Brain Injury Association of America, 105 North Alfred St., Alexandria, VA 22314, March 2001.

Chapter 2
1. Brain Injury Association of America, 105 North Alfred St., Alexandria, VA 22314, March 2001.
2. Rehabilitation of Persons with Traumatic Brain Injury, NIH Consensus Statement [1998, October 26-28]: 16(1): 1-41.

Chapter 3
1. Brain Injury Association of America, 105 North Alfred St., Alexandria, VA 22314, March 2001.
2. Brain Injury Association of America, 105 North Alfred St., Alexandria, VA 22314, March 2001.
3. Rehabilitation of Persons with Traumatic Brain Injury, NIH Consensus Statement [1998 October 26-28]; 16(1): 1-41.
4. Brain Injury Association of America, 105 North Alfred St., Alexandria, VA 22314, March 2001.

5. National Center for Injury Protection & Control, 2004.
6. Orthopaedic Sport Injury Statistics. www.mccg.org/childrenshealth/ortho/stats.asp.
7. Bicycle Helmet Statistics. www.bhsi.org/stats html.
8. National SAFE KIDS Campaign (NSKC), Sports Injury Fact Sheets, Washington (DC): NSKC, 2004.
9. www.aans.org/Patient%Information/Conditions%.

Chapter 4
1. Brain Injury Association of America, 105 North Alfred St., Alexandria, VA 22314, March 2001.
2. Brain Injury Association of America, 105 North Alfred St., Alexandria, VA 22314, March 2001.
3. Car, Mary, OTD, OTR/L. Disturbances of the Visual Pathways. Jcar@biausa.org.

Chapter 5
1. Brain Injury Association of America, 105 North Alfred St., Alexandria, VA 22314, March 2001.
2. Brain Injury Association of America, 105 North Alfred St., Alexandria, VA 22314, March 2001.

3. National Centers for Disease Control and Prevention, Dept. of Health and Human Services, Atlanta, GA.
4. National Centers for Disease Control and Prevention, Dept. of Health and Human Services, Atlanta, GA.
5. Bicycle Helmet Statistics. www.bhsi.org/stats htm.
6. Amusement Ride-Related Injuries & Deaths in the US: 1987-1999.

Chapter 6
1. Brain Injury Association of America, 105 North Alfred St., Alexandria, VA 22314, March 2001.

Chapter 7
1. Rehabilitation of Persons with Traumatic Brain Injury, NIH Consensus Statement Online [1998 October 26-28]; 16(1): 1-41.
2. Brain Injury Association of America, 105 North Alfred Street, Alexandra, VA 22314, March 2001.
3. Car, Mary. Disturbances of the Visual Pathways. Mcar@biausa.org.
4. FBIC: Fight Bad-faith Insurance Companies. http://badfaithinsurance.com/. 7/1/2004.

Chapter 8

1. Car, Mary. Disturbances of the Visual Pathways. Mcar@biausa.org.
2. Brain Injury Association of America, 105 North Alfred Street, Alexandra, VA 22314, March 2001.
3. Rehabilitation of Persons with Traumatic Brain Injury, NIH Consensus Statement [1998 October 26-28]; 16(1): 1-41.
4. Car, Mary, OTD, OTR/L. Disturbances of the Visual Pathways. Mcar@biausa.org.

Chapter 9
1. Car, Mary, OTD, OTR/L. Disturbances of the Visual Pathways. Mcar@biausa.org.
2. FBIC: Fight Bad-faith Insurance Companies. http://badfaithinsurance.com/. 7/1/2004.

Chapter 10
1. Eustice, Carol. Guide to Peripheral Neuropathy, Part 2 of 5. http://www.arthritis.about.com/od/nervepain/a/neuropathyguide.
2. Brain Injury Association of America, 105 North Alfred St., Alexandria, VA 22314, March 2001.

Chapter 11
1. Worden, Dr. Jeni, GP. Epilepsy—what are the causes?

http://www.netdoctor.co.uk/diseases/facts/epilepsycauses.
2. Car, Mary, OTD, OTR/L. Disturbances of the Visual Pathways. Mcar@biausa.org.
3. National Institute of Health at www.nih.gov/
4. Brain Injury Association of America, 105 North Alfred Street, Alexandra, VA 22314, March 2001.

Chapter 12
1. Perna, Dr. Robert B, PhD and Bordini, Ernest J., PhD. Cognitive Impairments in TBI: Pharmacological Treatment Considerations, TBI Challenge! (Vol. 5, No. 2, 2001).

Chapter 13
1. FBIC: Fight Bad-faith Insurance Companies. http://badfaithinsurance.com/. 7/1/2004.
2. Car, Mary, OTD, OTR/L. Disturbances of the Visual Pathways. Mcar@biausa.org.

Chapter 14
1. Reagan, Ronald. Presidential Statements, Letter to Congressional Leaders on the Social Security System, May 1981.
2. Car, Mary, OTD, OTR/L. Disturbances of the Visual Pathways. Mcar@biausa.org.
3. Car, Mary, OTD, OTR/L. Disturbances of the Visual Pathways. Mcar@biausa.org.

Chapter 15
1. Information available from any chiropractor or on the internet.

Chapter 16
1. Car, Mary, OTD, OTR/L. Disturbances of the Visual Pathways. Mcar@biausa.org.
2. Brain Injury Association of America, 105 North Alfred St., Alexandria, VA 22314, March 2001.
3. Pwu, Dr. Victor. Mississaugachiro. Your spinal column and nervous system. http://www.mississaugachiro.com.
4. Goldberg, Elkhonon. The new executive brain: frontal lobes in a complex world. 2009. www.books.google.com/books?isbn+0195329406.
5. State of CO., Dept. of Regulations. Unfair methods of competition and unfair or deceptive acts of practices in the business of insurance. Pursuant to Statutes 10-3-1104(1)(h)(III) and (IV), C.R.S.
6. Freedom Rights and Education for Everyone, 321 Sutherland Place, Manitou Springs, CO 80829.
7. FBIC: Fight Bad-faith Insurance Companies. http://badfaithinsurance.com/. 7/1/2004.

8. Prendergast, Alan. Hidden Damage, Denver Westword News, June 27, 2002.
9. Christensen Law Firm, PLLC. What Kind of Profits Do Insurance Companies Get? 2010. Insurance Profits of Car Insurance Industry, Salt Lake City. http://www.utahpersonalinjurylawfirm.com
10. Borkowski, Liz. Who's Paying for Gabrielle Gifford's Rehabilitation? Healthcare-Occupational Health and Safety, June 16, 2011. www.scienceblogs.com.

## Chapter 17

1. Raghupathi R, Graham DI, McIntosh TK. Apoptosis after traumatic brain injury. US National Library of Medicine, NIH. J Neurotrauma. 2000 Oct; 17(10):927-38.
2. Minambres E, Bellesteros MA, Mayorga M, Marin MJ, Minoz P, Figols J, Lopez-Hoyos M. Cerebral apoptosis in severe traumatic brain injury patients: an in vitro, in vivo, and postmortem study. US National Library of Medicine, NIH. J Neurotrauma. 2008 June; 25(6):581-91.
3. Freedom Rights and Education for Everyone (F.R.E.E.). Auto Claims, Insurance Companies & Courts, Truths & Myths. 321 Sutherland Place, Manitou Springs, CO 80829.

4. Bush, George W. Public Papers of the President of the United States, GW Bush, 2004…edited by the Office of the Federal Register (U.S.). (There were 59 articles about frivolous lawsuits by GW Bush).
5. Organization for Economic Co-Op and Development. Policy Issues in Insurance, Medical Malpractice-Prevention, Insurance and Coverage Options, No.11.
6. Shapiro, Alan. Presidential Election 2002: The Impact of Campaign Spending. http://www.teachablemoment.org.
7. Gottlieb, Emily and Doroshow, Joanne. The Money Vultures, Center for Justice and Democracy, NY.

Chapter 18
1. Borkowski, Liz. Who's Paying for Gabrielle Gifford's Rehabilitation? Healthcare-Occupational Health and Safety, June 16, 2011. www.scienceblogs.com.

Chapter 19
1. Brain Injury Association of America, 105 North Alfred Street, Alexandra, VA 22314, March 2001.
2. FBIC: Fight Bad-faith Insurance Companies. http://badfaithinsurance.com/. 7/1/2004.
3. NIH Consensus Development Conference on Rehabilitation of Persons with Traumatic Brain injury, 08/08/2006.

4. CommonDreams.org/.Oct 8, 2011/headlines04/1021-23.htm.
5. www.hhs.gov>homelessness, 2003.
6. Traumatic Brain Injury Common Among Homeless. Http: www.cbc.ca/news/health/story/2008/10/06/homeless-head-injury.htm.

Chapter 20
1. Swanson, Kara L. I'll Carry the Fork. Rising Star Press. Los Altos, CA, 1999.
2. Anonymous. Alcoholics Anonymous World Services, Inc., New York City, 1976.
3. Casdorph, Dr. Richard H, Walker, Dr. Morton. Toxic Metal Syndrome—How Metal Poisoning Can Affect Your Brain. Avery Publishing Group, Garden City, NY, 1995.
4. Pearce, Joseph Chilton. Evolution's End. Harper San Francisco, 1992.

Chapter 21
1. McKiggans, John. Traumatic Brain Injury Myth #3: A Normal MRI or CT Scan Means No Brain Injury. http://www.halifaxpersonalinjurylawyerblog.com/2009/08.
2. Myth #4. www.apmlawyers.com/lawyer-attorney-1346712.html.

3. Brain Injury Australia. Email: admin@braininjuryaustralia.org.au.

Chapter 27
1. Mild Head Injury and Posttraumatic Headache, http://www.neuropsychologycentral.com.

Indicative or Contributory Signs of Bad Faith. FBIC: Fight Bad-faith Insurance Companies. http://badfaithinsurance.com/. 7/1/2004.

# DISCLAIMER

I am not an attorney. All legal examples such as discoveries given in this book are simply examples of what was sent to me as the plaintiff only. Each state may have its own legal criteria. All legal contracts are examples only. Many of the examples can be found on the internet and re-worded to suit your own needs such as in the Durable Power of Attorney and Medical Directives.

Suggestions for therapies are just that—suggestions. Structure your therapy to fit your needs. Work with your therapists. If your gut says, "Don't do it. Don't do it."

Suggestions for preparing for your lawsuit or mediation are just that—suggestions. Structure your preparations to fit your needs. What I have written may be pertinent to your case and some aspects of your case may have been left out. Ask your attorney.

Suggestions for herbal supplements and alternative medicines are just that—suggestions. Check with your alternative health provider about what is best for you.

I am not a doctor. What I have written in the book was suggested to me by my medical providers.

If there are any errors in the Bibliography, I humbly apologize. At no time have I intentionally misquoted or not given the correct author credit. Once again, many of the quotes and reference material can be found in numerous internet articles. As far as the chiropractic aspect is concerned, the references can be found in most any chiropractor's office and on the internet as can information about MRI's, biofeedback, neuropsychology, etc..

Ironically, it is less of a chore for me to write what happened than to keep notes in any semblance of order. In brain injury fashion, I threw away the notes when I moved thinking that I had already put the notes in the computer. Of course I hadn't so had to wade through miles of internet information only to find that several quotes are no longer available on the internet. I felt that the information was so important that I left the information in the book and can only hope that I gave the right person credit. Often I changed the information completely as I found information that better demonstrated what I experienced.

Many names have been changed or left out of the book as this is a tort society. I left in the correct names of those who actually helped me.

It is time that we lower the veil of secrecy in the court system and allow people to tell the story of their legal outcome. I do not understand how newspapers can print how much someone gets awarded in a trial but others of us have to sign papers agreeing not to talk about how much we were awarded—as if it's a contest! I personally think it is because it's usually such a paltry amount compared to our pain, anguish and ongoing trauma that someone sitting at the head of the table of the insurance companies doesn't want people to know how little they are forking out for injuries versus what they are telling their customers.

And one last thing...don't you wish you had the same insurance as Federal Government employees?

Thank you for your patience and understanding.

# Author Info

The author has written one other book entitled *It's Time to Go Now—Our Journey Through the Veil* which is based on the December 17, 1973 Palestinian terrorist attack of Pan Am Clipper Flight #110 in Rome, Italy. The book will be available in December of 2011.

The following is an excerpt from the book:

On December 17, 1973 Pan Am Clipper Flight #110 was blown up by Arab terrorists while sitting on the tarmac at Rome's Fumicino Airport. Of the fifty-two people on board the plane that day, thirty-two people died. *It's Time to Go Now—Our Journey Through the Veil* is the story of what was, at that time, the "bloodiest hijacking to date" as told by one of the survivors.

What about the survivor? What happened after the attack? How does a survivor get through the guilt of surviving, PTSD, self-distrust, self-sabotage, drug addiction and alcoholism?

In 2001 the author was "killed" again in a roll-over car accident. She takes the reader on a journey of recovery from both near-death experiences and explains how souls work.

She answers her own questions about karma, spirituality versus religion, angels, dual souls, duality, the "other side", our veiled human consciousness, dream states, time lines, past lives, UFO's, IFO's, intuition, astrology, the archetypes, the activation of DNA, the chakra system, ego-states, how "thoughts are not my thoughts", the Mystery Schools, and how to decode the world we live in.

## It's Time to Go Now
### An Excerpt from Chapter Three

...Suddenly, an arm threw the curtain back. A plume of aircraft chunks, hair, and skin-riddled smoke exploded through the opening. I looked directly into the man's dark eyes and saw the machine gun leveled at our chests. The couple in the corner moved. The terrorist glanced to his left and saw the couple crouched in the corner. The man jumped up, grabbed his wife's hand and pulled her upright. He ran into me, knocked me and Muriel down then fell back onto the floor. The terrorist stepped on my back and ran down the aisle.

The couple jumped up again and attempted to go through the curtain into first class. When he yanked the curtain back, another plume of smoke burst through the opening. They immediately turned to run to the back of the plane. They tripped over me and followed the terrorist.

The smoke from the smoke bomb and the fire in the first-class section melded with the smoke pouring from the back of the economy section of the plane and my vision was completely gone. The spot fires were rapidly engulfing the plane. The burning material of the seats and the plastic hull of the plane were becoming a toxic poisonous holocaust.

I got back up on my knees and patted the floor with my hands, inch by inch, to try to find Muriel. I could not see more than two inches in front of my face. I kept feeling around. Where is she? Where is she? The only thing I could see in the wall of smoke were lazily drifting chunks that I dared not think about.

I was not about to leave that plane without her! I had to find her! …don't give up…I kept searching, searching…but Muriel was nowhere to be found. Where did she go? I kept asking out loud. Where did she go? It's like she fell into Alice's hole.

My lungs were choking. I could taste the acrid poison in the smoke. I gasped then gasped and gasped again. I was quickly melting down….

My head was spinning. My vision blurred. I was flat on the floor.

…and, just like that, I knew I was dead….

I watched as a sudden calm feeling ran through what used to be my body. It felt a tap three times on the shoulder and then in a blast I heard a voice whisper, "....

www.ingramcontent.com/pod-product-compliance
Lightning Source LLC
Chambersburg PA
CBHW060103170426
43198CB00010B/746